A Brief History
of
New York City

George J. Lankevich
and
Howard B. Furer

National University Publications
ASSOCIATED FACULTY PRESS, INC.
Port Washington, N.Y. • New York City • London

Manufactured in the United States of America

Published by
Associated Faculty Press, Inc.
Port Washington, N.Y.

Library of Congress Cataloging in Publication Data

Lankevich, George J., 1939-
    A brief history of New York City.

    (National university publications)
    Bibliography: p.
    Includes index.
    1. New York (N.Y.)—History.   I. Furer, Howard B., 1934-
    . II. Title.
F128.3.L36   1984   974.7'1   83-12487
ISBN 0-8046-9325-0
ISBN 0-8046-9326-9 (pbk.)

Preface

This volume presents the epic story of New York City, or as much of it as two urban historians could compress into a single book. Despite the thousands of monographs which deal with aspects of this metropolis, a short history based on modern scholarship has not been available. We hope that this volume fills that lamentable gap. The Big Apple's history is of course both desperate and elegant, and stretches from a few dozen courageous settlers founding an outpost of empire to seven million citizens of the world entering the post-industrial age. We can only hope that both the struggle and the glory emerge in the pages that follow.

The history we present clearly cannot deal with everything. Although it makes a concerted effort to avoid statistical or socio-logical analyses, it is not intended to be merely an uncritical compendium of amusing incidents. Rather, our purpose was to probe the nature of New York City's growth, to uncover some of its causes, and to synthesize the vast amount of information available on New York. A corollary goal was to explore the interrelation-ships between the City, the rest of America and the world. The sub-themes we emphasize are the political and economic style of New York (an amalgam of principle and pragmatism); the accul-turation function of the metropolis; and New York's pace setting role in fields as varied as communications, business methods, education, theater, ghetto life and urban services.

Certainly, no other American city has been more often de-scribed and written about than has New York. And, this is as it should be. After all, a third of all the people and products that came to this country entered through the Narrows. The urban environment of New York influenced all this immense "baggage" of history. The City has been and continues to be a magnet for the ambitious, a lodestone for both the talented and the oppressed. New York has been and still is the Mecca for Americans pursuing happiness, and, in this sense, the City sets the expectations for the remainder of the nation. The old question of whether New York is really part of America has in our view become an academic one, New York is America!

However, not everything in New York's past or present is bathed in sunlight. Down the broad vistas of its history there have been dark stains and shameful passages symbolized by the politicos, the corrupt elite, the character assassins and the wheeler-dealers in both high places and low. But, the City has been equally fortunate that every generation of its history has raised up leaders from Peter Stuyvesant to Ed Koch who somehow amplified the City's destiny.

Our historical portrait of New York has been divided approximately in thirds. The first third is devoted to events prior to 1825, the middle third to the remainder of the nineteenth century and the final third to the complex events of our own century. Such a division might at first glance appear overweighted in favor of the present, but we believe it is justified both by history and the themes we have developed.

We have depicted the growth of New York City as a three act play. In the first act, after a difficult childhood, our young hero will overcome a variety of obstacles (rebellions, wars, fires and revolution) to emerge as the dominant urban center of America. That triumph is consolidated and expanded upon in Act II, an age dominated by heroic figures (statesmen, bosses, reformers and merchant princes), enormous population increases (domestic and foreign immigration) and the achievement of commercial, financial and cultural supremacy. By Act III, the City, which has long set the tone for American urban life faces the grim realities of an ever-changing world. New York must now confront not only the historic animosity of a rural tradition, but also increased ethnic tensions, near-fatal fiscal stringencies and a national neglect unparalleled in more than three centuries. Whether the play will finally be a tragedy or a comedy is not yet decided, for both the plot and its chief character keep changing every day.

What New York's future is to be, and what part it is destined to play in the further development of the nation and the world, one can only guess. On the whole, however, we are inclined to be hopeful. This amazing city's characteristic resiliency, its material advantages, its great vitality and alertness, endow it with the tools that will enable it to maintain and improve its position as the premier city of the world.

We should like to acknowledge the interest and support of many of our colleagues. Our special thanks to Professors Leonard Dinnerstein, Samuel Ehrenpreis, David Felix and Arnold Rice who read and commented upon portions of the manuscript. Their help was substantial and errors remain our exclusive domain. Also, thanks are due to Mrs. Merilee Cohen, Ms. Faye Fishberg, Mrs. Sidney Furer and Mrs. Marge Hogarty who typed various drafts of the manuscript.

To our Wives and Children
for their
Patience and Fortitude

Table of Contents

I

New Amsterdam Becomes New York

THE MOST OUTSTANDING characteristic of the City of New York, from its primitive Dutch origins to the giant urban complex which it is today, has been continuous and rapid change. For over three hundred fifty years the City at the mouth of the Hudson River has been the critical center of American life, a funnel through which European peoples and culture entered this continent and a model which offered to an Old World, clues as to the nature of its offspring society. The developmental challenges which New York experienced were unique, yet they somehow achieved a larger historical impact than the same problems faced by other New World centers. By understanding something of the history of New York, we can obtain a more vital sense of what American was, is, and perhaps can become. Whether as a struggling trading post or as a financially troubled metropolis, New York has always made a larger-than-life influence on its times. It continues to have that same effect today.

Like the other Colonial settlements of America, New York City did not emerge as the result of deliberate and rational government planning. Its origins are to be found in the economic and religious turmoil which dominated European life in the wake of Columbus' voyages. It seems fitting that Dutch settlement of the

1

New York area began as a business enterprise which slowly took on other dimensions. The small trading post became a platform across which European civilization and its peoples could be transferred from Europe to America, an arena in which a myriad of cultures met and merged. The first of these formative infuences was Dutch, which is where the story of New York begins; but the larger reality of this metropolis should never be forgotten. New York is a "crucible of culture," the meeting place of the old and the new, a catalytic agent necessary to the process of a New World becoming America.

* * * * *

Early in the sixteenth century, no European yet had a firm conception of the size or the geography of the Western Hemisphere's land mass. Christopher Columbus had not touched North America, John Cabot had only briefly entered the frozen north where Norsemen had once sailed, and only Magellan had discovered a difficult passageway through the southern continent. Spanish explorers were examining and exploiting the Caribbean area, but there were still vast areas of unknown land, and perhaps somewhere there was yet to be discovered a sea passageway to fabled China. Certainly some such vision must have stimulated the mind of King Francis I of France when he hired an Italian sailor-explorer, allowed him to borrow a hundred-ton ship from the French Navy, and sent him out on the historic trip which gave France an early claim to much of North America.

It was on April 17, 1524, that Francis' Florentine captain, Giovanni da Verrazano, a genius of a navigator and also partly a pirate, blundered into what today is called the Narrows at the entrance of New York Harbor. Verrazano anchored the *Dauphine*, sent long boats into the bay, and noted the "very agreeable location situated within two prominent hills." The sailors rowing into the bay must have seen Manhattan Island because they caught a glimpse of a "great river" before sudden squalls forced them and the *Dauphine* to withdraw. Verrazano appears almost criminally incurious, however, for he sailed away and gave up his chance to be the first European man to set foot in New York. He named the upper bay after Sainte Margarita, sailed northward to Block Island and the Maine coast, and returned to France by July, convinced that an impassable continent stood between Europe and Cathay. The following winter, in January 1626, a black Portuguese explorer in the service of Spain, Esteban Gómez, also sighted the "great river" and named it the San Antonio, but he too sailed on. The memory of these early explorers might have been totally lost had not Verrazano's name been selected in 1964, to honor the world's largest suspension bridge which spanned the mile-wide Narrows. Even in their own day, it was only the story of a vast "Sea of Verrazano," fostered by the twin brother of the explorer, that served to stimulate other adventuresome captains. It was that rumored sea, perhaps still the passageway to the Indies, which brought the English navigator, Henry Hudson, to the fortieth degree of latitude in the year 1609.

Like his Italian and Portuguese predecessors, Hudson symbolized Europe's unflagging quest for an all-water route to the treasures of the Far East. A professional seaman, he sold his expertise to the highest bidder but, nevertheless, in the service of the Muscovy Company he had failed to find a northwest passage. The Dutch East India Company had hired him to try once again, and so, on March 25, 1609, he had sailed his eighty-ton galliot *Half-Moon*, out of Amsterdam and into the unknown. By September, he arrived at New York Bay and, pushing on through the Narrows, sailed into the world's greatest harbor. The vast "Sea of Verrazano" spread itself before him, a landlocked harbor south of Barcelona which would never ice over and which could easily accommodate the navies of the entire globe. The pride of discovery, the thrill of naming new places, and the challenge of further adventure, all mingled as the *Half-Moon* edged toward the "land surrounded by hills," the "place of the whirlpool," or the "land of mountains," which was to become Manhattan. Each of the foregoing has been offered as a translation for Manna-hatin, but no one knows with confidence what it meant to the Indians. What was certain, is that the epic of New York had begun.

Despite his bravery and daring, Captain Hudson probably deserved to be brought up on charges by his employers, for the company had clearly told him to sail east from Europe. Yet here he was, unmistakably west and certain that his gamble had paid off. Trading with the Indians, his crew obtained furs despite some unpleasantness in which boatswain's mate John Coleman was killed. Coleman thus gained the rather dubious honor of being the first white man murdered in New York. On September 11, the *Half-Moon* proceeded up the western river and advanced as far as the present site of Albany. Small boats went farther but the water had turned fresh, and the river they hoped would lead to Cathay had turned out to be only a gigantic estuary where the waters of the mountains met the encroaching Atlantic. The dream of a strait to the Far East once again had proven futile and, after some more trade, Hudson sailed away from both the harbor and the river which was to bear his name. Hudson returned to Europe with little to show for his efforts except some beaver furs, a well-written log kept largely by his mate, and historic immortality. His Dutch employers never saw him again, however, for when he put in at Dartmouth Harbor, the British authorities arrested him for serving under a foreign flag and confiscated ship, log, and furs. It is one of the strange ironies of history that both Hudson and Verrazano today are remembered as heroes by New Yorkers though both were convinced that their missions failed. Even more ironic was the fact that both would return to the New World to die—one as dinner for Carib Indians and the other in the frozen reaches of Hudson Bay.

Almost alone of the European states, the Dutch Republic seemed to recognize the commercial possibilities of the New World; by the summer of 1610, its vessels had established fur trade stations from Maine to New Jersey. By 1614, a rude fort had been constructed in the Albany area by Captain Hendrik Christiaensen and, during the winter of 1613–14, a group of Dutch sailors led by Adrian Block had wintered on Manhattan Island after a fire had destroyed their vessel. In the spring of 1614, in a makeshift craft named the *Restless*, Captain Block discovered *Hellegat*, where the present East River merges with Long Island Sound, and sailed on to find the Housatonic and Connecticut rivers. The *Restless* sailed on and charted Block Island, modestly named for the Dutch captain, and not for its original discoverer, Verrazano. Block's voyage proved that Manhattaan and Long Island were separate entities, the latter fact soon confirmed by Captain Cornelius May. The result of all of these trips was that the territory between the Delaware and the Connecticut rivers was claimed by the Dutch and called New Netherlands; the land would be theirs as long as they could hold it.

Early in 1614, the States General of Holland granted a three-year trade monopoly to thirteen Dutch merchants who formed the New Netherland Company. Colonization was part of their plans, but they completely failed in that venture. After the charter lapsed in 1618, the Dutch government looked for a group to undertake the difficult but potentially lucrative task of establishing a colony in the heart of the new continent's rich fur-trading area. A more permanent type of settlement than trading posts was needed since both Britain and France were known to have ambitions in the New World. On June 3, 1621; a twenty-four-year charter was awarded to the Dutch West India Company, a corporation modeled after its great East India predecessor. Thus, both of the world's largest corporations were Dutch and possessed at least ten times the capital of Britain's Virginia Company. Although the primary purpose of the new enterprise was expanded trade, it was decided in 1623 that in order to achieve that goal a permanent settlement must be created in the New York area. Rules for the new colony, an *Artikelbrief*, were drawn up in March of 1623, and a group of Walloon families led by Cornelius May was sent out in 1624 on the *Nieu Nederlandt*. Settlers were given strict instructions not to trade with foreigners and were scattered from Fort Orange (Albany), to Fort Nassau (Gloucester, New Jersey), to Nut Island in New York Bay. More settlers arrived in August of 1624, and soon huts were seen at Wallabout Bay on the Brooklyn shore, and at the southern tip of Manhattan itself. From these varied sites furs valued at 27,000 guilders were exported to Holland in 1624. By April 22, 1625, a settlement to be known as New Amsterdam was finally placed on Manhattan Island, and the Dutch period of New York's history can be said to have finally begun.

Although it was created relatively late in the Dutch ascendency, New Amsterdam rapidly became the heart of Holland's presence in the New World. Cattle, farm equipment, and additional settlers came from across the ocean and not even a rather inept leader named William Verhulst, who also diverted fur revenues to his private accounts, could hinder the settlement's progress. Kryn Fredericks, an engineer dispatched in 1625, designed Fort Amsterdam with star-shaped bastions and also selected the site for the State Street windmill, the town's most distinctive early structure. Land surveys for farms and roadways were initiated, and the Governor's House was placed inside the confines of the fort along with the company office; the latter, it was hoped, would always be filled with pelts. *Bouweries*, or farms, soon made their appearance as the employees of the Dutch West India Company settled in for what all hoped would be a self-sustaining and prosperous Colonial venture. Although there were competing English claims to the land, the Dutch had the advantage of occupancy on their side. For decades a rhetorical game of imperial and commercial bluff between New Amsterdam and what came to be called New England would continue, but in practice the Dutch settlement ended Colonial conflict for 40 years.

The goal of the West India Company was to send profits home to Amsterdam by bringing commercial order to New Amsterdam and its environs. Since it became increasingly apparent that Verhulst was a bungler, on May 4, 1626, Peter Minuit arrived as the new director of corporate interests. Not only did Minuit bring along some 200 more settlers, but he also carried instructions to strengthen the corporate claim to the land by purchasing Manna-hatin from the Indians. Within three weeks, a deal was made with the Canarsie Indians which gave the Dutch title to Manhattan's 22 square miles. The price, 60 guilders or $23.70, certainly marks Minuit as one of the shrewdest real estate operators of all time, for the land today is worth conservatively $30 billion. On the other hand, envious entrepreneurs should consider the fact that Manna-hatin was really "owned" by no tribe, and that the Indian chiefs provided Minuit with a worthless deed. The Canarsie lived on Long Island and used the island between the rivers only as a hunting and trading site. Ultimately, further purchase prices would have to be negotiated with tribes living near today's Washington Heights area; their claim to the land was at least equally cloudy.

Whatever the legalities, the Dutch company now held New Amsterdam, and under Minuit settlement slowly moved outward from the area under direct protection of the guns of the garrison. An inlet at Broad Street was widened to serve as the *Heere Gracht,* a canal which soon had bridges across its width and gave to the growing town a hint of Old Amsterdam. Some 30 houses along the eastern shore of the island were erected by the latest contingent of settlers, and farms grew food crops along the Hudson's banks. In November 1626, Minuit sent back to Holland on the *Arms of Amsterdam* a substantial cargo of beaver, mink, and other skins, as well as samples of New World lumber; it was hoped that the most profitable resource would be furs. New Amsterdam was, after all, the colony of a company which totally controlled its destiny; its only goal was profit. Unhappily, its population was neither so enterprising nor as loyal as Director Minuit might have liked. Nevertheless, by early 1628, he had built a town of 300 persons and had proudly been able to dispatch another 7,520 beaver skins back to Europe, where they soon graced the heads of German and Russian buyers.

In Amsterdam, the company directors were pleased with the early returns but came to believe that more rapid growth was necessary if New Netherlands was to effectively exploit its vast interior sections. It had become clear that the hired labor alone could not effectively colonize the enormous tracts of land held by the company. So on June 7, 1629, the Charter of Freedoms and Exemptions not only established the first frame of government for its colony, but also granted large tracts of land to rich Dutch investors who promised to settle 50 adults in New Netherlands within four years. Although these patroons would hold the land as a "perpetual fief," they purchased all Indian claims to the lands. By January 1630, five great patroonships had been organized but all, with the exception of Rensselaerswyck near Albany, would be commercial failures. Indeed, even after 1640 when the size of patroonships was reduced, the difficulties of attempting to transplant feudal attitudes into a virgin wilderness made the experiment a costly fiasco. By the end of the Dutch tenure in New York all but two of the grants had been repurchased and the word *patroon* itself stood as a monument illustrative of the futility of transporting European ideals into America. It should be noted however, that Michael Pauw's Pavonia grant, after its failure in 1637, was renamed Staten Island to honor the Dutch States General.

Although it ultimately accomplished little, the patroonship experiment demonstrated that the West India Company was concerned wth the future of its colony. But New Amsterdam was merely one aspect of corporate affairs and their man on the scene, in this case, Peter Minuit, was supposed to handle the details of development. In other words, the Governor had to produce profits, keep the colonists happy and working, secure the settlement against Indian attack, and be alert to potential incursion by other nations. All this was to be accomplished without adequate communication or support from home. Since any Governor's decisions were reversible once examined in Holland, the position of the leader was both tenous and vulnerable. Minuit was a shrewd and determined man who insisted that the Indians be treated fairly, but he had to be responsive as well to local public opinion. He knew that merchants in his town could complain about his decrees to the company, and he also knew he would have to cater to the wishes of the patroons from whose estates so much was expected. Although the company sent a minister in 1628 to see to the spiritual welfare of the settlement, Minuit never got the unstinting support he deserved. He was recalled in 1631 after being accused of overly favoring the patroons and of being unable or unwilling to halt the private trade in furs in which all sensible settlers clandestinely participated. Not for another fifteen years would as capable and loyal an administrator preside over New Amsterdam.

Minuit's first replacement was Bastiaen Jansean Krol, who proved to be no friend of the patroons in the brief year he ruled the colony. Accordingly in the spring of 1633, a new Governor arrived. Twenty-seven-year-old Wouter Van Twiller's primary qualification seems to have been that he was a nephew of the patroon Kiliaen Van Rensselaer. The new Director General brought with him 104 soldiers who rapidy completed work on a guardhouse, a new barracks, and the fort. The growing settlement soon boasted its first church, led by Reverend Everardus Bogardus, three sawmills, and a brewery. Moreover, trade expansion was indicated by the construction of Fort Good Hope on the Connecticut River, and by the ouster of a party of Virginians who had occupied the abandoned Fort Nassau. A garrison was stationed in the Delaware Valley to protect the trade of that region from foreigners, and the settlement of Long Island was begun in Flatlands, Brooklyn with the issuance of grants to Jacobus Van Curler and Wolfert Geritsen.

Van Twiller's New Amsterdam resembled its mother city in virtually every respect with gabled houses, bridged canals, solemn Dutch Reformed sermons, and pipe-smoking burghers part of its daily life. By 1636, the company laborers had constructed five large stone houses to be used as shops; its fort and windmill added to the illusion that it was a prosperous Dutch town. After

1633, some children attended Adam Roelantsen's school but he proved ineffective as a master and was soon reduced to augmenting his income by running a "bleaching ground" at the edge of the Fresh Water Pond where women could dry their linen. The area today is still known as Maiden Lane. The waterfront area predominated in New Amsterdam, but farms such as the ones run by Roeloff and Annetje Jans, Jacob Van Corlaer, and Maryn Adriaensen, sprang up beyond the town. Agriculture did not develop rapidly, however, because there was more profit to be made in furs, and raising crops in virgin land was hard, backbreaking work. The population was stagnant and increasingly apprehensive as English settlers from Connecticut were reported moving into eastern Long Island. New Amsterdam did have a few blacks among its population, and in 1635 it received its first Italian resident, a Venetian craftsman named Peter Alberti. In all it appears not to have advanced as rapidly as the company directors hoped. Although physically the town was "after the manner of Holland," in terms of ambition and profit it was very un-Dutch.

After all, the primary chore of the Governor was to produce money for his employer and in this regard Van Twiller was ineffective. It was true that during his tenure the value of exports grew to 134,925 guilders by 1635, but even though this represented a doubled return in a decade, it was a barely profitable sum for the company. Moreover, Van Twiller seemed far more adept at furthering his own fortune than that of his employers by purchasing lands from the Indians, especially Nut Island, and running a *bouwerie* using company labor. Nut Island today is known as Governor's Island as a reminder of Van Twiller's plantation, and still retains a vestige of his military power by serving as the site of a modern Coast Guard station. Van Twiller's greed extended to extorting money from visiting ship's captains. He feuded constantly with Dominie Bogardus as well. Ultimately, he was replaced because of his one-sided thrift, but stayed on in New Amsterdam where he had been so successful.

William Kieft, a vain, rough, and venal Amsterdam merchant, arrived on the company ship *Haring*, and replaced Van Twiller as Governor on March 28, 1638. His private brief from the company appears to have said "get tough" with the settlers and make New Amsterdam pay greater returns. Almost immediately, Kieft arrogantly ignored the populace and issued a series of edicts closing taverns, regulating the fur trade, and ordering the refurbishing of company property, such as the fort and the stone houses, which stood badly in need of repairs. He replaced local officials without consulting with any of the residents, who were soon complaining that "under a king, we could not be worse treated." Still, a ferry to Long Island was made operational, and a militia was organized, so perhaps all might yet be well. Those hopes were soon extinguished as Kieft instituted a series of measures designed to raise both revenue and population. A tax was levied on tobacco and residents of New Amsterdam were told they would need official documents in order to leave and enter Manhattan. A revision of the patroonship system in 1640, was issued so as to encourage new settlements, and in 1641, a large land grant was awarded to Jonas Bronck, a Danish Lutheran farmer whose name later became famous as the Bronx. Kieft also appeared to encourage Englishmen to settle within Dutch territory, a policy his burghers found incomprehensible. Most critical, however, was Kieft's mismanagement of Indian affairs as shown in his attempts to tax friendly tribes while antagonizing all others. In the summer of 1640, after a few pigs had disappeared from Staten Island, the Governor rashly decided that the Raritan Indians—who hated his levies on their corn—were responsible for the loss. Subsequent investigations showed that company seamen had expropriated the swine, but the militia Kieft sent to Staten Island killed a few Indians instead. An uneasy calm settled on the province until the following summer, when an Indian brave of the Wecquaesqeek tribe, who years before had witnessed the murder of his uncle by Dutch white men, took sudden and fatal revenge on an innocent wheelwright, Claes Swits. When Kieft demanded the immediate surrender of the warrior, the Wecquaesqeek sachem refused, which emboldened the Raritans to attack and avenge their honor as well. For the next year a series of skirmishes made New Amsterdam's life extremely perilous. In desperation, Kieft agreed to consult with twelve men, representatives of families, rather than elected officials; the former would serve as his advisory council for the course of the war. The Twelve met on August 29, 1642, and gave their consent to a campaign against the Indians of the lower Hudson Valley, the Algonquins, as well as Raritans and Wecquaesqeeks. The effort proved abortive, and a year's truce was finally negotiated under the auspices of Jonas Bronck. The Indians did promise to "inflict justice" upon Swits' murderer, but as far as anyone knows, that pledge went unkept.

With the temporary end of the Indian threat, Kieft faced a demand from The Twelve for a reorganization of the local governmental structure. In a petition on January 21, 1642, The Twelve put forth a proposal for the creation of a five-man council to advise the Governor, greater freedom of movement for settlers, and restrictions on the importation of both English cattle and new Englishmen as well. Such impertinence could not be tolerated by Kieft, who informed his council that its services had been required only "to give advice respecting the murder of the late Claes Swits." On February 8, he thanked them for that service and for their unsolicited advice, but ordered them not to hold any further meetings. A brief but important step toward representative government had been taken, yet the unchallenged authority of the company director was restored. And Kieft used that authority to perpetrate an atrocity beyond anything that had yet occurred. Mohawk Indians, armed by traders at Fort Orange who gave them guns for furs, had been pressing southward against the tribes of the lower Hudson Valley and had forced many of them to seek refuge among the Dutch settlers at Pavonia (New Jersey) and upper Manhattan. Against the advice of several burghers and Dominie Bogardus, Kieft decided to use the West Indian Company militia to deliver a crushing blow against the refugees, presumably on the theory that all Indians would ultimately be his enemies. On the night of February 25–26, 1643 over a hundred twenty Indians were massacred and most of the bodies thrown into the rivers. A coalition of tribes was immediately created and it was only with the greatest luck and tact, the latter not supplied by an unrepentant Kieft, that another truce was arranged in April.

By September of this terrible year, the apparently never-ending Indian troubles once again erupted into open war. Kieft was not accountable for this conflict, which began in Connecticut and spread into the Hudson Valley, but that was little comfort to those settlers who lost their lives or property. Refugees flooded into lower Manhattan where Kieft once again decided to convene an advisory commission, this time labeled "The Eight" (two of whom were English). Cornelius Melyn, patroon from Staten Island, served as president of this new council which decided to attack only the Algonquin tribes and to seek peace with those Indians from Long Island. More importantly, The Eight and Kieft decided to hire an English Indian fighter, Captain John Underhill, and to build a line of defenses that generally followed the line of today's Wall Street. Nevertheless, the prospects were gloomy indeed; in a letter to the States General on November 3, The Eight reported that "almost every place is abandoned . . . we are not safe even for an hour . . . all of us who will yet save our lives, must of necessity perish next year of hunger." Among the many who lost their lives in this tragic warfare were Mistress Anne Hutchinson and her family, but almost against expectations New Amsterdam survived. Successful raids led by Captain Underhill resulted in the virtual massacre of hundreds of Indians in Connecticut and Westchester and the danger of being overrun by the uprising passed. A settlement with many of the warring tribes was signed by Kieft in April 1644, and the province turned to the tasks of rebuilding and assigning blame.

In the opinion of The Eight, it was Governor Kieft who bore the responsibility for bringing fire and tomahawk against the Dutch colony. Yet the peace agreement had only seemed to confirm him in his autocratic ways. In June, the Governor decided that the task of reconstruction demanded that direct taxes be levied upon the settlers, but according to the tradition of the Republic he would have to obtain their approval. Thus he convened a session of The Eight for the first time since November's crisis yet overruled their objections; the town detested most of all Kieft's levy upon the good Dutch beer brewed and consumed by colonists of all ethnic backgrounds. Manhattan's population now included English auxiliaries, Dutch reinforcements from Brazil and Curaçao, Swedes from the Delaware, blacks, Indian allies, and a myriad of others. When Father Isaac Jogues, a Jesuit missionary rescued from the Mohawks in 1643, recuperated in New Amsterdam, eighteen different languages were spoken in the town; that number if anything increased as a result of war. The total population was probably only seven hundred but in the bedlam Kieft saw opportunity. He opened his own distillery and loosened the strictures he had originally placed on taverns. Soon one of every four structures was a tavern of sorts and the Reverend Bogardus was moved to condemn another Governor's actions as he had done with Van Twiller. Since the Governor rarely attended church, he retaliated by having the town militia drill and play their drums during Bogardus' services. It was all too much for The Eight, who in August and again in October 1644 secretly petitioned the States General for the recall of their testy Governor.

Yet Kieft's tenure still had two years to run and it was not to be without accomplishment. On August 30, 1645, a general treaty was signed with all of the tribes inside the fort at New Amsterdam, a peace sealed by smoking a pipe "under the blue canopy of heaven." There was much rebuilding of farms and villages to be done and the Dutch presence on Long Island from Gravesend to Flushing was restored. Settlers moved once again northward toward Connecticut and inevitably came into conflict with the authorities in English New Haven and in the United Colonies of New England. The Governor's correspondence with New England's leadership, largely carried on in Latin, is interesting, but his lack of wise diplomacy made it only a record of erudite failure. New Amsterdam's political, moral, and business leaders seemed ever more united against him as were the increasing numbers of English settlers to his north and east. He himself was aware that his authority was about to be ended, and so informed Governor John Winthrop of Connecticut in April 1647. He set about putting his papers and his defense in order and, less than a month later, formally greeted his successor under the walls of Fort Amsterdam. It is a vast loss to history that Kieft's defense was never to be heard, for on his return trip to Holland, he, Dominie Bogardus, and several other officials were lost at sea when their ship *Princess*, sank in a gale in the Bristol Channel.

"Lord General" Peter Stuyvesant took command of New Amsterdam on May 11, 1647. Tall and spritely, he previously had lost a leg in the service of the company and was prepared to liberalize the restrictive trading regulations in hopes of stimulating the colony's agriculture, commerce, and ambition. He had already enjoyed a distinguished military career and references to his silver-banded wooden leg disturbed the clean-shaven Governor not at all. He had moral strength, efficiency, and a scholarly intelligence, and honestly believed he could set New Amsterdam right within three years and move on to his next assignment. Thus, in his first address to the townspeople he promised that all his actions would be "as a father to his children, for the advantages of the Privileged West India Company, the Burghers, and the

Country." Certainly there was much to be done, not only in effecting a smooth transition, but also because cows and goats were grazing on or around the walls of the fort. Discipline had to be restored, malcontents punished, repairs made, and the town spruced up to Dutch national standards. A general reform seemed imperative and Stuyvesant set to work with an imperious will. He ordered taverns to close after nine, issued harsh new regulations to end the smuggling Kieft had countenanced, and decreed that wines, liquors, and furs should be taxed to pay for civic improvements. He ordered that a dock be constructed (it was finished in 1648), that the hodgepodge of growth be regulated by a systematic land survey, and on September 25, 1647, created a board of nine advisors from the burgher population. Although closely controlled by Stuyvesant, this body was soon to assert its independence and in many ways deserves to be called the first real legislative government in New Amsterdam. Their advisory position was of course dependent on cooperation with the Governor, but his obstinate and proud nature made such a course difficult for both sides. There was in Stuyvesant a lamentable tendency to shout down his opposition and, despite all the evidence of "building, laying masonry, making, breaking, and repairing," it was his job to serve the corporate interest first. The inevitable misunderstandings and conflicts over what really served the public interest soon led to political conflict.

In July of 1649, The Nine dispatched a Remonstrance of their grievances to the States General of the United Netherlands. They claimed that New Netherlands had been ruined by the mismanagement of the Dutch West India Company and by the series of ineffective administrators that it had sent to preside over the colony. The document argued that only a takeover by the national government would solve the "very poor and most low" situation, and that local governmental authority should be given to the burghers. The petition requested greater security from "the insufferable arrogance of the natives," a condition that was honestly ascribed to the still too meager population. If the town was exempted from duties and taxes and if the company authority should be lifted, then New Netherlands would prosper and all Holland would benefit. Although the Remonstrance was not primarily directed against Stuyvesant, it clearly condemned his paternalistic attitude as a contributing factor to the problem. The petition was of course opposed by the company and vigorously denied by a representative sent by the Governor, but it did stir the States General to action. On May 25, 1650, it issued an order easing immigration curbs to New Netherland and calling for a reorganization of government, but Amsterdam refused to accept the task of running the colony. The government's decree made it clear to the corporate directors that concessions would have to be made but they decided that Stuyvesant, the man on-the-scene, could be trusted to keep the situation under control. Meanwhile, they appeared each day before the States General and argued vehemently against the recall of their Governor. After two years of delay the company was ordered to grant a municipal government structure to New Amsterdam, although the recall of Stuyvesant was avoided due to the outbreak of war with England. Accordingly, on February 2, 1653, Stuyvesant granted a form of burgher government to New Amsterdam; the Governor named the two *burgomasters* and five *schepens* ("aldermen"), as well as the new *schout* ("sheriff"), but in fact he now presided over the first municipal council in America. Great and small burgher-rights were established requiring payment of fees to do business in the City of New Amsterdam. A City Hall was established in a tavern once owned by Kieft and work on the fort and on the City's protective wall was intensified due to the fact of war. By summer, a 2,340-foot palisade had been completed along with 6 water towers and several gates; it never had to be used. The European war was won by England, but it never spread to America, where New Amsterdam survived as a small Dutch island in a virtually English sea. The year 1654 ended therefore not only without war, but with mutual toasts of friendship between Stuyvesant and his council.

Stuyvesant was to rule New Amsterdam for a total of 17 years, although he hoped to reform it in 3 years, and in that time he achieved many improvements in his domain. Although the City never extended northward more than 600 yards from the Battery, he was in time able to produce a far more livable and efficient town than the battered and decrepit one he took charge of in 1647. The survey he had ordered managed by 1656 to give order to the 120 houses and to properly align the streets. Under the new municipal arrangement the *burgomasters* took control of further highway construction, and new streets were added as the population grew beyond 1,000. By 1664, two dozen streets and seven major arteries cut through the expanding seaport. They were given names, and a series of rudimentary traffic regulations were adopted for the protection of pedestrians as well as cart and wagon drivers. The Dutch municipality also made a concerted effort to clean the streets and as early as 1647, the Governor decreed that fines were to be levied on residents who allowed their pigs, goats, sheep, or cattle to stray; the next year any goat caught wandering without a keeper was ordered confiscated. Cleanliness was a perennial issue and in 1657, the City authorities prohibited the dumping of rubbish or litter into the streets, and passed ordinances which placed responsibility for cleaning that portion of the street fronting on one's house upon the individual home-owner. Constant attempts were also made to abolish or at least restrict the common practice of allowing bands of hogs to roam the streets at will. Pigs served a useful purpose as scavengers, but they also caused congestion and additional filth in the streets. Although ordinances were enacted to regulate this nuisance, they proved to be unsuccessful, and the "ubiquitous hog" continued to vex municipal authorities. Contemporaries frequently com-mented on the "noxious odors" emanating from the town, and the municipality was forced to come to grips with the problem. Part of the difficulty stemmed from the fact that residents dumped their garbage in the *Great Gracht* which ran through the center of town, and so in 1657, five locations were designated as garbage dumps. From time to time, other ordinances were passed regulat-ing privies, slaughterhouses and cemeteries. Although these laws somewhat helped the sanitary condition of the City, New York was already acquiring its reputation for filth.

Medical facilities, too, lagged behind the growing needs of the town. Although at least five trained physicians practiced in New Amsterdam, most were little more than barber-surgeons more adept at their tonsorial activities than in healing the sick. A small hospital opened in February 1659, but generally, institutions of this kind were lacking. After the English took possession of the City, a number of doctors arrived and medical facilities improved.

The City also had to contend with problems fundamental to any growing urban center; primary among these were the spheres of fire and police protection. The municipality in 1653 enacted a series of building regulations designed to combat the chief causes of fire, and by 1658, the codes extended to roofs, chimneys, and walls. In addition, Stuyvesant and his councilors began purchasing fire-fighting equipment. Buckets, ladders, fire hooks and storage sheds were acquired by 1660, and a few years later several fire wardens were appointed to care for and repair the apparatus. The Governor also issued a directive requiring every homeowner to keep a bucket at his doorstep to be used in case of fire. Of equal importance was the City's need for increased police protection. In the early years of the port's existence there had been little need for such services because New Amsterdam's Dutch were basically law-abiding and everyone lived in fear of the Indians. Drunkenness was not infrequent but robbery, rape, and murder were almost totally unknown. As the port's commerce increased, however, so did the outbreak of brawls and violence as sailors from ships other than the company's became frequent visitors. In 1638, a law had forbidden ships' crews from remaining in town overnight but by Stuyvesant's time it was virtually ignored. "Old Silver Nails" organized in 1649 a foot patrol to walk the streets at night, but the burghers found it expedient to avoid service. Yet as more and more servants, slaves, sailors, and soldiers came to New Amsterdam, more formal policing institutions were clearly necessary. In 1653, a jail was opened in the fort and soon the *schout* and the *schepens* who served as justices of the peace had much to do. By August 12, 1658, a Rattle Watch was again created to police the streets at night. Though temporarily disbanded in 1660 for want of funds, it was resurrected in 1661, and continued to perform its job until the English conquest; the few constables of the watch really constituted America's first police department.

The problem of poverty and the burden of relief for the poor likewise caused difficulties. During the settlement's early years the Dutch Reformed Church, rather than the company or the town, accepted charitable responsibility for the indigent. When New Amsterdam was granted municipal status, the council appointed "orphan masters" to care for children. When another Indian war in 1655 created additional orphans, the town officials established a permanent "Orphan Masters Court." In the same year, the Dutch Reformed Church opened a poor house and a poor farm. As the problem mounted, the municipality issued a "poor code" in 1661, but continued to subscribe to the principle that private philanthropy and religious charity were the best means to provide aid to the indigent. With the exception of these meager beginnings, little attention was devoted to this growing problem.

The civic development of New Amsterdam was intimately tied to trade and commerce and as these grew so did the wealth, population, and problems of the port. A produce market had been established at Pearl Street in 1648, and Tuesdays and Saturdays were recognized as market days throughout the Dutch era. The construction of Stuyvesant's dock had somewhat eased the off-loading of cargoes but, since it was the only pier, the coming and going of goods remained slow, haphazard, and almost unregulatable. As a result, New Amsterdam, despite its unrivaled harbor, never came close to competing with Boston in commercial importance during most of the seventeenth century. Nevertheless, many burghers increasingly believed that trade was the key to the colony's future and never lost their eye for the quick deal. Until 1664, Manhattan served as point of entry for all the commerce of the province and ships were required to unload their cargoes and pay the required duty. In theory, the town controlled a vast and rich economic hinterland but there were far too many holes in the system. Since the 1630s packet service was available to farms and towns along the Hudson up to Fort Orange, and in Stuyvesants's tenure the variety of goods carried in trade expanded. Meats, dairy products, furs, and liquors were all important. Despite complaints from Manhattan burghers that trade languished as a result of economic subordination to the West India Company, business was good.

Manufacturing and retailing were also growing. In 1637 when two windmills were operating and grinding flour for export, several bakers set up shops in the town. By 1664, ten bakeries were selling their fragrant twisted breads and sugar cookies to an ever-growing clientele. Other retail establishments increased just as rapidly—so much so that in March 1648 the Governor and council were forced to issue regulations concerning fair prices, weights and measures, and competition. Nonresident merchants, as a result of these new laws, were prohibited from doing business in the seaport. These rules were expanded in 1657, when Stuyvesant required anyone wishing to engage in "trade or commerce" in Manhattan to obtain "burgher right." Counted among the artisans and tradesmen serving the residents at this time were several tanners, ten bakers, twelve butchers, a number of brewers, half a dozen grocers, a glazier, and three silversmiths. The common laborer, so crucial to a growing City, seems to have been in short supply. Company attempts to recruit workers were unsuccessful because other opportunities in the New World dissuaded them from taking or remaining in menial jobs. Nevertheless, ordinances were passed that regulated working hours and salaries for those who depended on ordinary labor. Another source of labor was available after 1646, when the first shipload of slaves arrived. Last, but certainly not least for traders, Stuyvesant was responsible for creating a more regularized monetary system, replacing the diverse wampum/beaver/gold/silver/trust system which had hindered commercial arrangements until his administration.

By the middle years of the seventeenth century the outlines for a more sophisticated and urbane society were beginning to emerge in New Amsterdam, but such a world could hardly be uncritically welcomed by the struggling municipality to which diversity meant danger. To the already present babble of tongues and blend of races, a new element was added in September 1654. Asser Levy led a group of forty-three Jews into the City. Dominie Johannes Megapolensis, representing the power of the established Dutch Reformed Church, tried to have them expelled because, like Stuyvesant, he held the bigoted belief that "the obstinate and immovable" Jews would only bring confusion to New Amsterdam. But since the company wanted the Jews to stay and augment the population, protests were of no avail. The Jewish community celebrated Rosh Hashanah in secret in September 1654, and within two years they had been granted permission to have their own burial ground, a mile outside the defensive wall; part of that plot still remains in Chatham Square and is the oldest existing cemetery on Manhattan Island. It took three years before permission was granted for Jews to buy land, but soon they were even permitted to join the Rattle Watch as good citizens. Levy's group joined the numbers of Puritans, Lutherans, Catholics, and Quakers who worshipped their God in the privacy of their homes, for no denomination beside the Dutch Reformed was yet permitted its own public place of worship. The official church even expanded its authority beyond the East River to Flatbush in 1655, after the settlers there found that attendance at Sunday services in Manhattan was impossible. The Governor worked out an arrangement whereby the Flatbush community obtained their own pastor but only on the condition that he preach on Sunday afternoons at Stuyvesant's farm as well. The personal chapel that Stuyvesant constructed stood on the site of St. Mark's Church, where the bones of "Old Silver Nails" now rest.

The single most infamous example of Stuyvesant's personal bigotry and distrust of nonconformists was his feud with the Quakers. These inoffensive but highly principled people were found not only among the population of New Amsterdam, but in large numbers in Long Island villages as well. In the fall of 1657, a twenty-three-year-old Quaker, newly arrived from England, was arrested for preaching his gospel in Hempstead and sentenced to a public whipping, after which he was confined to his cell without food, and even hung by his thumbs until the Governor's own sister intervened. Robert Hodgson was then exiled to a more permissive Rhode Island. But Stuyvesant's troubles with the Quakers were not yet over, for in direct violation of his prohibition, the John Bowne family in Flushing had held services. The Governor's decision to banish them precipitated one of the earliest struggles for religious liberty in America. Claiming that they had been guaranteed freedom of religion in their town charter (1645), both the Dutch and English residents of Flushing united in protest when one Henry Townsend was fined and imprisoned for his denunciation of the Governor's edict. The citizens refused to persecute Quakers or to prosecute one of their own because in their town they upheld liberty of conscience and the motto, "Let every man stand or fall on his own." When the Flushing sheriff delivered the Remonstrance to Stuyvesant, the enraged Governor dismissed him as *schout* and ultimately banished the unrepentant man. Stuyvesant, not one to forgive opposition, in 1663 returned John Bowne to Holland only to be mortified once again when a letter from the company directed that he "shut his eyes" to the offensive worship.

Although the Governor's authority was absolute in theory, there were many areas in which compromise was obvious during Stuyvesant's reign. In the realm of foreign policy, however, there was no sharing of authority, for dangers threatened the small colony on all fronts. Sandwiched between two groups of English colonies, there was constant tension in regard to the boundary lines. Moreover, Swedes had settled on the Delaware in territory claimed by the Dutch. Yet the Governor, for all his emotional nature, showed a vast delicacy in his dealings with his neighbors. He realized that his decisions were controlling, for he received precious little help from the West India Company; he was instructed to live as peacefully as possible with everyone. During the Anglo-Dutch War of 1653–54 only his adroit diplomacy and the reluctance of Massachusetts to go to war had spared New Netherlands. In 1655, however, the loyal Governor saw an opportunity to expand his domain and put an end to one of his problems. He conceived and led a sudden expedition against New Sweden on the Delaware and captured Fort Christina on September 25, after a siege of ten days. But even as the surrender took place, the mind of Stuyvesant had to be in New Amsterdam, for during the siege he had received word that the Indians, for the first time in his tenure, had taken to the warpath.

Just as New Netherlands had the bad fortune to lie between English colonies, so too it separated Indian confederations whose enmity spanned centuries. In September, while the Governor was off conquering New Sweden, hundreds of Hudson Valley braves from at least three tribes appeared in New Amsterdam on their way to attack their enemies, the Canarsies, on Long Island. Many helped themselves to edibles from the *bouweries* along the shore and in the process a farmer named Hendrick Van Dyck shot and killed a squaw who was stealing peaches from his orchard. By the morning of September 15, hundreds of angry Indians roamed Manhattan and were convinced to withdraw only by the narrowest of margins. New Amsterdam's luck turned into tragedy on Staten Island, however, and for three days the angry Indians ravaged that area. Stuyvesant returned from the Delaware to discover that the "Peach War" had cost at least 40 deaths, led to the captivity of 100 women and children, and caused the destruction of 28 farms. The financial cost was put at 200,000 guilders. Not for two years were all the captives returned by the Indians and then only after the Governor had supplied a powder and lead ransom. Although Stuyvesant was not present when the war began, he showed great strength by refusing to wage a retaliatory campaign. To prevent further bloodshed, he issued a proclamation forbidding further settlement of the Bronx in order to placate the tribes to his north. Not until all of the captives were returned did the Governor permit new settlement in northern Manhattan. In 1658, he allowed a contingent of families led by Hendrick de Forest to move into that area; those settlers named their town New Haarlem to honor their home area.

In retrospect, the late 1650s can best be seen as a time of peace and contentment for the Dutch City. As the Indian menace receded, social life became quite lively and picnics and fishing parties along the edge of the Fresh Water Pond once again took place. Within the town, dancing, bowls on the green, or "pulling the goose" amused the young, while gossip was enjoyed by all. There were more slaves than ever to do the hard labor, though after 1658, no one could whip his slave without specific permission from the officials. Children, when they were not attending the Latin school established in 1652, had a choice of listening to exotic tales of Africa, or playing the games of old Holland. New Amsterdam loved holidays as well and had celebrated the colony's first Thanksgiving Day in August 1654, when news came of the cessation of hostilities with England. The City loved all its holidays, however, and the Christmas season was both a solemn and joyous time. One of the grandest legacies of the Dutch era is the "Sinter Klaus" figure, much modified by modern America, who distributed presents to small children on St. Nicholas' Day. The now defunct custom of making New Year's calls was also a Dutch practice, and New Amsterdam's well-attired young women sat in front parlors to greet amorous young men. May Day was so enthusiastically celebrated that, after 1655, erecting Maypoles was prohibited and liquor sales were limited. The edict did little good, for New Amsterdam was a hard-drinking town and the social supremacy of the tavern "was contested only by the church, whose influence did not reach equally to all classes of people." Licensed taverns made up the single largest contingent of shops, and illegal grog was of course easily available to the enterprising searcher. In 1657, the reconstruction of major roads began with Stone Street, and by the last years of Stuyvesant's rule the most frequented avenues were all paved. Paved streets alleviated dusty conditions but raised the issue of how the town should deal with speeders. Incidentally, given Stuyvesant's character, it was not surprising that seven streets were named after members of his family. The Governor even gave up his residence within the fort and reestablished himself at a mansion named Whitehall, a name which still identifies a downtown Manhattan street. By 1660, the City had 342 homes, a population somewhat over 1,500, and presented an overwhelming Dutch impression to the ships that regularly entered its busy harbor.

But the essential fact of New Amsterdam's weakness in relation to the growing number of Englishmen in the New World could not be denied. Despite all the hopes and efforts of the company and the States General, the town's population grew too slowly. Hundreds of Englishmen lived within the boundaries of New Netherland, in Connecticut, Westchester, and Long Island. In 1650, Stuyvesant had negotiated a boundary settlement for the latter territory on a line running north and south through Oyster Bay, but its provisions had been largely ignored. New England Colonial patents overlapped Dutch lands everywhere and boundary disputes were an inevitable part of the Governor's agenda. Stuyvesant tried desperately to maintain good relations with his neighbors and signed a trade agreement with Virginia in 1660, only to have it annulled by Parliament. The only real protection he could conceive of was to physically possess the land, and so in 1661 he issued charters to the towns of New Utrecht and Rust Drop (Jamaica). The Dutch remained, however, little more than a third of the population of Long Island. Additional factors which caused friction with the English were the Dutch trading monopoly with the Iroquois and the Mohawks, and the high import-export taxes levied at the port of New Amsterdam. The Governor, by strenuous efforts, might maintain his colony, but in his heart he must have realized that its future depended on events far beyond his control.

The heart of the matter was that New Amsterdam was only a pawn in the great commercial rivalry between England and Holland which dominated the last half of the seventeenth century. The City was of necessity involved in such conflicts because all seamen now recognized that it occupied the most critical port area on the eastern coast of North America. Whatever Stuyvesant's other failings might have been, a strategic myopia was not among them, and he insistently implored the company to send more supplies and soldiers for his use. Instead of aid, the company sent only encouraging letters and the news that its monopoly charter privileges had once again been confirmed by action of the States General on January 23, 1664. Rather foolishly, the

Dutch tempted fate by asking the British Parliament to confirm the Hartford Treaty establishing a Long Island boundary which Stuyvesant had negotiated fourteen years ago. Two hundred soldiers were ultimately dispatched to the colony but, with Connecticut encroaching into Long Island and with a burgher population less than anxious to take arms in its own defense, the prognosis was not favorable. Stuyvesant soon learned as well that on March 22, 1664, King Charles II of England had granted to his brother James, Duke of York and Albany, a vast tract of land consisting of "all of Maine between the Croix and Kennebec rivers and from the coast to the Saint Lawrence, all islands between Cape Cod and the Narrows, and all land from the western boundary of Connecticut to the eastern shore of Delaware Bay." The gift included the power to govern, subject only to the reservation that judicial appeals might be taken to the Crown.

James acted quickly, and dispatched a task force of four frigates under Colonel Richard Nicolls to capture New Netherland. Learning of the approach of the English fleet, Stuyvesant and his council ordered new defenses and fortifications which were constructed in late June and early July 1664. James' fleet did not arrive off Gravesend until August 26, but when it did, the English settlers of eastern Long Island proved willing to furnish both information and volunteers. To oppose the English, Stuyvesant had only four hundred soldiers and an inflexible determination to perform his sworn duty. On September 1, when Colonel Nicolls and Governor Winthrop demanded his surrender on rather generous terms, the old war-horse refused to even show the conditions to his burghers. Although outgunned and outnumbered, Stuyvesant was determined to hold on and proposed on September 2, that both sides do nothing until they received orders from Europe. On September 4, Stuyvesant defiantly tore up yet another surrender demand but his ability to even contemplate resistance was rapidly fading. The letter was pasted together and on September 5, ninety-three leading citizens and members of the council asked that he surrender in order to spare the City "absolute ruin and destruction"; among the signatures proud "Old Silver Nails" found the name of his own son.

Although the Governor had sworn that he "would rather be carried to my grave" than surrender, there were simply no options left. On September 8, 1664, a treaty of twenty-three articles was signed at his farm and without the firing of a shot, and even before a formal declaration of war between Holland and England, New Amsterdam had fallen. Under the generous terms Nicolls granted, the Dutch were allowed freedom of religion as well as property and inheritance rights. Direct trade with Holland was permitted for another six months, but in reality continued until 1668. In addition, Dutch municipal officials would stay in office for a year until arrangements more suitable to Duke James could be made. On October 20, after all of the citizens of the City, Stuyvesant among them, agreed to take the oath of allegiance to the British Crown, the conquest was complete. In the interim, Nicoll's forces had completed their mission by gaining control of all the outlying Dutch garrisons. Thus it was that the report that the West India Company submitted to the States General on October 24, was more correct than it could know. The English had taken "the whole of New Netherland" and "immediately called the same by the name of York." New Amsterdam was no more and the first scene in the drama of New York City was over.

* * * * *

The first forty years of New York's existence had been exciting ones. Many of the patterns that the City was to follow in later years were established by the few but enterprising Dutch. Characteristics which were to be associated with New York in the future—cosmopolitanism, heterogeniety, materialism, specialization, and even impersonality—clearly manifested themselves during these early decades. The City had even developed a modicum of sophistication and urbanity, qualities not ordinarily found in a young, raw society. Of course Boston, the heart of New England, possessed these traits as well and later in the century, Philadelphia equaled, and in several ways surpassed, the future mighty metropolis on the Hudson. But New York's power would not, and could not, be denied. As for the Dutch, they remain a minor ethnic group in a melting pot that was soon to accommodate peoples from every corner of the globe. New Yorkers today owe a debt of gratitude to these courageous people, for they bequeathed a powerful and enduring heritage—a legacy of robust commercialism, basic tolerance, and an immense zest for life, qualities that exemplify the reality of the modern Empire City.

BRIEF BIBLIOGRAPHY

Bachman, Van Cleaf. *Peltries or Plantations: The Economic Policies of the Dutch West India Company in New Netherland, 1623–1639.* Baltimore, 1969.

Boxer, C. R. *The Dutch Seaborne Empire, 1600–1800.* New York, 1965.*

Bridenbaugh, Carl. *Cities in the Wilderness: The First Century of Urban Life in America, 1625–1742.* New York, 1938.*

Condon, Thomas J. *New York Beginnings: The Commercial Origins of New Netherland.* New York, 1968.

Goodwin, Maude W. *The Dutch and English on the Hudson.* New Haven, 1920.

Innes, John H. *New Amsterdam and Its People.* New York, 1937.

Jameson, J. Franklin, ed. *Narratives of New Netherlands. 1609–1664.* New York, 1909.

Kammen, Michael. *Colonial New York: A History.* New York, 1975.

Raesly, Ellis L. *Portrait of New Netherland.* New York, 1945.

Van der Zee, Henri and Barbara. *A Sweet and Alien Land: The Story of Dutch New York.* New York, 1978.

Van Rensselaer, Marianne. *History of the City of New York in the Seventeenth Century.* Vol. I. New York, 1909.

Weslager, C. A. *Dutch Explorers, Traders and Settlers.* Philadelphia, 1961.

*Paperback

II

English Town to American City

THE NEXT SEGMENT of New York's history was to last for a century, and would end as it began, with the clash of arms. The seizure of New Amsterdam by the private fleet of James, Duke of York, was only a prelude to the Second Anglo-Dutch War of 1665–67. In that conflict the Dutch embarrassed Charles II and the royal Navy by defeating it at Lowestoft in 1665, and, after two years of further conflict, culminated their exploits by raiding the docks of London itself. The battles drained the treasuries of both nations, however, and the two countries were relatively content with the peace signed at Breda on July 10, 1667. Each party was left with the "places, cities, and forts" taken during the war, but the Dutch considered this a victory because it maintained their dominant position in the East Indies and forced the English to recognize their possession of Surinam. But the seizure of New Amsterdam was confirmed and its career as New York began. The war itself had no direct effect on Manhattan, now ruled by Richard Nicolls on behalf of his liege lord Duke James. Nicolls was both popular and efficient and, in time, even the cantankerous Stuyvesant became his friend. He had the good sense not to mandate a completely new set of regulations; indeed he kept on most of the local officials, but slowly English ways of administration and law were imposed. The City was now New York, and a sense of stability as well as an awareness of its role in the imperial system would permeate the town for the next century. Time would prove that rule from across the ocean, be it English or Dutch, was an unworkable ideal and in the end New York would join with the other colonies in waging a Revolution against an island which had built the world's greatest Empire. These pages trace New York's growth and development until it became part of America's struggle for independence. In that process, the City on the Hudson would obtain the experience and self-confidence which would soon make it the premier urban center of the United States.

* * * * *

The City that Nicolls conquered in 1664 was three quarters Dutch, but the population proved quite adaptable to the change of rule. It was not simply that Anglican services, as of September 1664, were held in public, but rather that the company employees who had accepted the autocratic rule of Stuyvesant now saw unexpected personal opportunity as the primary result of English rule. It is significant that not a single Dutch resident took advantage of the free passage home offered by Nicolls; only the garrison of ineffective Fort Amsterdam had to be repatriated. A spasm of construction work led to new homes, churches, and shops, and in February 1665, the town officials named their successors according to the local practice during the last Dutch years. Probably the most significant change was the issuance by Governor Nicolls of the Duke's Laws on March 1, 1665. As compiled by Mathias Nicolls, these laws consisted of civil and criminal codes based on New England models, arranged for the election of overseers and a constable in each town within the colony, set up a provincial organization of the courts and the militia, and assured freedom of conscience for all. Approved on March 11, 1665, by a meeting at Hempstead of thirty-four delegates from seventeen towns, these articles became the law of the colony. New Netherlands had never had a real legislature, and even though the pious platitudes of the Duke's Laws could be set aside by gubernatorial edict, the experience of even limited self-rule was heady. The Governor maintained his privilege of naming officials, however, and in June 1665, he appointed Thomas Willett to serve as New York's first Mayor. Official English customs and language thus superseded the Dutch heritage, though in actual practice Nicolls maintained in office and drew on the expertise of such powerful burghers as Nicolas Bayard, Jacob Kip, and Johannes de Peyster. In essence he tolerated the domination of local affairs by the wealthy Dutch oligarchy, but forced them to govern by English rules.

Such enlightened tolerance is not to suggest that the Governor did not establish firm control of his colony. Nicolls confiscated the farms and property of the West India Company on the grounds that its absentee directors had "inflicted all sorts of injuries on His Majesty's subjects." Again, during the Second Anglo-Dutch War he confiscated all the property of Dutch owners who had not yet taken the oath of allegiance. At first, Nicolls' actions did not seem to bother the citizens: after all, Thomas Willet, the first appointed Mayor of the City, was an honest man and aldermen chosen by the Governor were outstanding and upright men. Nicolls' need to raise revenues for his duke soon fostered a change in the attitude of the Dutch. They were not alone, however, for New Englanders who migrated to Long Island in search of better land were angered by the high patent charges ordered by James. They resented, as well, the duke's arbitrary power to appoint magistrates over them.

Perhaps the greatest single difficulty that the British administrators encountered was their inability to understand Dutch pride. In March 1668, when Francis Lovelace succeeded Nicolls as Governor, he expressed shock that the people of New York, though drawn from many ethnic groups, had nonetheless the "breeding of courts." Though Manhattan's society was far from democratic, its Dutch leadership was united in opposition to patronizing attitudes by their new English masters. In many ways they lived in greater luxury than their conquerors and thus social as well as political tensions existed.

Such Dutch prominence must have irritated Lovelace beyond measure, for he saw the colony as a means to make his fortune. Unlike Nicolls, who was a soldier and one of the few governors who left poorer than when they arrived, Lovelace had come to New York with two brothers who shared his ravenous desire for wealth. He found it immediately expedient, however, to continue his predecessor's conciliatory policy and the City, which was the heart of the province, continued to flourish. Expansion of settled territory seemed to be the major priority, and in May 1668, John Arcer was given permission to settle families in the area of the

Bronx which by 1673 became the town of Fordham. For the sixth and last time, lands were purchased from the Indians and their latent threat now vanished. Moreover, the first ferry between the Jersey shore and the island of Manhattan began operations. But the most important permanent acquisition of Lovelace's administration was securing the Duke of York's title to Staten Island, an area much disputed between his colony and New Jersey. In 1665, Nicolls had reaffirmed James' claim to the land by naming it Richmond, after a bastard son of the not always pious duke. In 1670, an agreement was concluded between the two provinces which allowed New York to retain title over all the islands in the harbor which could be cicumnavigated in a twenty-four-hour period. In April, Captain Charles Billop accomplished the tricky task of circumnavigation and saved Staten Island for the future City. Billop was rewarded with a vast manor centered on present-day Tottenville, which he named *Bentley* in honor of his sturdy vessel. On April 13, a glowing Lovelace took official possession of the island for his province and by 1700 at least two hundred families had settled in the rolling hills where large apartment house complexes rise today.

Lovelace's tenure brought other tangible proofs of progress as well. A wagon road was completed to Harlem, and a ferry connection to the remote Bronx was established. The Lutheran congregations so long oppressed by Stuyvesant were allowed to open a church in the house of Cornelius Pluvier (1671), while the commercial community was encouraged to expand its informal Merchants Exchange. Trade remained the key of City life and ships constantly were docking and sailing from the harbor. Early in 1672, however, an oceangoing vessel brought the unwelcome news that the temporary alliance between Holland and England had been shattered and that the old adversaries were once again at war. In July, therefore, Lovelace ordered construction of new defense works and established postal service between New York and Massachusetts. He had no wish to share the inglorious end of Stuyvesant and sought to assure quick access to reinforcements from New England.

Yet despite the preparations, Lovelace's New York was still surprised when a Dutch fleet commanded by Cornelius Evertsen suddenly appeared in New York Harbor on August 8, 1673. The Governor was not even in the City and his deputy, Captain John

Manning, had been so lax that Dutch sympathizers had been able to spike his best cannon. Once again the greatest prize in the New World was to change hands, for Manhattan could not be defended. The Dutch burghers declared their neutrality, reinforcements from Long Island amounted to only a dozen men, and the remaining guns of the fort were rusted. At the cost of only a single English death, Captain Anthony Colve, leader of the Dutch landing force, took possession of Manhattan; on August 12, he was designated Governor-General. The rest of the province was reoccupied, Dutch officials were appointed, and the province and City of New York was renamed New Orange. While the Dutch destroyed old Fort Amsterdam and built new defenses at the tip of Manhattan, Europe once again settled the fate of New York. Colve was to have little time to prove his talents, for it was during European peace conferences that the future of New Orange was decided. The insignificant City counted for little within the conflicting goals of Holland, England, and France; in the complex negotiations the territorial claims of the West India Company were totally ignored. By the terms of the Treaty of Westminster on February 9, 1674, the English were again confirmed in their possession and the Dutch gave up forever their claims to North America. Charles II generously reconfirmed his brother's grant on July 9, 1674, but James, a bit peevish at the colony's lack of preparation, recalled Lovelace, after arranging for that avaricious yet inept man to forfeit his English lands. He now sent out to New York an experienced military man to serve as his Governor. On November 10, 1674, after a hiatus of fifteen months, James' ducal flag once again flew over the City which so far had brought him little return, though he hoped for better performance in the future.

New York's new governor, Major Edmund Andros, was an honest but unlucky bureaucrat. After reissuing the Duke's Laws, he divided up official appointments between Englishmen, Dutch, and other ethnic groups, reorganized the ineffective militia, and set his goal on increasing the trade of the City. Andros recommended as well that an elected provincial assembly be created, but the duke's adamant refusal to even consider such an innovation quickly brought the initiative to an end. The decision did cause some dissatisfaction, particularly among the well-to-do merchants of the town and, for a time, they declined to pay import duties in protest. In other spheres, however, Andros was able to report substantial gains. In November 1675, he granted to the City the English equivalent of burgher right, and fostered new construction that included a Lutheran church (1676), an insane asylum (1677), better wells, and the first night lamps (1679). More important was the completion by 1676, of a Great Dock at the foot of Whitehall Street, a structure which served the port until 1750. Even more crucial was Andros' decision to grant a bolting concession to a few major merchants in the hope that they could increase both the production and demand for fine Dutch flour. In the long run this was a wise policy but it led to no immediate revenue gains and James was impatient to see results. On January 7, 1680, the Bolting Act formally mandated that all the grain for export from the New York area should be sent to the City for grinding, processing, and packing. Moreover, the Governor decreed that the port would be the sole port of entry for the province. The result was a sudden spurt in prices, ship clearances, and revenues, particularly among the favored merchants. Those who were not part of the monopoly charged Andros with favoritism, profiteering with the Dutch, and official corruption. By 1681, he was forced to return home where he won both exoneration and a knighthood. His economic legacy was the first real boom in New York's history; the flour monopoly was primarily responsible for a tripling of the City's wealth and population before the end of the century. It was the start of a long list of firsts that the metropolis would carve into American history.

The bolting monopoly revenues benefited the City's merchant elite far more than they enriched James, however, and were one factor which convinced the duke that he must grant his colony more self-government if he hoped to turn a profit. Both Andros and William Penn advised James that an assembly might produce both cooperation and revenues and the duke reluctantly decided to follow their counsel. On January 27, 1683, James named Thomas Dongan as his new Governor and furnished him with instructions to create an elected assembly and to revise the tax structure of his province. When Dongan arrived in New York in the fall, he authorized the first provincial elections in which all freeholders were entitled to vote. On October 27, the first General Assembly, an elected body of seventeen men from ten counties with the power to pass laws and raise revenues, subject always to Governor Dongan's approval, convened in Manhattan. Within three days the representatives produced a Charter of Liberties and Privileges calling for cooperation between the "Governor, Council, and the people" and asserting their rights to self-government, self-taxation, freedom of worship, trial by jury, and other privileges enjoyed by Englishmen. The tone of the charter presaged the far more strident Revolutionary voice of future English colonists. James at first gave his consent to the charter but later, after his accession to the throne and the transformation of New York into a royal colony, he declared it abrogated.

Dongan proved to be both a strong and a skillful executive. There had been some initial distrust of him since, as a Catholic, he had arrived with several Jesuit priests who presided over the first public masses in New York. The basically tolerant attitude of New York rapidly overcame that uneasiness, however, especially since the community leaders recognized the vast privileges Dongan brought. The new Governor deftly wooed the merchants by confirming both New York's bolting monopoly and sole port of entry privilege; he added to these an exclusive right of transport on the Hudson. New York served as the provincial capital and in December was granted a new municipal charter by the canny Governor. It provided for the division of the City into six wards (North, South, East, West, Dock, and Harlem), an elected alderman and assistant for each ward, and an appointed Mayor and Recorder. These fourteen officials would constitute a Common Council, which was empowered to enact ordinances for the City in accordance with the statutes of England. In addition to the Mayor and Recorder, most of the other municipal officials were also appointed by the Governor. Annual ward elections and a local court system were features of a second Dongan Charter which became operative on April 27, 1686. The Governor and the merchant class who filled City positions soon settled down into a comfortable working relationship. The legal basis for real estate titles and wharfage rights was settled amicably and long years of cooperation and prosperity seemed secure. Yet despite all these real improvements, the City was to revolt in 1688, and zestfully join in the Glorious Revolution.

The origin of that sea change in English and American life was the sudden death of Protestant King Charles II on February 6, 1685, and the accession of his Catholic brother as James II. James' own imperious nature as well as the advice of his Lords of

Trade convinced him that the Crown must exert greater authority over all the colonies. In New York, therefore, he canceled the Charter of Liberties and recalled Dongan. He ordered Andros out of retirement and appointed him to rule as Governor over a consolidated provincial unit composed of New York, New Jersey, and all of New England. This Dominion of New England was envisioned as a solid bulwark against the French and as an effective means of forcing all the colonies to adhere to imperial trade regulations. Merchants throughout America resented James' actions, but it is at least arguable that New York suffered more than other cities since law enforcement threatened the trade revival which was underway. Thus, like Massachusetts and Connecticut which had lost their charter rights, the City was anxious to see "tyranny" rejected.

Once again it was politics in the Old World that stimulated events in the New. The gentlemen of England were as angered at James' religious excesses and political insensitivity as were his Colonial subjects, and, they in 1688, carried out the Glorious Revolution which expelled him and his offspring from Britain. Almost as swiftly, Governor Andros found himself imprisoned in Boston by mid-April of 1689. His deputy in New York, a tactless martinet named Francis Nicholson, was thus left without orders or guidance. A foolish remark by Nicholson made some merchants fear that he might burn down the City rather than surrender; rumors began to spread that he would even deliver the port over to the hands of Catholic France. A surge of popular anger erupted, a Committee of Public Safety was selected, and a well-to-do merchant named Jacob Leisler was prevailed upon to take charge of the militia. Leisler had earlier made something of an instant reputation for himself by refusing to pay duties on a cargo of wine on the grounds that the collector of the port was a papist. He thus emerged as a symbolic champion of freedom against autocracy, Protestantism against Catholicism, the Dutch against the English and, perhaps most importantly, the popular hero against "grandees." On the night of May 31, 1689, Leisler's militia seized control of the City and soon Nicholson, former Governor Dongan, and the few priests in New York, were expelled. Acting in the name of the people, Leisler proclaimed the reign of William and Mary, abrogated the flour monopoly, and ruled as virtual dictator. Immediately, he granted the City its only opportunity during the Colonial period to choose its chief magistrate, and on October 14, Peter Delanoy, a man from Haarlem, became New York's first elected Mayor.

There was no legal basis to Leisler's regime although the harried merchant always believed he had acted as an instrument of the popular will. In terms of constitutional authority, however, Leisler based his authority to rule on letters that had arrived from England in December 1689, addressed to Nicholson or to "such other person [who] for the time being may be in authority." He naturally interpreted this to mean himself. He pledged his loyalty to William and Mary, but embarked upon a ruthless policy of throwing into prison all who opposed him. The aristocratic families of New York bitterly resented Leisler's actions and their envoys, including Nicholson, soon appeared before William and Mary to denounce this "son of the people." The new monarchs, influenced by these reports, appointed Colonel William Sloughter to replace Leisler as Governor. Sloughter's lieutenant, Richard Ingoldsby, arrived in the City ahead of the new Governor but with no official documents to prove his legitimacy. An increasingly paranoid Leisler thus refused to transfer authority and subsequently there occurred clashes between his militia and Ingoldsby's troops. Sloughter's arrival in March of 1691 finally put an end to the farce and Leisler dutifully surrendered the City to its legitimate Governor. His acquiescence came too late, however, for his reign had offended both English officialdom and the ruling class of New York. Leisler was accused of treason, arrested, and tried before a specially commissioned court of oyer and terminer; both he and his son-in-law, Jacob Milbourne, were condemned to death. Despite impassioned pleas that King William show mercy, both men were hung at the Manhattan end of today's Brooklyn Bridge on May 16, 1691.

The execution of Leisler was interpreted by ordinary New Yorkers as a vengeful act by the elite on a man who served the people; it was nothing less than judicial murder. By 1694, after Leisler's supporters convinced Parliament that a great wrong had been committed, his property and good name were restored to his heirs. But the memory of the class struggle that his rebellion signified, continued to have a political impact across the next half century. The Leislerian legacy was an expanded franchise, although property requirements kept the very poor from voting, which represented a continuing threat to merchant supremacy. So implacable were the passions aroused that Sloughter felt compelled to call a representative assembly which met in a tavern on Pearl Street on April 9, 1691; the Governor even reissued the Charter of Liberties after Leisler's execution. The confusion of authority between the king, ethnic groups, and wealth was compounded when Sloughter died suddenly in June 1691, after a drinking bout. With the Treasury depleted, classes in conflict, and Europe once again at war, New York faced at best an uncertain future. In this situation, the City turned once more to a verity that its entire population shared—it was good to make money.

In the spring of 1692, another royal Governor arrived in New York. Colonel Benjamin Fletcher was an Episcopalian who established the Anglican Church as the official religion and built the first Trinity Church with the donations of rich New Yorkers. Like many of his predecessors, he hoped to discover his fortune in New York and so made common cause with rich merchants whether they were English or Dutch. The Bolting Act had been repealed and there now was a representative assembly, two conditions which many had earlier expected would cause the City's ruin; but now neither condition disturbed the elite's prosperity. Fletcher, citing the passage by Parliament of further Navigation Acts regulating trade, made it his business to tightly control the harbor and to collect fees from the legitimate ships and even more exorbitant ones from pirates. In return for substantial bribes, he permitted buccaneers to enjoy the safety of the port for relaxation and for the repair of their vessels. Merchants, with the tacit cooperation of Fletcher, were encouraged to engage in smuggling to that haven for all pirates, Madagascar; he claimed that wartime conditions justified such laxity. Among the many legitimate traders who cooperated with the venal Governor was a certain William Kidd, whose free-booting activities led to his subsequent hanging in 1701. Many still believe that a mythical treasure from Kidd's pirating will one day be found on some sandy beach, perhaps Gardiners Island, near the City. Land grants were yet another avenue of wealth for a Governor who was famed for lining his own pockets, though in the process he enhanced the prosperity of New York. New brick mansions soon filled the area below Wall Street and oil lamps made their first appearance on New York streets in 1697, Fletcher's last full year as Governor. Due to complaints from the Leislerians, combined with the incontestable fact that New York was not producing enough royal revenues, Fletcher was replaced early in 1698.

Richard Coote, the Earl of Bellamont, ruled New York from 1698 to 1701, and on balance, was not a bad Governor. He realized that he owed a debt to the Leislerians, and filled his administration with ethnic Dutchmen. Moreover, he attempted to provide more public services by building the King's Bridge to the Bronx, and ordering yet another effort to clean the streets. Construction began on a second City Hall at Wall and Nassau streets, the site of the Subtreasury in modern New York. The ceremonial opening of Trinity Church under Rector William Vesey made New Yorkers proud regardless of their religion, since without taxation it could not have been built. Even in such arcane areas as the provisioning of troops, the Earl of Bellamont mediated with various groups to reach acceptable and nondivisive accommodations. Coote's sudden death in 1701 led to the advent of Edwin Hyde (Lord Cornbury) a man of a totally different persuasion. As Governor of both New York and New Jersey until 1708, Hyde established a level of corruption and arrogant maladministration over the 4,500 New Yorkers that has never been equaled. A transvestite and a thief, Hyde owed his position to the fact that he was a nephew of Queen Anne. He was probably not responsible for the visitation of yellow fever which swept the town in 1702, the first of many such plagues, but New Yorkers were willing to blame everything else upon him within a few years. In one case, he simply put into his own pockets the money that the assembly had appropriated to renovate the Narrows defenses. So flagrant were his personal excesses that New Yorkers of every political faction united to send to the queen a formal listing of their grievances and Cornbury was removed in disgrace.

The tenure of Lord John Lovelace and his successors as New York Governor up to the time of the American Revolution, was made far more difficult because, after 1708, the assembly maintained its right to vote annual appropriations for the colony and its officials. Henceforth, all governors would of necessity be constrained in their actions, because they realized that their salary payments depended upon preserving good relations with the legislature. In Manhattan, Abraham de Peyster was named City treasurer, a post he would hold for the next 46 years, and under his prudent guidance municipal finances were regularized and showed steady improvement. Lovelace, who died in 1709, was not Governor long enough to have problems but the salary issue clearly emerged during the tenure of Major General Robert Hunter who arrived to take his post in 1710. Hunter is almost always accorded the palm as the "best" Colonial Governor, and he did preside over improvements in the municipality's finances, ferry services, and street construction. A large influx of refugees from the German Palatine swelled the City population to almost 7,000 during his tenure. Yet despite his popularity, for years Hunter went without his salary in protest against the assembly's control of the Governor's purse. He insisted that long-term assignments of money be appropriated and it was not until he left that an admiring assembly settled his personal accounts.

The Hunter years also saw the first significant racial troubles in New York, an issue which was to cause agony in future centuries. The City included among its population not only free blacks, but a large number of Angolan-born slaves who occupied the lowest strata of society. Some accounts suggest that as much as a fifth of the City was black and the general consensus was that far too much freedom was allowed them to congregate and perhaps plot insurrection. In early April 1712, a series of unexplained fires focused public attention and subsequent madness upon the black minority and for two weeks virtual terror reigned. That some kind of organized violence was planned is clear, for ten whites died before order was restored. Several blacks fled the City, others committed suicide, and nineteen more were executed by order of Governor Hunter. The details remain sketchy and unclear, but the mania first released in 1712, was to reappear often later on in the City's history.

Most of the men sent to govern New York after Hunter were inexperienced, ill-informed, greedy, and unsuited to the office they held. Yet none could deter the growth of wealth and power in the great marketplace at the mouth of the Hudson. Hunter's successor was William Burnet (1720–28) whose major policy initiative was an attempt to regularize the fur trade by negotiating direct contracts with the Indians. This statesmanlike program was later to be achieved by Sir William Johnson, but in the 1720s it only alienated the New York fur aristocracy. They defeated him in the assembly and isolated him from the commercial wealth that before the end of the decade enabled less populous New York to outstrip the exports of Boston or Philadelphia. A notable event of Burnet's tenure occurred on November 1, 1725, when New York's first newspaper, William Bradford's *Weekly Gazette,* made its appearance. Colonel John Montgomerie, a genial Scottish crook, succeeded Burnet in the spring of 1728, and reigned over New York for the subsequent three years. A friend of King George II, Montgomerie allied himself with the merchants against the popular party led by Judge Louis Morris. He solidified City revenues through the use of quit rents and license fees and is most remembered today as the Governor who granted the municipality a charter which lasted for a century. That document of February 11, 1731 cost the burghers a pretty bribe, but extended the boundaries of the City and expanded the lawmaking powers of its council. Probably even more concessions would have been obtained from Montgomerie for cash had not he and 500 other New Yorkers been victims of a smallpox outbreak which devastated the City in the summer of 1731.

Rip Van Dam, head of the council and a shipowner with 15 children, administered New York until a replacement for Montgomerie arrived some 13 months later. William Cosby was typical of the officials who hoped to make a personal fortune out of their public service. He had been appointed Governor of the Leeward Islands and actually was en route there when he received word of the far more lucrative opening in New York, a position he obtained in January 1732. He arrived in the City in August, was given an assembly gift of £1,000, and immediately alienated much of his potential support by claiming that Van Dam owed him half the salary he had received as Cosby's gubernatorial stand-in. The new Governor created a Court of Exchequer to hear his claim for the cash and was mortified when that handpicked body refused to grant him a decision. Cosby blamed his humiliation and financial loss on Chief Justice Morris, and on August 21, 1733, removed him for "partiality, delay of justice, and oppression of the people." Morris used his removal as a campaign issue to rebuild the power of the popular Leislerian party. He won election to the assembly while his partisans swept the City aldermanic elections in 1734. The old class rivalries, long thought buried, suddenly reemerged due to Cosby's greed and authoritarianism. The Morrisite faction even founded their own newspaper in November 1733, to promote their version of electoral controversies. The paper was the *Weekly Journal* and its editor was a German immigrant named John Peter Zenger.

During the next year, Zenger's paper delighted in satirizing the pretensions, the power lust, and the avarice of Governor Cosby. The stream of fables and sly wit that appeared in Zenger's paper finally convinced the Governor that harsh repression was in order. On November 2, 1734, copies of the *Journal* were publicly burnt and two weeks later Zenger himself was arrested for libel; he was kept in jail by means of extraordinarily high bail. The charges against Zenger not only stirred New York, but also had reverberations throughout the colonies. The prognosis for Zenger became extremely bleak, however, when Chief Justice James de Lancey, a Cosby ally, disbarred local attorneys who might have defended the printer. When the trial finally began on August 4, 1735, the defense was led by Andrew Hamilton, the most gifted of Pennsylvania's attorneys. The hinge of Zenger's defense was that the facts he had printed about Cosby were true. "It is not the cause of a poor printer, nor of New York alone which you are now trying," Hamilton told the jury. "No! It is the best cause; it is the cause of liberty, both of exposing and opposing arbitrary power by speaking and writing the truth!" Hamilton convinced the jury that Zenger had published only facts and therefore could not be convicted of libel. The jury agreed and Zenger was acquitted. The trial proved that government officials can be freely criticized if the accusations are truthful. Zenger and Hamilton reigned briefly as social lions, but far more important was the spirit of civil disobedience which reigned in New York until the Revolution. Freedom of the press had been vindicated; could other rights of Englishmen now be denied?

In 1737, the population of New York had reached 10,664 and it would continue to grow slowly in the 40 years preceding the Declaration of Independence. Commercial activity remained the prime arena of money-making, but the garment industry as well as the printing and publishing trades had their origins in this period. Fortunes continued to be made in the fur trade and not even a series of wars with France halted the curve of prosperity. Perhaps most importantly, New Yorkers maintained the ability to pay their Governors an annual salary and so kept them on a short rein up to the time of the Revolution. Finally, in 1756, the British government itself conceded that New York's assembly did have the right to vote annual appropriations to officials as well as to supervise provincial expenditures. It was another victory won by New York in defense of the rights of free men.

Significant changes took place in the City's political, social, and cultural history as well. The Montgomerie Charter established the fundamental principles of municipal administration, but while "freemen and freeholders" could vote, they had to pay for the privilege. The municipal government, moreover, granted suffrage grudgingly until the late 1750s, when it finally began to reduce fees. As a result, the percentage of eligible white voters in the City increased from 7 percent in 1731, to barely over 10 percent by 1761. Women and blacks were excluded, as they were everywhere else in Colonial America. In local elections the economic power of the merchant aristocracy usually prevailed, but New York's elections were lively events. On Election Day, the enfranchised citizens in each ward voted for their candidates by a show of hands. These ward elections were supervised by the aldermen who frequently manipulated them to help favored associates. Such political machinations were often criticized by New Yorkers, but the assembly did not see fit to change the electoral procedure until 1771, when it ordered the appointment of special election officers in each ward.

During this period, the Common Council began to accept greater responsibility for pressing questions of urban services. It enacted ordinances concerned with fire and police protection, the regulation of wharves and docks, the operation of public markets, and the improvement of health and sanitary conditions. Its greatest weakness was its inability to tax without the permission of the provincial assembly. This gap in authority caused difficulties and considerable protest, especially since by 1760, New Yorkers were contributing one third of all the colony's taxes although they numbered only one fifth of the total provincial population. Services beneficial to the City's welfare could not be adequately funded and, as in later times, the ultimate pain was borne by the citizenry. Yet, despite these problems, real advances in some public services took place. To protect the City population of 10,000 from imported disease, the council, in 1738, ordered a quarantine on all incoming ships until visited by a City physician. In 1744, it passed a further series of ordinances designed to

improve health and sanitary conditions within the City limits. By
1758, a pesthouse had been constructed on Bedloe's Island, and
demands for a hospital were met on May 28, 1771, when the New
York Hospital, the oldest in the City, was incorporated.

Manhattan was also required to take care of its indigent citizens since the provincial government would not. In 1735, the first
almshouse in New York was opened in what is now City Hall Park.
It was a two-story brick building which housed not only paupers,
but also beggars, tramps, and loafers convicted of vagrancy. The
authorities treated the unfortunates as minimally as common
decency would allow; thus private philanthropy and church charity continued to shoulder the greatest share of this work. The
City's treatment of criminals and prisoners was even worse.
Reflecting the brutal practices common in this period, prisoners
in Manhattan's jail were subjected to all sorts of indignities. Until
October 1, 1759, the basement of the City Hall was used as a jail,
but on that date, a new structure was opened on the Commons;
all prisoners were removed from the jail and incarcerated in the
new building. Despite the new surroundings, medieval conditions continued. The maintenance of law and order was always
difficult as a result of the old problem of sailors on leave in a port
City. In addition, large numbers of soldiers, slaves, and criminals
prowled the streets. Press gangs for the King's Navy, on the
lookout for prospective seamen, sometimes clashed with residents and contributed still further to the disorder. The large black
population in Manhattan also caused anxieties among the citizenry because of suspected violence as exemplified by the so-
called Negro Plot. According to rumors, blacks intended to burn
the City. The resultant hysteria, very much like that of 1712,
lasted this time between May and August 1741, and before it
ended, 13 blacks were burnt at the stake, while 16 were hanged
along with 4 whites. More than 70 blacks and a few whites were
permanently banished from British North America in the wake of
a "conspiracy" which may never have existed.

The need to maintain order in the streets, a matter that concerns all urban centers, rose increasingly to the forefront of
municipal action as the eighteenth century advanced. Gambling,
prostitution, and drunkenness remained the most common
crimes, but robbery, assaults, and murder were not infrequent.
The Common Council established a watch and, technically, all

residents were required to serve on night patrol; each ward elected annually two men to supervise their respective domains. Beginning in 1734, the municipality created a paid standing guard of two squads, but in 1742 it was disbanded and a citizens' watch was reinstated with every able-bodied man required to take his turn. Although this system lasted for twenty years, it was totally inefficient. In 1762, the Common Council reestablished the system of a paid standing force and expanded the system of oil lamp posts on the City's streets.

The most feared danger to every American City was fire, and New York's officials enacted more stringent building regulations, though enforcement proved sporadic and lax. In December 1731, the City's first two fire engines arrived from London and gradually thereafter additional equipment was purchased and distributed among the wards. In 1737, the Common Council approved the creation of volunteer fire-fighting companies and thirty men were selected as the first contingent. Eleven companies served the City by the time of the Revolution and the informal system lasted beyond the Civil War. Closely connected to fire protection was the question of water supply. The many springs and private wells of the seventeenth-century City were clearly inadequate to service a population beyond 10,000, and the municipality had to dig public wells; residents paid the cost of such projects by means of special assessments. Pumps for the wells were provided by the City beginning in 1741, the most celebrated of these being the Tea Water Pump at Chatham and Pear streets. However, the Common Council recognized the need for a more efficient water supply and in 1774, authorized Christopher Colles to draw up a detailed proposal for the creation of a new public water supply system. Colles' plan was approved and the first stage of the system was begun when a reservoir was built on the east side of Broadway. The project was interrupted by the outbreak of the Revolution and the City continued to suffer not only from inadequate water supplies, but also from the many diseases that resulted from contaminated drinking resources.

The fact of the matter was that New York's pretension in the mid-eighteenth century always seemed just a bit beyond its re-sources. It mattered little whether royal governors were named Clinton, Osborn, Delaney, or Hardy; they simply succeeded each other too quickly to master all the problems of the emerging metropolis. The myriad of ferry lines, for example, continued to expand in both the Hudson and East rivers, but their operators often failed to pay fees to the City. Public musical concerts began in the thirties as did the professional theater, but performers had to be brought in from Boston or Great Britain. The almshouse, the pesthouse, and the jails always seemed to be too little, too late. Educational facilities weren't much better and in a City which boasted of its great social mobility, it was nonetheless true that a large majority of the children went uneducated. Even the children of the wealthy minority received inadequate educational training. A few evening schools were established, especially to familiarize apprentices with the three Rs. The Dutch Reformed Church in the City continued to operate the elementary school it had established before the English conquest. Children in all of its classes were instructed in the Dutch language until 1772, when the use of English was finally permitted by the church board. Some religious sects operated charity schools for the poor, and a few wealthy families hired itinerant private tutors, but the bulk of the middle class usually sent their children to private schools or academies set up by individual masters. Probably the single most important educational achievement of this time was the chartering in 1754 of King's College, now Columbia University. This institution obtained its original endowment from public lotteries and was constructed on land donated by Trinity Church. The sixth college in America, the goal of Kings was to "prevent the growth of republican principles" and its charter stipulated that it must be led "forever and all time" by an Anglican president. Its first presidents, Samuel Johnson and Dr. Myles Cooper, indeed did their best to make the college a bastion of conservative thinking, but during the Revolutionary years a number of Patriot leaders emerged from the student ranks; the chief such luminary was Alexander Hamilton. As the 1760s ended, however, the radical promise of Columbia was yet to be proven.

In other aspects of cultural life New York clearly lagged behind both Boston and Philadelphia although its elite class was always reluctant to admit this. In truth, however, the merchants were far more concerned with their pocketbooks than with their souls. They spent their leisure time in "pleasures of the field" such as hunting or boating rather than in cultivating their minds. The City's first theater opened in December 1732, and a subscription

library was established in 1754, but neither was overly successful. Not until 1753, did Manhattan enjoy a full season of drama,
and then it was provided by the Hallam Company of London.
Architecture, music, and painting too imitated English models.
Architecture, for instance, followed the Georgian style, and the
best examples could be found in the homes of the wealthy. Inside
the homes, too, the furniture and furnishings were imported
from England. Portraiture was the most popular form of art in the
City, and merchants and government officials, vying with each
other to display their prominence, commissioned such able artists as Robert Feke, Benjamin West, and John Singleton Copley to
have their likenesses preserved for posterity. Although the study
of science advanced in Colonial America, New York could not
boast of a single scientist as distinguished as Philadelphia's
Benjamin Franklin. Probably the most outstanding New Yorker in
this field was Cadwallader Colden, a professional physician, but
an amateur historian and philosopher. Lower-class New Yorkers
had no time for such diversions and took their relaxation in the
many taverns and grogshops scattered throughout the City. It is
estimated that by 1772 there was one tavern for every 55 residents in the population of 22,000.

New York continued to thrive in other areas as well and was
probably the single most important commercial center in British
North America at the time of the Revolution. Docking facilities
had been expanded in the 1750s as the Empire recognized and
more ably utilized the magnificent harbor. Manhattan's merchants opened up the hinterland of the Hudson Valley, exchang-
ing agricultural products, meat, flax, hemp, potash, and naval
stores for manufactured goods. A lucrative "triangular trade"
between the City, the West Indies, and Great Britain itself became
established. The Acts of Trade and Navigation which supposedly
tied the colonies to the Mother Country market were largely
ignored as the City elite built fortunes. For almost a century the
merchant community had carried on a lucrative but illegal trade
with Holland. It sold flour, meat, and lumber to the French and
Spanish Indies and earned the specie necessary to pay for British
manufacturers. Trade was trade regardless of belligerency, and
during the French and Indian War (1756–63) New York merchants carried on so extensive and profitable a commerce with the
enemy that it became America's second largest City. Most mer-

chants sold their products on both the wholesale and retail levels, although by 1760 some specialization within retailing procedures began to be seen. Several artisan-shopkeepers sold specialty items over-the-counter at retail prices, but most merchant establishments remained in the "general store" category. Complaints were already being heard about the myriad of local ordinances since Common Council rules regulated the price of meat, the size of bread, and the operation of the public markets. But despite all outward signs of commercial prosperity, the City's business often fluctuated wildly as a result of an unstable currency and an unfavorable balance of trade with England. In addition, New York's business community continually suffered from a lack of specie to carry on normal business operations. Occasional paper money issues helped somewhat, and when the British government refused to allow further issues in 1764, Manhattan's merchants became enraged. Out of that anger would emerge an intensified Revolutionary spirit.

Across three thousand miles of ocean Parliament began to lose patience with colonies that refused to accept their proper role in the imperial system. It seemed to English politicians that their American plantations wished all the benefits and none of the responsibilities of being British. During the French wars Colonial merchants had openly violated the Navigation acts and New York had compounded that guilt by refusing to vote adequate moneys for defense. Yet England's first attempt at regulation had led to a monumental legislative debacle, since from 1762 to 1764 not a single measure had been approved by that colony's recalcitrant assembly; not until peace was made in 1763, was the impasse allowed to end. New York and the other colonies must be brought to heel and the laws must be obeyed!

Thus Parliament, victorious over France and secure in its might, in 1764 passed the first of the series of acts whose purpose was to end its "salutory neglect" of the colonies and bring them into a proper relationship with their homeland. In itself the Sugar Act was a judicious piece of legislation, for it reduced the duty on foreign molasses from sixpence to threepence per gallon, allowed only the importation of British rum (which was admitted duty free), and levied new taxes on non-English West Indian imports. New York's merchants, alarmed at the damaging prospects to their rich West Indian trade because of a more determined British effort to enforce the new act, protested to the Board of Trade. Some of the more radical even suggested a boycott of British goods but were convinced instead to circumvent the act in time-honored fashion. The fact that revenues from the tax would be used to support the British military presence in North America was troubling to all. In the midst of the uneasiness surrounding the Sugar Act came even more distressing news. Parliament had passed a Stamp Act imposing fees on forty-three categories of the colonies' ordinary life, from marriage licenses to playing cards to newspapers. At issue now was not only merchant prosperity, but rather the rights of all.

Significantly it was New York which took the lead in opposing the law (which was to become operative on November 1) and which orchestrated the colonial protest. James McEvers was appointed stamp collector for the City of New York, but would resign his post fearing violence from his fellow citizens. Whig Republican merchants who opposed the act formed the majority of the assembly in the summer of 1765, and they sent a formal protest to the king. At the same time, this group entered into communication with the General Court of Massachusetts and together they initiated a Stamp Act Congress to meet in New York City to discuss the situation. From October 7 to October 15, that congress, made up of delegates from nine of the colonies, met in New York City. This meeting, to the delight of the local citizenry, roundly denounced the Stamp Act, and adopted a Remonstrance drawn up by three New Yorkers, John Cruger, Leonard Lispenard, and William Bayard.

During the month of October 1765, the Sons of Liberty made their first appearance in the City. Ultraradical, they advocated forcible resistance and on October 22, when the British merchant ship *Edward* arrived in the harbor with the first cargo of stamps, the Liberty Boys, led by Isaac Sears, John Lamb, and Alexander McDougall, threatened to start a riot; the stamps were therefore removed to a British warship. From there, they were taken to the fort where they were locked up under guard. On October 31, a group of merchants meeting in Brown's Tavern drew up a Nonimportation Agreement by which they bound themselves to boycott English goods until the Stamp Act was repealed. Moreover, the angry traders established a Committee of Correspondence to exchange information and plans with Virginia and Massachusetts. In the most unexpected fashion, a national consciousness was beginning to be apparent.

On November 1, the day that the act became operative, the Sons of Liberty ruled the streets of New York. Vessels in the harbor lowered their flags, business was nonexistent, and some newspapers were published with a skull in the spot where a stamp should have been evident. No stamps were sold, since the vendors had resigned, and that evening a mob burned first the effigy and then the coach of Lieutenant Governor Cadwallader Colden. All port activity virtually ceased for almost two weeks until the arrival, auspiciously timed, of a new Governor. Sir Henry Moore was the only Colonial-born Governor ever to rule New York and he not only invited all the City to his inaugural, but also on November 13, suspended the operation of the Stamp Act. Although the Sons of Liberty seized and burned yet another load of stamps when it arrived two weeks later, Moore's wise action put an end to the crisis and the City continued its business without using the hated stamps. The embargo on imports continued, however, until Parliament retreated by repealing the act in March 1766. At the same time it revised the Sugar Act by making all molasses, both British and foreign, subject to the duty of only one penny. The Americans had won! When word of Parliament's retreat arrived, the triumphant New York Assembly ordered that a statue of King George be constructed. The radical factions represented by the Sons of Liberty erected their own memorial by raising a "liberty pole" on May 20.

Although the Stamp Act crisis had been settled, many outstanding issues remained to excite tensions. In 1765, Parliament had mandated that New York bear the costs of quartering British troops, a demand which many saw as yet another tax without Colonial consent. Under intense official pressure, the assembly had provided a building but declined to deliver straw for bedding, firewood, cooking pots, or rum. Fights and insults between the angry garrison and the Sons of Liberty became common and on August 10, angry soldiers cut down the iron-banded liberty pole, the first of six such incidents. So tense did the situation become that George III himself labeled the City "rebellious," and a semblance of urban peace was not restored until the assembly voted supply money in December.

The calm that prevailed in New York during 1767 was akin to

that which precedes a great storm. Parliament's decision to enact new import duties—the Townshend acts—was not immediately opposed. Governor Moore took some comfort from the fact that merchants organized themselves into a Chamber of Commerce on April 5, 1768, the first such organization anywhere, but he did not understand that such a group might be useful for Revolution- ary as well as trade purposes. By the end of the year renewed demands for boycotts were being heard. Political battles over assembly appropriations, and physical ones around the liberty pole once again disturbed the peace. Months of clashes reached a climax on January 19, 1770, when the Sons of Liberty fought British regulars in a riot sometimes called the first battle of the Revolution. Casualties were few in the Battle of Golden Hill, which preceded the Boston Massacre by two months, but after it ended British soldiers were permitted to walk the streets of New York only in pairs. In April, Parliament retreated by repealing all of the Townshend duties except for the tax on tea and also granted to New York the right to issue £120,000 in paper currency to help the merchant community. It seemed that peace had been achieved and the Sons of Liberty did not even object when the statue of George III was dedicated on August 16, 1770.

For the next several years New York returned to its pursuit of trade and commerce. Now the second largest City in America, it accepted a new Governor, William Tryon, in 1771, and exulted when over 700 ships cleared the harbor in 1772. But the issues of imperial control would not be ended so easily. The next outbreak over the issue of taxation came in 1773, when Parliament ap- proved the famous Tea Act. This "concession" to American feel- ings gave to the British East India Company a monopoly of the tea sold in the colonies. New York merchants might lose some reve- nues as a result of the measure, but since the fees were minimal, they had little real objection to the act and were as surprised as Parliament at the results it produced. In fact, events were now moving beyond the control of elites anywhere as a fervor for greater independence manifested itself. The Sons of Liberty reorganized and led a public meeting which pledged to repel any tea ships that appeared in the harbor and to boycott any New York establishment which purchased East India Company tea. When Bostonian "Mohawks" dumped 342 cases of tea into their own harbor on December 16, the resolve of the radicals in New York was strengthened. When the tea ship *Nancy* appeared in the Narrows, the firing of cannons and a massive protest rally convinced its captain to depart without unloading. It was obvious that the merchant elite no longer was in charge of the anti-imperial movement. When a reckless consignee elected to receive his cargo, the obviously migratory "Mohawks" struck once more. On April 22, 1774, New York had its own tea party as 18 boxes were unceremoniously dumped into the waters of New York Bay. Radicalism was now ascendant and when Parliament punished Boston with a series of Intolerable Acts, New York's action went far beyond sympathetic indignation. On May 16, even before news arrived of the closure of Boston's port, a Committee of Fifty-One chaired by Isaac Low, was organized. The majority of this group represented conservative, even pro-English opinion, but was nonetheless resolved to act against the British outrages. Low's group suggested that a meeting of all of the colonies be held so as to decide upon a common course; one of the prime speakers advocating such a policy was a 19-year-old college boy named Alexander Hamilton. The still conservative merchants of New York thus became the first of many public groups to call for the inter-Colonial congress which eventually did convene in Philadelphia on September 5, 1774.

It would not be useful to once again detail the road that led the colonies toward independence. But it should be clear that in New York radical elements increasingly came to the fore and deposed those who favored accommodation with Britain. In the late summer of 1774, the delegates of New England on their way to Philadelphia were greeted tumultously, and it was John Jay, a delegate from New York, who wrote the Declaration of Rights adopted by the First Continental Congress. That body also decided to follow a policy of nonintercourse with England, and established a Continental Association whose authority was enforced in New York by the Committee of Fifty-One. By November, the Fifty-One were transformed into a more radical Committee of Sixty elected by all the males in Manhattan. When the regular assembly failed to sanction the work of the Continental Congress, it was the Committee of Sixty which organized the movement for a provincial convention which named delegates to the Second Continental Congress. As war clouds gathered, the British government, aware of the crucial position of New York, proposed that the City be subject to no trade restrictions whatsoever, but that offer was overtaken by events. On April 23, 1775, a messenger from New England arrived in Manhattan with the news that battles had been fought outside Boston. The radicals now took command! A mob led by Isaac Sears and John Lamb seized muskets and organized a militia. By May 1, a radical Committee of One Hundred was placed in charge of the municipality and by the end of the month a Provincial Congress was convened in Manhattan; it authorized both the raising of troops and plans for defense of the City. But protest was not yet war and loyalism was still powerful in New York. Governor Tryon, who had been away in Britain, returned to cheers and when he ordered the evacuation of British troops to ships in the harbor, his decision was lauded. However, Colonel Marinus Willett and the Sons of Liberty did intercept the departing column on June 6, to "liberate" some supplies.

The Provincial Congress appointed a Commission of Safety which continued to function throughout the war, often making its headquarters in the Christopher House on Staten Island. City merchants continued to supply the British troops in the harbor in hopes that some reconciliation of interests could be accomplished, although such a result seemed increasingly less likely. On August 23, when the militia repositioned several cannon, shots were exchanged between the opposing sides, and the warship *Asia* loosed a broadside against the City. As in Massachusetts, blood had been shed and tempers were high. By the end of the summer, the entire City was in patriot hands and Governor Tryon was attempting to rule the rebellious province from his military headquarters on the British man-of-war *Halifax.*

The path to independence was a difficult one for many Americans, but no colony was as sorely tried by the experience as was New York. As the foregoing events showed, the City was becoming increasingly radical and attempted to speak for the entire province, much as Paris did for France in its revolutions. But commercial and sympathetic ties with England were strong and, in early 1776, a Loyalist uprising in Queens generated by Governor Tryon had to be repressed. The City elections of February 1 resulted in a rout of Loyalist groups and the City now prepared to meet the test of real war. It is interesting to note that about a third of all Revolutionary war battles took place in crucial New York State, but its first experiment with the might of the Empire was to be most lasting. The City was to be so ravaged that the scars would take a decade to be erased.

By mid-March 1776, General George Washington had forced the British to evacuate Boston, and then made his triumphant way to New York, where it was clear that England's retaliatory blow would fall. The general and his entourage arrived on April 13 and established themselves in the DePeyster Mansion on Pearl Street. Washington considered New York to be of "infinite importance" and, though the City itself extended little more than a mile north of the tip of Manhattan, the entire area had to be defended. Forts and redoubts were constructed in New York and along Brooklyn Heights but the strategists among the rebels must have recognized the difficulty of defense. Much attention therefore was focused on the City of Philadelphia, where members of the Second Continental Congress were discussing the weighty question of a formal break with England. The weak role played in those deliberations by the New York delegation is well-known, for the Provincial Congress had told them not to approve independence. As a result, the New York delegation abstained during the critical votes on the Declaration. When word of Congress' action reached New York, however, it was lustily cheered. On July 9, 1776, Washington ordered the Document read to soldiers and citizens on the Commons, and when the news reached White Plains, the Provincial Congress gave its belated approval. The still new statue of George III was pulled down and recast into 42,088 bullets as the City wildly celebrated its freedom. The exhilaration ended on August 22, when word came that Lord William Howe had landed his army, the largest expeditionary force ever raised by England, on the south Brooklyn shore. The City, which already had lost a sizable part of its population as Loyalists fled to British protection, now had to put easy cheering aside and face the reality of war.

The test of battle proved unkind in the extreme for the defenders of New York. Washington had been obliged to disperse his limited forces to protect against a series of potential threats, and Howe had the inestimable advantage of mobility provided to him by the Royal Navy. Most of the defenders had been entrenched along Brooklyn Heights, a position that was now meaningless given Howe's presence in their rear. Only 7,000 Americans, and they largely militia, were in a position to defend New York against an advance by 20,000 British regulars. On the night of August 26, the British offensive began, and by ten o'clock the next morning the Patriot forces were driven back all along their lines. General Washington arrived on the scene in the afternoon and found the morale of his troops at a very low ebb. The battle of Long Island had been a crushing defeat for America. Almost 2,000 men had been lost and the British juggernaut had not been dented. Only Howe's lassitude saved the Americans, for after a day's respite Washington successfully extricated his defeated army by using John Glover's "Marblehead Mariners." By August 30, Washington's beaten forces had been withdrawn to Manhattan without further loss.

Events now became temporarily static as an attempt was made to settle the conflict by diplomatic means. On September 11, John Adams, Benjamin Franklin, and Edward Rutledge met British representatives at the Billip House on Staten Island—but the negotiations floundered on the fact of America's declared independence. Thus on September 15, the battle for Manhattan began as Howe's Navy opened a tremendous bombardment along the East River, routed the militia stationed at present-day Thirty-fourth Street, and leisurely advanced across the Island. Most American troops escaped northward, however, and on September 16, a British probe was repulsed by the Patriot forces. The Battle of Harlem Heights was not much of a victory but it did much to restore sagging morale.

Once again Howe's lethargy benefited the American Army. Inexplicably, his advance halted and Washington decided that information on Howe's intentions must be obtained. A volunteer named Nathan Hale entered the City as a spy but was captured before he could reach American lines. At the same time, a fire broke out in the City and destroyed fully a quarter of its homes. Howe believed the fire was started by the rebels and dozens of New Yorkers were arrested as suspected arsonists. Perhaps Hale also may be considered a victim of the blaze, for on September 22 he was condemned as a spy and hanged near the Dove Tavern. Hale's last words, "I only regret that I have but one life to give for my country!" have thrilled generations of Americans ever since.

Certainly there were good reasons for Howe's suspicions since for months there had been rumors that the rebels would destroy New York rather than see it turned into a British base. Although the Continental Congress had explicitly ordered that the City should not be destroyed, that declaration could have been only a public relations ploy for there were British reports of men caught with rosin-tipped matches and of dark figures scrambling across rooftops. Washington was quoted as saying that "Providence, or some good honest fellow, has done more for us than we were disposed to do," and he doubtless was glad that Howe occupied a ravaged City. In the meantime, the pursuit of Washington's army continued and the General, leaving a force under Colonel Robert Magaw at Fort Washington (183rd Street), retreated into Westchester. On October 12, at Throgs Neck and again at White Plains on October 28, his troops were defeated, leaving no hope for the few Americans remaining in Manhattan. Four columns of British troops now converged on Fort Washington, its outpost at Kingsbridge was seized, and harsh surrender terms were transmitted to Magaw. On November 16, the last American stronghold on Manhattan fell to the enemy. New York remained in British hands for the next seven years, until November 25, 1783.

For the duration of the Revolution, New York served as a British military headquarters and as its base for frequent sorties against the coastlines of the colonies. Like most occupied towns, New York suffered indignities; its resources were plundered to supply the troops; its trees cut down to fuel their fires; its commerce stagnated under wartime restrictions. The streets were patrolled by Hessians and cavalry of the Light Horse, but not even the most stringent precautions could prevent the calamity of another major fire on August 3, 1778. Over 100 more homes were destroyed and military rule was made even more strict. Governor Tryon was replaced by General James Robertson, who presided over a City wracked by high inflation, rumors of espionage conspiracies, and a rather large and grasping corps of prostitutes. New York also became the major detention center for prisoners of war and the British treated all captured rebels quite harshly. At first an old sugar house on Liberty Street was converted into a dungeon but its capacity was soon exceeded. Ultimately, American prisoners were put into naval hulks anchored in the harbor; the *Jersey* in Wallabout Bay was the most notorious of these ships, and due to privation and unsanitary conditions it is estimated that almost 11,000 soldiers died. Death carts rumbled daily through New York streets, or at least through those that remained passable after the conflagrations. On the streets, all residents were required to tip their hats to British officers and were constantly subject to search. Although the City population might have reached 30,000 early in the war, by 1781, when it became obvious that Britain was seeking peace, Manhattan's total including the garrison could hardly have exceeded 12,000. Despite its long-term occupation, however, the City continued to cement its trading patterns with the West Indies and Europe. Privateering ventures could lead to quick profits, and many Tories in Manhattan made their fortunes during these years.

Lord Cornwallis' surrender to Washington at Yorktown in October of 1781 brought an end to the military phase of the Revolution; by chance, Prince William Henry was visiting safe New York at that time. However, it was not until April 1783, that the City received word that George III had proclaimed that the hostilities were ended. Manhattan itself was not to be free of British troops for another seven months. New York thus became the setting for the last act of the American Revolution when General Knox's troops took posession of the City on November 25, 1783. His forces escorted General Washington and Governor George Clinton into the City as the British withdrew to Staten Island. As a parting gesture, the English tars had greased the flagpole from which the Union Jack fluttered and a young American had to make a perilous climb by nailing cleats to the staff. He tore down the British colors and unfolded the American flag as the crowds cheered. The Revolution was over!

* * * * *

During this second stage of its history, New York secured its position as the most important urban center in North America in terms of its commercial and strategic value. Already it was a gateway for immigration, a City which offered greater opportunity to ambitious men than any other. During the long century of British control it had overcome inept leadership by developing liberal institutions of government; constant tension between governors, the assembly, and the popular will was the result. In many respects the part taken by New York in the events and controversies which led up to, and culminated in, the Revolution, were of more than ordinary import. Perhaps this is the more remarkable since many of its citizens were of non-English descent and were struggling for rights to which they were unaccustomed. In opposing the Stamp Act, for example, Manhattan's citizens were particularly active and successful and, in 1770, it was found that although Colonial America had sworn not to trade with England, New York City alone was really observing the agreement. This was peculiar indeed for a City whose prosperity rested primarily upon commerce. When war finally broke out, New York's exposed position forced her to bear the brunt of attack. No other City endured so long a period of occupation by the enemy; no other City suffered more for the cause of independence. Its commerce had been considerably disrupted, two disastrous fires had destroyed large numbers of buildings, and its population had decreased from 25,000 or more before the capture, to about 12,000 at the time of evacuation. Its currency was unstable, its trade connections were diminished, and inflation hampered recovery. George Washington bade farewell to his staff at Fraunces Tavern on December 4, 1783, and then the task of reconstruction, this time as America's capital City, began.

BRIEF BIBLIOGRAPHY

Abbot, Wilbur C. *New York in the American Revolution*. New York, 1912.

Archdeacon, Thomas. *New York City, 1664–1710: Conquest and Change*. Ithaca, 1976.

Barck, Oscar T. *New York City During the War for Independence*, New York, 1931.

Bliven, Bruce. *Battle for Manhattan*. New York, 1964.*

Bridenbaugh, Carl. *Cities in Revolt: Urban Life in America, 1743–1776*. New York, 1955.*

Brown, Henry C. *The Story of Old New York*. New York, 1940.

Earle, Alice M. *Colonial Days in Old New York*. New York, 1937.

Edwards, George W. *New York as an Eighteenth-Century Municipality, 1731–1776*. New York, 1917.

Harrington, Virginia. *The New York Merchant on the Eve of the Revolution*. New York, 1950.*

Peterson, Arthur E. *New York as an Eighteenth-Century Municipality. Prior to 1731*. New York, 1898.

Reich, J. R. *Leisler's Rebellion: A Study of Democracy in New York, 1664–1720*. New York, 1953.

Wertenbaker, Thomas J. *Father Knickerbocker Rebels*. New York, 1948.*

*Paperback

III

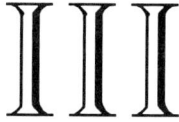

National Capital City

DURING THE REVOLUTION, New York was occupied by the enemy longer than any other American City. Although it had been only briefly a focus of fighting, it remained a center for rebel espionage efforts and a mainstay of British supply. After 1783, its well-established commercial ties to England were still the strongest in the new nation, and the fact that independence had been achieved did not alter those existent patterns although the actual traders changed from loyalists to Americans. Some idea of the scope of this transformation was given on April 27, 1783, when almost 500 Tory families sailed from the City to Shelburne, Canada, where they would build a new life still under the aegis of the Crown. Such substantial losses of population and expertise hurt New York's commercial development just as substantially as the great fires had devastated its physical structure. The City was therefore to face a myriad of difficulties before it could capture the palm as the undoubted leader of the nation. The British fleet did not finally leave the harbor until December 5, 1783, and it left behind a City whose population had been reduced to 12,000, whose elite corps of business executives had been shattered, whose municipal system was in ruins, and whose people were deeply scarred and divided by memories of the occupation. Yet within a generation all of these difficulties were proven to be transitory. New York was to reign triumphantly not just as a national (1789–90) and state capital (1783–96), but also as the greatest of all American urban centers, a position it was never again to relinquish. By the end of the War of 1812, it was straining the limits of its island and seeking an even greater stage for its aggressive business community. Commerce remained predominant during the first half of the nineteenth century, but in parallel areas such as finance, industry, and even intellectual activity, the City was to make spectacular strides. Yet with all its varied growth, the single creation that determined New York's future more than anything else was the political club soon known to the nation as Tammany Hall, a name which in time became virtually synonymous with City politics. As much as its ships, banks, and factories, the style of New York would be created by this unique institution. All these changes lay ahead for the New York of the 1780s, yet within 40 years the rebuilding and recovery would be accomplished and the metropolis on the Hudson would be the true heart and capital of the nation. How that transformation was achieved is the story of these pages.

* * * * *

America's first priority after 1783 was the creation of stable mechanisms of government. On the national level the search proved to be an arduous task, and the difficult road that led to the Constitutional Convention of 1787 is well known. Transforming Colonial institutions into state governmental forms was the second major area of development, and in this sphere New York was more fortunate than other states, for it was led by one of the great "unknown" statesmen of American history, George Clinton. From 1777 to 1795 Clinton served as Governor and, consistent with his advocacy of states' rights, established the basis for New York's prosperity in the nineteenth century. Part of the English heritage that continued to operate after 1783 was the right of the Governor to appoint New York City's Mayor, and so Clinton selected a prominent attorney named James Duane to serve in the post and to preside over the reconstruction of the City. As Duane took his oath in February 1784, the legislature proclaimed that New York would also serve as the state's capital, a position it was to hold until 1796. In addition, the Articles of Confederation Congress, which had been convened in Trenton, declared that as of January

1785, the national capital would be located in New York as well. City Hall in Wall Street was offered to the nation to serve as its Federal Hall, and after 1785 three levels of government were centered in lower Manhattan. The ravaged metropolis, which encompassed less than four square miles, was now recognized as the most crucial area of the nation and would remain a focus of politics during the nation's formative years.

Duane occupied the Mayor's chair for five years, and his major accomplishment during that time was the rehabilitation of the City. The post of Mayor was an unsalaried one; its incumbent received as compensation only revenues gained through the issuance of tavern licenses and excise stamps. Since Duane was already quite wealthy, the lack of a fixed income was not distressing to him. Working closely with the governor and with City Recorder Richard Varick, Duane supervised a rebuilding effort which proceeded at an almost unbelievable pace. The task was not simply one of renaming thoroughfares—Crown became Liberty Street, Queen became Cedar, and King was transformed into Pine Street—but also creating a suitable urban environment for the major ornament of American society. A federal customhouse was opened in 1784, the same year that the Anglican Church was disestablished and that Kings College officially became Columbia. Moreover, the first bank in the City opened for business on June 9, and boasted that Alexander Hamilton was one of its leading sponsors. As commerce was revived, the population increased as well, and by 1786 the City's total had virtually doubled. But the problem of wartime loyalty remained a vexing one for New York. The Chamber of Commerce had professed its loyalty to King George III during the conflict and now the returned American merchants displayed little sympathy for their fellow traders. Moreover, the Duane administration confiscated a substantial amount of Tory property, regardless of whether or not the owners had actually fled in the exodus, and used the proceeds to finance the building program. Tories were also subjected to higher tax levies as well as social ostracism. Initially, the law courts ignored Tory claims to legitimately owed debts. Hamilton defended and secured Tory legal rights and argued as well for the primacy of a national treaty in the landmark case of *Rutgers* v. *Wadington* (1784), and this helped ease what was becoming an explosive social and legal conundrum. As in the aftermath of any civil war, the battered survivors had once again to learn to live together—this time as Americans.

The basic, undeniable strength of New York in the 1780s was the inventiveness and expertise of its merchants. Immediately after the peace treaty there had been some trade dislocations because America no longer received favored treatment within the Empire and because of some dumping of British goods into the starved American market. But within a few years traditional lines of trade had been reestablished. Not until the 1790s, however, did the value of exports reach pre-Revolutionary levels. New areas had to be developed and the restive merchants of the City were quick to accept the challenge. It was a New York merchantman, *The Empress of China*, which became the first vessel to transport American products to the Far East; it thus initiated the dream of a "China market" which launches daydreams and attracts investors to this day. But China and the East represented at best a minor commercial gain. The basic market loss engendered by the Revolution was America's exclusion from trade with the West Indies and Canada. Only with time and gradually improved relations with Britain could this gap be bridged, for no amount of smuggling could make up for the loss of normal commerce. However, in a move to expand coastal trade with other states, the City merchants began to transship some Southern farm products, the first steps toward the creation of the future "cotton triangle." A Society of Merchants and Tradesmen was chartered in 1786, and within a year it had extended its membership to encompass thirty distinct mercantile areas. Thus, although commercial treaties with foreign nations and settlement of relations with England were yet in the future, the basic strength and resilience of New York's mercantile position was apparent. This is not to imply that New York and its environs did not suffer economic pangs during the Confederation period. Perhaps the bleakest and most depressed year was 1786, a factor of some significance in the calling of the Constitutional Convention, but by the early years of the 1790s conditions as well as expectations had significantly improved. By the time that the great European wars of the French Revolutionary period began in 1793, the American nation and its greatest port would be in a strategic position to benefit from those conflicts.

The major factor which enabled the United States to surmount the difficulties of its infancy was the creation of a Constitution in the summer of 1787. No amount of economic gain was comparable to the stability and order implied by an agreement upon the frame of government. In the 1780s, those political and business leaders with the ability to look beyond parochial state concerns believed that the American experiment might fail unless a more effective central government could be created to lead the federal system. The result of the herculean labors of the Founding Fathers was the Constitution, and the significant role that Alexander Hamilton played in convening the convention is well known. Equally important is the critical role that this New York attorney played during the struggle to obtain state ratification in 1788. The contributions that Hamilton made during the actual drafting of the Constitution in Philadelphia were minor, but most scholars agree that George Clinton's New York would not have ratified the Constitution had it not been for the genius of Hamilton, ably abetted by James Madison and John Jay, who explained the document to America in their *Federalist Papers.* The delegates who convened at Poughkeepsie in 1788 to consider ratification of the Constitution were at first overwhelmingly anti-Federalist, but slowly the ardor and logic of Hamilton and his associates changed their minds. Not an inconsiderable factor in the deliberations was that New York City acted as a united bloc of support for the Constitution; its business community saw in a stronger central government the stability it needed in order to prosper. Some Federalists whispered and John Jay was reputed to even have voiced the threat that unless the Poughkeepsie delegates approved the Constitution the metropolis would secede from the state and join the Union on its own. Whether it was brilliance or logic or expedience that won ratification is still debated, but finally New York decided to join America as its "eleventh pillar." Even before that formal acceptance, however, the City had expressed its commitment by organizing the greatest parade in the history of Manhattan. On July 23, over 5,000 New Yorkers marched to demonstrate their support of the Constitution, and the line of celebrants extended more than a mile. The City's message was clear and the Poughkeepsie convention, in a sense, was only ratifying the will of the people when on July 26 it narrowly, by a 30–27 margin of victory, gave New York State's approval to the Constitution of the United States.

One of the unstated but very real lures that helped transform the anticonstitutional majority at Poughkeepsie was the fact that New York City would certainly be selected as America's first capital city. Once ratification was secured, Major Pierre L'Enfant arrived in town to remodel the City Hall into a suitable meeting place for Congress. All that fall and winter his workers busily redecorated the structure along Grecian lines, and City officials pondered how they were to pay his bills. Municipal officials finally decided that some of the common lands north of present-day Thirty-second Street should be sold off in five-acre parcels and that individual building lots farther downtown should also be offered to buyers to raise cash. Neither sale brought in much revenue, the purchasers often defaulted and failed to improve the land, and sadly, Major L'Enfant wound up being cheated on his fees. Nevertheless, the Federal Hall was ready for the First Congress by March of 1789, although the House of Representatives did not actually achieve its quorum until April 1. By the sixth, the electoral vote had been officially compiled and George Washington was notified that he had been unanimously chosen as America's first President. On April 23, Washington arrived in New York aboard a ceremonial fifty-foot barge and was escorted to the first presidential mansion, the renovated Samuel Osgood home at 3 Cherry Street, a site now beneath a pier of the Brooklyn Bridge. After a week of formal dinners, balls and final preparations, the great day arrived. On April 30, Washington was inaugurated President on the balcony of L'Enfant's Federal Hall and the United States finally had an executive. John Q. A. Ward's great statue of our first President still gazes out at downtown New York from the steps of the Sub-treasury Building which now occupies the site. New York was not long destined to serve as the national capital; the famed "deal" between Hamilton and Thomas Jefferson would soon give the nation both a financial plan and a capital along the swampland of the Potomac River. It seems fitting, however, that as the birth-place of the American government our leaders should have in-stinctively selected the future national metropolis as the only suitable capital for the new nation. The strength and energy so powerfully felt in 1789 was to intensify throughout the rest of the nation's history.

It was inevitable that leaders from New York City, men who shared the Federalist faith which dominated the first decade of our national existence, should figure prominently in the Washington administration. The greatest of these figures was Alexander Hamilton, whose service as the first Secretary of the Treasury established the financial and credit systems which allowed the nation to achieve respectability. But it is too often forgotten that John Jay served as the first Chief Justice of the United States, that Mayor James Duane was appointed the first federal district judge for New York, and that Samuel Osgood was the first man to fill the position of postmaster general of the United States. Richard Varick replaced Duane as Mayor of New York, and filled that post with distinction for the next twelve years, a record not matched until the twentieth century. Like his predecessor, his major preoccupation remained the reconstruction of the City but to this he added the task of keeping it a bastion of the Federalist cause. Varick was to succeed admirably in both of these endeavors. Varick's metropolis was no longer to play host to the national government, however, for in August 1790, the capital was transferred to Philadelphia, where it remained for a decade. Perhaps the most telling comment on that hegira was that of Abigail Adams, a woman known both for her judgment and candor. Writing of the move to Philadelphia she resolved to make the best of it but "When all is done," she concluded, "it will not be Broadway."

There no longer could be any doubt that Broadway and its surrounding City were rapidly recovering from the effects of the occupation. The first federal census completed in 1790 showed a population total of 33,131, still some 9,000 behind Philadelphia but growing much more rapidly. There was a sense of vigor and implacability in New York which the Quaker City could never match, and there were few even in the 1790s who doubted which would be the ultimate winner of this urban competition. The systematic reconstruction of the previous decade had increased New York's housing stock by 4,000 homes, and the first City directory had to be issued in 1790 to document the changes; by 1793 continued construction would force the introduction of a house numbering system. It seemed that every year created a new landmark structure. In 1790, the rebuilt Trinity Church was dedicated by its congregation, and in 1791, New York Hospital reopened. A second, naturally Federalist controlled, bank opened for business that same year. In 1792, an institution which in the minds of some Americans is still synonymous with New York was organized by the brokers of the City. Since 1790, they had congregated to do business under the branches of a buttonwood tree on Wall Street, where they bought and sold government securities; on May 17, 1792, they formed an association for such activity. By 1793, the stock traders met regularly in a newly constructed Tontine Coffeehouse and much financial history was made in those cozy rooms over the next decade. In any event, the "Buttonwood Agreement" was an important precedent for the creation of the general stock exchange which was to be organized in 1817. In the year 1794, Bellevue Hospital for the treatment of contagious disease opened, as did also the sumptuous City Hotel, for long the finest hostelry in New York. So rapid was the pace of construction that the old Dutch and English fortifications along the Battery shoreline had to be razed to meet the demand for advantageously located commercial sites; a new set of defensive works were soon placed at Fort Jay on Governor's Island. An inventor named John Fitch tested a steamboat on the Collect Pond in 1796, but failed to obtain the financial support the project deserved. When the vessel was pillaged after an accident, it broke Fitch's heart and the glory of steamboat travel was to be gained by Robert Fulton early in the next century. A total of nine newspapers already were available to City readers in 1790, but as the population virtually doubled to 60,489 in a decade their number too increased; by 1807, over 20 papers were available and New York had won its spurs as the premier news center of the nation. The City was on its way to greatness and all events now seemed to contribute to its prosperity. Revolution might convulse France, war might engulf Europe, an influx of immigrants from sites as varied as Ireland and Santo Domingo might arrive in the port but everything and everyone thrived in the City.

During this decade of fantastic growth New York was identified with the cause of Federalism. Even after Alexander Hamilton's retirement from the Cabinet in 1795, he and his supporters dominated the political life of both Manhattan and the nation. It is somewhat surprising, therefore, that the course of the City's political future was being prepared not in Federalist salons but rather in the slow growth of a private club, the only such club in American history to act as a political organization. The club was the Lodge of Tammany and its development into Tammany Hall is one of the marvelous stories of American urban history. It was in 1783, the year of Revolutionary triumph, that the officers of Washington's army had organized themselves into the Society of Cincinnati, a benevolent association whose primary function was to aid the widows and orphans of veterans. The Cincinnati did in fact also seek greater state cooperation during the 1780s, and was a staunch supporter of the constitutional movement. In terms of membership the organization was inherently elitist, and within only a few years a New York upholsterer named William Mooney created a lodge with similar fraternal purposes but whose membership would be limited to common soldiers; the first meeting of this lodge was held on May 13, 1788. Mooney sometimes called his creation the Society of St. Tammany, or the Columbian Order, and quite naturally most of the early meetings of the group were held in New York taverns. The namesake of the society was a Delaware Indian chieftain whose real character somehow merged with that of a mythical Tammenend, a figure whose exploits were responsible for the Great Plains and Niagara Falls, among other deeds. Mooney's hope was to build a "national institution," and the original constitution of the society claimed that members held as their goals "the smile of charity, the chain of friendship, and the flame of liberty, and in general whatever may tend to perpetuate the love of freedom or the political advantage of the country." By 1789, Grand Sachem Mooney led a society with branches in thirteen states, and the organization boasted a national existence until early in the nineteenth century, when events and leadership changed its focus to one that concentrated on New York City. All members were assessed an institution fee of $1.25 and contributed $1.00 for charity each year. In return, they were able to attend patriotic lectures, march in parades, and know that their money was indeed being used to help widows and orphans. The group even opened a museum in 1790, and the Indian artifacts displayed there ultimately became part of the collections of P. T. Barnum.

In the 1790s the social and philanthropic purposes of the Society of St. Tammany slowly were overshadowed by increasing political activity, the first stirrings of the machine which would dominate New York politics for the next century and a half. The architect of the change was not to be William Mooney, however, but rather one of the great "lone wolves" of American politics, the war hero and brilliant attorney, Aaron Burr. Burr boasted a distinguished family background—his grandfather was Jonathan Edwards, and his father the president of Princeton—but in the familial and Federalist politics which dominated New York in the 1780s Burr was an outsider. He longed for political success to match his thriving law practice. When Mooney was replaced as Grand Sachem of Tammany by William Pitt Smith—there was some suspicion of a scandalous misuse of funds intended for poor relief—Burr saw in the weakened leadership an opportunity to become the voice of common New York men against the aristocrats. Burr's cadre of personal satellites entered Tammany, they were later called his Tenth Legion, and began to change its orientation from charity and fun to more serious political concerns. The Burrites argued that the aristocratic Federalists who dominated the City displayed little concern for the common worker, that they conspired to prevent a widening of the suffrage in local elections, and that only by an alliance with George Clinton and his upstate supporters could ordinary New Yorkers ever hope to receive the benefits of democratic government. Even after New York City was reapportioned into seven wards in February of 1791, the society protested that a thousand such restructurings would not help poor workingmen because voting lists had not been expanded. There is some inconclusive evidence that Burr consulted with Thomas Jefferson and James Madison during their famous "botanic" expedition of May 1791, when supposedly the foundations of a national opposition party to Federalism were created. However, there is not now, nor is there ever likely to be, exact confirmation of what the three men discussed. A major political change that aided the new coalition was Aaron Burr's appointment as senator from New York, a post he obtained because of his alliance with the upstate Clintonians. He returned that favor in 1792 by preparing the legal brief which invalidated the election of the Federalist candidate and secured for Clinton his sixth consecutive term as Governor of the State of New York. It was Burr who slowly yet effectively changed Tammany's destiny in the early 1790s and made Mooney's social club into a dynamic part of the rising Republican coalition both in New York and the nation. Gradually the lesser merchants and artisans adopted the views they heard preached by the legionnaires of Tammany, and these echoed the opinions of Aaron Burr. The process of leadership is somewhat mystical as well as intensely personal, and something new was occurring in Tammany, a development which was to impact fundamentally on all of America's urban history; Aaron Burr was becoming the "Boss" of a political machine.

At first, Burr's organization attained precious little success in a New York City dominated by Federalists and Alexander Hamilton. As Secretary of the Treasury, Hamilton was the heart of the Washington administration and in local matters felt it "a religious duty" to oppose the career of the pragmatic, amoral Burr. In any event, during Burr's senatorial years in Philadelphia, Tammany made few gains in New York City. Not until 1793, when great issues of foreign policy convulsed American society, was there to be a significant change in party development. In June of that year, the French frigate *Ambuscade* anchored in New York Harbor and brought news of the French declaration of war against Great Britain. An extraordinary wave of enthusiasm burst forth from French sympathizers, and still-fresh memories of the Wallabout prison ships made it difficult for any citizen to remain neutral. Jeffersonian groups professed strong support of France in its struggle against Britain, a point of view intensified when America's old enemy began impressing seamen from our neutral vessels into the Royal Navy. New York City Federalists, on the other hand, favored Great Britain. The violence of the Reign of Terror convinced them that the French experiment in "democracy" was running amok. The Washington administration decided that continued peace with Great Britain was its major priority and sent Chief Justice Jay to negotiate a trade agreement with our former enemy. The resultant treaty was hated by advocates of France but gratefully accepted by merchants who still dominated the politics of the City. By a margin of 60–10 New York's Chamber of Commerce endorsed the Jay Treaty on July 1795, in the expectation that it would increase the port's cargo trade and stimulate its shipbuilding capacity. In Philadelphia, however, Senator Burr condemned the pact and voted against it, an act which helped to cost him his Senate seat. Burr's southern ally, Jefferson of Monticello, also opposed the treaty and in 1796, both Republican leaders ran for the presidency on the basis of their shared opinions. The electoral results only confirmed Federalist control of both the nation and New York. Burr, however, did amass the fourth highest electoral vote and thus perhaps qualifies as Tammany Hall's first national candidate.

From the parochial viewpoint of New York, the national Republican defeat in 1796 was significant because the Clintonian-Burrite alliance lost control of the state legislature. Early in 1796, therefore, Burr was refused reelection as a United States senator and temporarily lost his role in national politics. He was almost immediately elected to serve in the state assembly, however, and was to spend the next three years preparing the way for Republican victory in the next elections; the mechanism he used to achieve this goal was a strengthened Tammany vote. Burr understood that so long as Federalist-sponsored property requirements for voting limited New York's electorate, the chances for Republican victory were small. A system had to be designed to reduce aristocratic control of the voting lists and to broaden the opportunity to vote. Whether Burr really had much sympathy with the common man is questionable, but in 1798 he worked a bill through the legislature which enabled foreign citizens to own land in New York State; by 1800, some of those foreigners were certain to be Americans. Even more significant was Burr's sponsorship of the famous Manhattan Company. New Yorkers knew that both yellow fever and cholera plagued their City, and each year lives were needlessly lost to diseases which doctors suspected had a direct connection to the impure drinking water. The Republicans had supported a proposal to pipe pure water from the Bronx to Manhattan, and since everyone recognized that the growing metropolis needed a more adequate water supply, on April 2, 1799, the legislature granted a utility charter to the Manhattan Company. This private corporation promised to provide "pure and wholesome water" to the City, and so clear was New York's interest that a municipal representative would serve on the corporate board of directors for a century. Quickly beginning its operations, the new corporation sank a well on Spring Street, ultimately laid about six miles of wooden pipes and supplied over four hundred homes with water. In time the wooden pipes proved to be ineffective and unsanitary, and even after iron pipes were substituted in 1828, the quality of the water hardly improved. In fact, in the sphere of water supply New York lagged far behind its great rival, Philadelphia, during the first four decades of the new century. Nevertheless, the Manhattan Company continued to pump water until 1900, lest it lose its most precious possession, not customers, but its charter of incorporation.

The Manhattan Company charter not only established a public utility, but also granted to that corporation the privilege of investing its surplus capital in "monied transactions or operations." Burr and the Republicans saw in that innocuous clause the opportunity to break the Federalist financial monopoly of banking in New York, and to create a bank that would serve the democratic interest. The investment clause of the charter allowed Republicans to create the Bank of the Manhattan Company, an institution which broke the Hamiltonian stranglehold over Manhattan's development. Burr's relatives and members of his legion ruled the Manhattan Company board, and there is a belief that several Federalists provided votes for the utility charter in order to get themselves in on the ground floor of a good business deal. Whatever the real motivations were, the Republican interest now had their bank, though the company never was to draw a drop of water from the faraway Bronx River. Rather, the bank provided mortgage loans to men of democratic persuasion and these new property owners were enfranchised in time for the next national elections. Tammany also encouraged its members to band together, buy 40 shilling freeholds in common, and thus qualify to vote for assemblymen. Thus by several expedients, as well as the normal course of economic growth, the Republican voting lists were expanded before the crucial election of 1800.

The election of Jefferson in 1800 is sometimes called a Revolution, but if so, it was a Revolution made in New York City and successfully orchestrated by Aaron Burr. As leader of Tammany, Burr not only mobilized his new voters, but also put together a slate of candidates so studded with important and aristocratic names that it swept to victory. Control of the state legislature guaranteed Republican presidential electors and the party's margin of national victory was provided by the vote of New York State. Few historians have appreciated the irony that the victory of Jefferson in 1800 was due to the vote of an urban center, though all know that he saw cities only as "sores." The Tammany campaign of 1800 is one of the most dramatic stories of our history, but it is often ignored in the attention given to Burr's purported attempt to wrest the Presidency itself away from Jefferson after both Republicans finished in an electoral tie. Burr's historical reputation is so bad that almost all books agree that the attempt was made, but there is no proof that Burr actually tried to sway the House deliberations. In any event, after Jefferson became President, Tammany Hall claimed credit for his victory. Burr served as Vice-President until 1805 but to Jefferson he was ever after only a "crooked gun." When Clintonians regained control of the state, they froze Burr out of local patronage and the genius of the Revolution of 1800 bitterly contemplated the ruins of a career. Knowing he had no future in Washington, Burr ran for Governor of New York in 1804 only to be defeated, in part due to the intervention of Hamilton, who had great influence and considered Burr "a dangerous man." The frustrations and anger of the two City leaders culminated on July 11, 1804, in the most famous duel in American history. On the cliffs opposite New York Hamilton was shot and died the next day. Burr fled, leaving Tammany temporarily in total disrepute. Another leader now emerged from the chaos and would preside over the City's continued maturation.

The man who dominated New York City for the early decades of the new century was the strong-willed nephew of the Governor, DeWitt Clinton. In October 1803, Clinton resigned from the United States Senate to begin his reign as Mayor, a position he held with only two yearlong interruptions until 1815. Few mayors have done more for the City; during his tenure New York achieved first place among American municipalities. The list of significant firsts associated with the Clinton years is long and varied. The Mayor assisted John Pintard in organizing the New York Historical Society in 1804, and cooperated with Jedediah Peck and Thomas Eddy to create a public school system. On February 19, 1805, the Free School Society was founded and opened classrooms on Chatham Street in 1809. The public schools of the City remained under the benevolent dictatorship of the society until 1853. The first black congregation in New York was organized by members of the Methodist Episcopal Church, an American Academy of Art was founded, and the Mayor served as chief patron of both the Orphan Asylum and the City Hospital. Perhaps symbolic of the rising confidence of New York in these years was the progress of a new City Hall. The cornerstone of the John McComb/Joseph Magnin structure had been set in place on September 20,

1803, just before Clinton took office, but all during his tenure it gradually took on the graceful lines which make it one of the most significant of urban governmental buildings. Completed by 1812 at a cost of $500,000, New York's City Hall was at that time so far uptown that its northern side was not faced in Massachusetts marble as were the other three facades; no one really expected that the northern side would ever be visible to the public. Nevertheless, the City Planning Commission appointed in 1807, was less dubious about the future and insisted on surveying a grid of potential streets which stretched northward beyond the village of Harlem. Another first of these years was Washington Irving's use of the term *Gotham* to describe New York, a title it has borne proudly ever since 1807. When Irving then published his *Knicker-bocker History* (1809) that burlesque account of Dutch New York gave the City a literary cachet which also set it apart from all rivals.

The growth of the City remained inextricably tied to the sea and the incessant European wars between France and England stimulated the rise of America's, but particularly New York's, merchant marine. A federal naval yard was established along the East River in 1801, and Clinton presided over a large increase of City dock capacity to handle the increase of traffic. Britain's naval presence was palpable outside the harbor and the threat of sailor impressment or even violence was always present; in April 1806, for example, H.M.S. *Leander* killed an American sailor during a chase off Sandy Hook. The Common Council and the Mayor, alarmed at the prospect of war or occupation should the British attempt to blockade shipments to France, ordered the construction of new defensive works on Governor's Island and on the tip of Manhattan. The Southwest Battery built in those years was called Castle Clinton and played a significant role in the City's future social history. No one really wanted war, however, for there was too much money to be made in commerce and the threat of American retaliatory action soon eased. The farsighted among the merchant community were already beginning to speculate about the impact of steam on their profession, for on August 17, 1807, many of them had seen Robert Fulton's *Clermont* begin its epic trip to Albany. The age of steam navigation thus began and in time would bring new leaders, such as Cornelius Vanderbilt and new names, such as the Black Ball and Cunard lines, to prominence in the port. New York was never hesitant to adopt innovations that added to its sea-going greatness.

By 1807, the value of goods exported from New York City exceeded that of any other American city or state, and the prospects of its continued increase seemed certain. It was with consternation therefore that the City learned that Congress, responding to the beliefs of President Jefferson, had, on December 22, 1807, declared a total embargo on all goods shipped to European belligerents. Frantic efforts by owners and captains launched a veritable fleet of ships by 8:00 A.M. the next day, but the prospect of hard times suddenly faced the City whose prosperity depended on the sea. By April, "grass had begun to grow on the wharves," and idle seamen had to be given food and shelter at the Navy Yard and at a specially created "soup kitchen." Some displaced sailors and unemployed carters were given jobs on the construction gangs building City defenses, but in large part a Washington-caused depression settled on Gotham. In 1809, over 1,300 merchants would be jailed for debt, and another 1,050 suffered the same fate in 1810.

The end of Jefferson's administration brought an end to the embargo, but the alternative adopted by James Madison gave little relief to the beleaguered merchants of New York. The Non-Intercourse Act banned trade with both England and France, but offered to reopen normal commercial relations with the nation which first withdrew its orders and decrees against American traders. A measure of America's commercial panic, Non-Intercourse lasted only fourteen months and was replaced by an even weaker measure. By the end of 1810, the port once again displayed the "busy hum of its daily life, and the sound of saws, axes, and hammers at the shipyards." Merchants obviously believed that even limited commerce, carried out under wartime conditions and costing huge insurance fees, returned them sufficient margins of profit. New York was against any war or any law that hurt its boom and its prospects.

Physically the City now extended almost two miles north of the Battery, but it remained relatively unimposing. A traveler commented, however, that there was "such a rapid increase of building as to make the City seem perpetually new," a comment still heard in the 1980s. City population reached 96,373 in 1810, and seized first place from Philadelphia. Most of the larger homes were

still located near the Battery and beyond these ranged a constantly growing number of well-stocked shops. Broadway was
New York's chief attraction and its constant activity was enhanced by the many poplar trees which "lent an ornamental and
somewhat suburban note to the City's principal thoroughfare."
City Hall, finished and occupied in 1811, was immediately recognized as one of the "most superb" buildings in the United States.
The City Hotel and its main rival, Washington Hall, once again
were filled to capacity and in 1812, the first building called
Tammany Hall was completed at Nassau and Frankfort streets.
Taking advantage of the times, the Hall served as a hotel as well as
a political meeting place and maintained this function until after
the Civil War.

War in 1812 was thus the least welcome news that the City
could have received, yet war was declared on Great Britain on
June 18. Trade conscious New York wanted peace but one of the
prime reasons for war was the imprisonment of American sailors,
an inconvenience to which the City seemed reconciled. Making
the most of a catastrophe, a series of swift and strong privateers
immediately put to sea to prey on British shipping around the
globe. Dividends were high from such trips, though the thin line
between privateer and smuggler made some New York merchants
flirt with treason during the next two years. The actual battles of
the war on both land and sea were far from New York, but when
Captain James Lawrence, whose *Constitution* had captured His
Majesty's frigate *Resolution*, visited the City late in 1812, he was
accorded a hero's welcome. When Lawrence was killed later in the
conflict, his remains were placed in the Trinity churchyard near
those of Hamilton. Many New York-based ships stayed at sea for
the duration of the war, an extended journey caused by the fact
that from 1813 the port was effectively closed by a strict British
blockade; ordinary sea trade ended as effectively as it had during
Jefferson's embargo. The closest that the City came to conflict
was on August of 1814, shortly before the burning of Washington,
when a British invasion fleet appeared off Sandy Hook and the
City girded for a repeat of Howe's invasion of 1776. Mayor Clinton
organized the defense and thousands of New Yorkers and even
volunteers from New Jersey worked on the fortifications. Tammany Hall competed with the Freemason Society to see who could
build the strongest ramparts along Brooklyn Heights while the

entire student body of Columbia College fortified the defenses at 123rd Street. "Let us die in the last ditch," trumpeted Clinton, rather than "tamely and cowardly surrender this delightful City."

By November, however, it became apparent that the blockading squadron had no intention of attacking New York and the bristling defenses were never to be used. Life returned to a semblance of normality, schools reopened, and the militia and volunteers returned to their neglected businesses. On February 11, 1815, news arrived that America's team of negotiators had arranged a peace settlement at Ghent, a treaty which expediently ignored almost all of the causes for the war and merely restored the *status quo ante*. Nevertheless, New York greeted the pact with "expressions of tumultuous joy"; the port could now be reopened, and the City could once again trade with the world. Behind the ship that brought news of the peace came a virtual fleet of British ships which, from April to June, "dumped" enormous quantities of goods into a ravenous market. New York's auctioneers made fortunes, the customs house took in unprecedented amounts of revenue, but the well-calculated dumping caused a business depression by the next year. America's domestic woolen and cotton manufacturers were almost wiped out, and the nation's first truly protective tariff had to be enacted in 1816, to prevent further damage to the economy. New York also felt the impact of the recession and it is estimated that between 15 and 20 percent of its population had to receive public assistance by 1820. But the City economy weathered this brief storm magnificently and, with its commercial houses, port facilities, and manufacturing capabilities undamaged by conflict, the course of its prosperity was hardly deflected by the war or by its aftermath.

Phenomenal growth became the hallmark of New York life in the decade following the Peace of Ghent. Already the largest urban center in the nation, the 1820 census showed a population of 123,706 and the City was often referred to as the London of America. Peace opened the commerce of the world once again to its merchants and, despite the best British efforts to hinder trade, the inventiveness and initiative of these entrepreneurs soon proved to be irresistible. More and swifter ships were demanded and the naval builders responded magnificently. In 1817, a group of Quaker merchants decided to initiate a new type of commercial venture, and within a year they had created the *Black*

Ball packet service. For centuries, ships had sailed from ports only when they had full cargo holds and when the tide was right. *Black Ball* packets carried both cargo and passengers, but left New York for Liverpool on a specific day, whether they were full or empty and even in the face of a gale. The *Red Star* line and the *Blue Swallowtail* line soon followed, and service was expanded to both London and France by 1824. Perhaps even more significant was the maiden voyage of the steam-driven, ocean-going *Savannah*, which made the trans-Atlantic voyage to Liverpool in 1819. Although this first trip proved to be a failure (there was too little cargo space and the machinery was inefficient) the future of commercial enterprise was clearly indicated. For many years to come, sailing ships remained the stalwarts of the Atlantic trade, but once New York merchants broke the Livingston-Fulton steamboat monopoly in 1824, the metamorphosis to steam shipping was inevitable.

Reliable packet service was of vast importance to the port in yet another sector of its economy. During the years surrounding the War of 1812, New York merchantmen had become dominant in the coastal trade of the nation, and far more vessels were engaged in this type of commerce than in the more glamorous oceanic trade. The enormity of New York Harbor allowed ample anchorages for those vessels bringing foreign imports and for those engaged in collecting the products of the eastern seaboard as well. In a methodical and unexciting fashion, New York assumed the essential factoring role in America's cotton export trade and soon dominated the trans-shipment of Southern cotton to European manufacturers. Many New York-owned ships sailed directly to Europe from the South filled with cotton, and returned via New York laden with textiles, manufactured goods and immigrants; they then refilled their holds and coasted southward to begin the triangle once more. Many other ships simply brought cotton to New York and the annual output of cloth manufactured there rose dramatically from only 3,000 yards in 1812, to well over 1,000,000 in 1825. In 1832, George Opdyke would build the City's first important clothing factory, selling his goods largely to Southern plantations, and creating the basis of a new industry. By their expertise and by their initiative, New Yorkers had forced oceanic cotton trade some 200 miles from its normal course, and had made their City the cotton broker to the world. The control of

coastal trade in conjunction with packet service to Europe solidified New York's trade dominance. When coupled with the City's
control of hinterland trade routes along the Hudson and Mohawk
rivers, the economic primacy of New York had been assured even
before the completion of the Erie Canal.

The extraordinary growth of foreign commerce necessitated the
creation of the entrepreneurial tools essential to such an expansion—insurance, banking, and auctioneering. Men such as
Philip Hone and John Haggerty made their fortunes by clearing
goods from the docks and getting them to the wholesalers and
retailers who marketed them across America. The primitive stock
arrangement of the Buttonwood Agreement was regularized into
a permanent exchange in 1817, and a series of new savings banks
were chartered to provide the capital that drove expansion. Specialized insurance companies were developed and soon ended the
traditional British monopoly of marine underwriting; by 1820,
the New York Board of Underwriters was created and soon built a
worldwide system of agents. Sailors of a dozen nations filled the
streets and drank and whored at the 2,500 saloons which served
the population's needs. Righteous and God-fearing merchants
and manufacturers might lament the presence of such men and
waterfront dives, but the phenomenon was as much the product
of their activity as was the increasing wealth of the City.

Urban land speculation also offered lucrative opportunities for
instant wealth, and men of all stations maneuvered unceasingly
for the possession of choice City lots. Those fortunate persons
with the skill or just plain dumb luck to acquire New York
property during these years made fortunes. Shrewd purchases of
New York real estate made the merchant John Jacob Astor one of
the richest men in America. During these years, the City was
selling its property at ridiculously cheap prices, but Astor correctly reckoned that continuous urban growth would sharply
increase property values. As a result, between 1800 and 1818, he
bought $35,000 worth of New York real estate annually. In addi-
tion to choice waterfront property, the fur entrepreneur acquired
acreage located on the outskirts of the City. These made him a
millionaire many times over when in subsequent years his holdings formed the heart of midtown Manhattan. When Astor died in
1848, his real estate holdings alone were worth an astronomical
$20,000,000, and were destined for an even greater rise in the

future. Other large investors in Gotham real estate were the Wendel, Goelet, and Rhinelander families, who systematically expanded their lands in anticipation of New York's future greatness.

The frantic expansion of the postwar decade was bound to leave many ragged edges in the wake of its growth, but the tendency was to dismiss these as only the "carelessness" of youthful development. Visitors were almost unanimous in condemning New York's dirty and crowded streets, its smelly docks, and its ever present pigs. John Palmer, an English traveler, complained in 1817, about ". . . the number and nuisance of the pigs permitted to be at large," while Baron Axel Klinckowstrom of Sweden, who visited New York in 1818, wrote:

New York is not as clean as cities of the same rank and population in Europe; in spite of the fact that the police regulations are good, they are not enforced and one finds in the streets dead cats and dogs, which make the air very bad; dust and ashes are thrown out into the streets, which are swept perhaps once every fortnight in the summer, only, however, in the largest and most frequented streets, otherwise they are cleaned only once a month. . . . The drinking water in New York is very bad and salty. Even the so-called Manhattan water, . . . is not good.

Filth and bad water combined to make disease as rampant as money-making. In 1815, the Board of Health urged New Yorkers to be vaccinated in order to prevent the spread of smallpox which had appeared in the City. Early in 1816, the Common Council appropriated $1,000 for free vaccinations, while Bellevue Hospital, formed from the Murray, Livingston, and Kip estates along the East River, expanded its facilities. A public institution for the Instruction of the Deaf and Dumb was incorporated in 1817, and this step was followed in 1818 by laying the cornerstone of the Bloomingdale Hospital for the Insane. Despite all these advances, however, yellow fever reappeared in 1819 and 1822; the epidemic of the latter year was the worst that the City had yet endured. Over 1,000 people lost their lives before the frost came in October, and those who could afford to do so fled the crowded City for the suburban safety of Greenwich Village or Harlem. Victims were interred in an open field, now Bryant Park, because the advancing City was encroaching upon the old potter's field near present-day Washington Square.

Growing pains could not mask the burgeoning cosmopolitanism which was to mark New York's future. In 1815, the first St. Patrick's Cathedral opened on Prince Street, tangible proof of the growing influence that Catholic immigrants were having in the City. Most of these unlettered newcomers were quickly incorporated into the labor market but some few of their offspring did manage to attend classes offered by the Free School Society; by 1824, more than 5,000 students would be enrolled in the society's six schools, while thousands of other youngsters were still privately educated. The City, while not yet ready to challenge Boston's cultural primacy, did display vitality in several other areas of intellectual life. It had already surpassed Philadelphia in the volume of its printed materials, and had become the center of the printing and publishing industry. Bookstores and reading rooms were opened by several of the more enterprising printers, and in these confines patrons could examine new editions or read one of the City's two dozen newspapers. Library societies were a praised innovation, and in 1820, both the Mercantile Library Association and the Apprentices Library were established to provide books on a circulation basis to people of moderate income. Indeed, to many observers, by the mid 1820s the City had surpassed both Boston and Philadelphia to become the literary capital of the nation. Books by such authors as James Kirke Paulding, Washington Irving and James Fenimore Cooper were published in the City and won large audiences. Morever, Manhattan was becoming a literary mecca for other authors; William Cullen Bryant and Fitz-Greene Halleck now called New York home.

While the City could not yet boast of major accomplishments in sculpture, music, or architecture, in the realm of painting some important things were achieved. By 1825, art was maturing in the United States, and many of the country's leading painters moved to New York. Portraiture was still the most popular means of earning a living for the artist, and many of the outstanding canvases of successful merchants, bankers, and government officials that have come down to us today date from this period. Painters from Europe also gravitated to the City, and the works of Fevret de Saint Mémin and Francis Guy attest to the attraction Manhattan held. "Tontine Coffeehouse" by the latter, depicts the bustle of commerce so characteristic of lower New York. Native New Yorkers, too, practiced their art in the 1820s. Samuel F. B. Morse displayed extraordinary talent, but his primary interest lay elsewhere; he is remembered today not for his paintings, but rather for his inventive genius. Perhaps the best resident artist in New York was John Trumbull. A student of the expatriate Benjamin West, Trumbull became the first important artist to establish a studio in the City. The New York Academy of Fine Arts, the first of its kind in the nation, encouraged artistic endeavor and Trumbull served as its president. His influence was much reduced when his artistic rivals created the even more prestigious National Academy of Design in January 1826.

In the artistic field with which New York particularly is identified, the theater, the early years of the century clearly foreshadowed the present. Even in 1815, the variety of dramatic and popular entertainments available to resident and visitor was already noteworthy. The Park Theater, under the management of Steven Price, was the showplace of the City and began the practice of bringing Europe's best-known performers to the United States. These tours invariably began in New York and then "went on the road" under Price's direction. Audiences were almost always more intrigued with the actors rather than with the plays, and America's leading performers of stage, song, and dance all gravitated to New York, where a reputation could be made. In 1821, a rebuilt Park Theater, accommodating 2,500 persons, opened and other large houses soon were constructed in a City which seemingly had an insatiable desire for more theater. The first grand opera in the United States, Rossini's *Barber of Seville*, was produced at the Park in November 1825. In 1823, the federal government added to Manhattan's cultural mix when it ceded the battlements of the old Southwest Battery to the City; after extensive remodeling, Castle Clinton became Castle Garden and balls, receptions, and plays were regularly held there. In 1824, when the Marquis de Lafayette, on the invitation of President James Monroe, returned to the land he had served during the Revolution, citizens of all classes thronged Castle Garden to honor the old warrior. The occasion was a triumph, but the indistinguishable nature of the crowds puzzled Lafayette greatly. He is reported to have asked Mayor Philip Hone, "But where are the people?"

Lafayette's question identified perhaps the most striking aspect of New York society; it was a City in which rigid class lines had begun to blur and in which opportunity beckoned to everyone. The class separations of the past had fallen and the metropolis had already entered the age of the common man, a more democratic society in which equality seemed psychologically present. To be sure, New York's "identifiable society" was still dominated by its commercial aristocracy and they lived graciously and well, yet the gap between classes seemed not insurmountable. The vigor of City business now derived from the myriad of activities carried out by its middle classes, and they in turn were constantly aware of entrepreneurial pressure from below. Life for the laborers, sailors, apprentices, and blacks was hard, but in this booming City there always existed the expectation of upward mobility. This belief in opportunity is as apparent in modern New York as it was a hundred fifty years ago.

This pervasive sense of egalitarianism had been extended into the arena of politics before the national Jacksonian revolution. In 1821, a Constitutional Convention met in New York and drastically altered the definition of those citizens entitled to the suffrage. The old Constitution required strict and heavy property qualifications for the right to vote in state or local elections. The new Constitution abolished the Council of Appointment, scattered the appointing power, and greatly increased the suffrage. To a very great extent the new document created, for white voters at least, almost complete universal manhood suffrage. Moreover, in 1817, Governor Daniel Tompkins had signed a measure which abolished slavery in New York as of July 4, 1827. Relatively few blacks could vote, but their physical freedom added to a general sense of optimism which infused New York life. The extension of the suffrage made politics less a gentleman's preserve than in the past and, as events proved, it provided the impetus for the rebuilding of Tammany Hall's power. Constitutional change had expanded the number of potential electors sixfold, and these new voters had to be led and counseled and organized. The extension of the suffrage was bitterly opposed by conservative men such as Chancellor James Kent, who feared that the City was on the brink of becoming a copy of Europe, where nations were dominated by urban capitals and by their mobs. "New York is destined to become the future London of America; and in less than a century, that City, with the operation of universal suffrage and under skillful direction, will govern the State." Kent deeply resented the presence in New York of large numbers of recently arrived immigrants, whose untapped voting potential could be opened through naturalization. Tammany also recognized this opportunity, and in the 1820s, it began to develop the techniques which would soon give it control of the City. The Constitution of 1821, by enacting into law an ideal of equality and democracy, fostered a bloodless Revolution which was to alter the history of the City and the nation. New York thus ushered America into its era of the common man.

By 1825, the City of New York had achieved commercial dominance in a rapidly growing America. The port handled almost half of the national imports and fully a third of its exports; 500 new business ventures had opened in the course of this single year. Over 3,000 new houses had been constructed in 1824, to meet the needs of a population soaring beyond 165,000, and the capital available in banking establishments had passed the unprecedented level of $25,000,000. Yet all this seemed only preparatory to the great event of the age; the long-awaited Erie Canal, DeWitt Clinton's "Big Ditch," was about to open. Clinton's services to the City as Mayor have been noted, but surely his greatest contribution to the greatness of New York was made during the years he spent as chief barrel-thumper and planner for a Canal which would tie his City to the western heart of the continent. After his last term as Mayor ended in 1815, Clinton won appointment to the Canal Commission of the state and in 1817, became Governor. On July 4, 1817, Governor Clinton turned the first spade of earth for the Canal project, and during its construction phase he remained its driving force. It is not pertinent here to repeat the prodigies of labor and engineering skill which built the 363-mile, 83-lock Canal "by guess and by God" over the next 8 years. Opponents charged that "Clinton, the federal son of a bitch, taxes our dollars to build him a ditch" but the Governor held firm; without his vision the Canal would never have been completed. Suffice it to repeat the judgment of one eminent historian that the project was "the longest Canal in the world, built in the shortest time, with the least experience, for the least money, and to the greatest public benefit." New York City was to benefit the most, however, for it became the essential middleman between the farmers and trappers of America's West and the civilization of Europe. Suddenly, New York's hinterland included the entire Middle West as well as the reinvigorated cities of Buffalo, Rochester, Syracuse, Utica, and Albany. The Canal guaranteed that New York and not New Orleans would be the outlet port for the produce of mid-America and it ended forever Philadelphia's faint hopes of overtaking New York as America's metropolis.

Finally the great day arrived and the Canal was opened. On October 26, 1825, the *Seneca Chief* entered the Canal at Buffalo; a series of cannon shots brought word of its entry to New York City some 81 minutes later. Not until November 4, did the barge and Governor Clinton arrive in Manhattan, but as he poured Lake Erie water into the Atlantic Ocean the Governor knew that he had achieved a miracle. When even some New York merchants opposed his scheme as "upstate improvements" he had held firm; when voters rejected him because of the higher taxes enacted he had persevered; and now the dream had become reality. The commerce of virtually the entire United States would now flow toward New York. Already the metropolis was America's greatest City, but in the next 30 years it would take its place as one of the great world centers. As much as one man may be responsible for such a historic change, the credit should go to DeWitt Clinton.

* * * * *

The keynote of New York life during the first quarter of the nineteenth century was rapid growth. The physical expansion of the City was evidenced by the following newspaper item: "Greenwich is no longer a country village. Such has been the growth of our City that the building of one block more will completely connect the two places; and in three years' time, at the rate buildings have been erected the last season, Greenwich will be known only as a part of the City, and the suburbs will be beyond it. . . ." Progress and change characterized Manhattan during these sometimes troubled, but mostly spectacular years. The City had become the nation's leader in population, commerce, finance, manufacturing and culture. Its development had been swift, but so solid were the foundations laid down during this period that few doubts remained as to its national preeminence or its future world destiny. The organizational and entrepreneurial skills displayed by the City's business leaders set the standard for urban communities throughout the nation, while the incredible success of the Erie Canal insured New York's primacy. Walt Whitman's later judgment was correct. New York is "the great place of the Western continent, the heart, the brain, the focus, the main spring, the pinnacle, the extremity, the no more beyond of the New World."

BRIEF BIBLIOGRAPHY

Albion, Robert G. *The Rise of the New York Port, 1815–1860.* New York, 1939.

Duffy, John. *A History of Public Health in New York City, 1625–1866.* New York, 1968.

Gilchrist, David T., ed. *The Growth of the Seaport Cities, 1790–1825.* Charlottesville, Virginia, 1967.

Ginsberg, Stephen F. "The Police and Fire Protection in New York City: 1800–1815." *New York History,* 52, April 1971.

Guernsey, R. S. *New York City and Vicinity During the War of 1812–1815.* 2 vols. New York, 1895.

Kaestle, Carl F. *The Evolution of an Urban School System: New York, 1750–1850.* Cambridge, 1973.

Mohl, Raymond. *Poverty in New York, 1783–1825.* New York, 1971.

Monaghan, Frank, and Lowenthal, Marvin. *This Was New York: The Nation's Capital in 1789.* New York, 1952.

Osgood, Samuel. *New York in the Nineteenth Century.* New York, 1910.

Pomerantz, Sidney I. *New York, An American City, 1783–1803.* New York, 1938.

Shaw, R. E. *Erie Water West: A History of the Erie Canal, 1792–1854:* New York, 1966.

Spaulding, E. Wilder. *New York in the Critical Period, 1783–1799.* New York, 1963.

IV

Building a Modern City

THE SUCCESSFUL COMPLETION of the Erie Canal guaranteed New York City's future prosperity. By 1835, the total costs of the project had been repaid and the upstate cities along its route had grown by an average of 300 percent. Canal traffic, only 218,000 tons in the first year of operation, would be 1,417,046 tons by 1840, and more than double again by 1850. City merchants, even those who had shortsightedly opposed the original plan, now basked in the prosperity that the "Big Ditch" created, and never ceased to compete for America's constantly widening Western markets. Additional areas were added to the metropolitan hinterland each year. In 1828, for example, the coal fields of Pennsylvania opened to New York when the Delaware and Hudson Canal was completed. Railroads such as the New York and Harlem were built, and in 1836 construction of the Erie Railroad along the Hudson began. Cleveland (1835) and Toledo (1840) were soon tied into the expanding New York network. Although most consider the story of the Erie Canal to be a nineteenth-century saga, it is somewhat shocking to recognize that the high point of tonnage carried was not reached until 1951. But the Canal was merely the most obvious of the many forces that were combining to make New York a metropolis in a class by itself. With its commercial and manufacturing firms, and its adventurous entrepreneurs and tremendous energy, the City seemed the natural base for those who sought to organize modern enterprise. A practical electric telegraph and transmission code existed by 1837, and various other inventions that presaged a new kind of urban society were being exhibited in New York; among them were pumps, submarine devices, and continually improving steam engines. Each in time would demand hundreds of laborers for production work, and each would play a role in the building of America's most modern City.

Manhattan by the 1840s was growing at such a phenomenal rate that it would soon contain more people than Baltimore, Philadelphia, and Boston combined. Immigrants from Europe poured in by the tens of thousands, making New York ever more cosmopolitan and heterogeneous. Gulian C. Verplanck, an old New Yorker, remarked that his native City had become a "sort of thoroughfare where almost every remarkable character is seen once" in the course of one's life. The great waves of immigration which characterized the 1840s came after the government of the City had been reorganized on a more democratic basis by the removal of property qualifications for voters. City offices were now elective, and politicians could use the votes of new citizens to acquire control of the government, and then manage municipal affairs for their own profit. Yet New York's municipal government, while far from perfect, was greatly improved. And despite the manifold problems created by the inrush of newcomers, a richer, more productive and culturally diverse City was created.

*   *   *   *   *

Five years after the Erie Canal opened, the population of New York was only 202,589; it was to quadruple in the next 30 years. A rising birth rate combined with the influence of thousands of European immigrants to produce this demographic explosion, a phenemenon enhanced by the fact that large families were commonly accepted as natural by all classes during that era. Far slower growth characterized the 2.5 percent of City residents who were black, a percentage far smaller than that of the Colonial period. Blacks suffered both *de jure* and *de facto* discrimination within New York State. In order to vote they had to fulfill a property qualification higher than that required of whites; property qualifications were still required for blacks long after an 1826 law removed this stipulation from white voters. An attempt to grant blacks full equality in suffrage was defeated in 1846, as it was to be in 1860 and 1867. Not until the passage of the Fifteenth Amendment in 1870, was the property requirement eliminated in both the state and the City. Moreover, blacks were subjected to both social and economic discrimination as the century progressed and soon lost their traditional position in the job market to new white immigrants. As Irishmen flooded into the City after 1820, they took on menial carting and wharf jobs which blacks had held, while their women soon expelled blacks from domestic service as well. This displacement process was simply one aspect of the vast sea change in City life which occurred in the decades before the Civil War.

European immigration remains one of the dominant themes of American history, and no urban center is as identified with that procession toward a better life than is the City of New York. Despite the immigrants from France, Santo Domingo, and Ireland who had already been incorporated into its fabric of life, the City of 1825 was still largely dominated by native-born citizens; only some 11 percent of its population was alien born. Yet Europe's 1830s were a time of deteriorating economic conditions, to which would be added political unrest in the next decade. Both situations led to the uprooting of populations, especially in the countries in the north and west of the continent. Artisans displaced by the Industrial Revolution and farmers who had lost their lands came to America by the thousands. In Ireland and Middle Europe, disastrous potato famines caused starvation and economic decline unmatched in the nineteenth century. In Germanic lands, the failure of the liberal Revolution after 1848, led to the exodus of an educated and privileged elite as well. Hundreds of thousands of economic or political refugees made their way to Atlantic ports, and crossed the ocean to seek advancement and security for themselves and their families. To these most determined and ambitious of refugees America offered possibilities not to be obtained in their native lands. Irish and British immigrants rose from 267,000 in 1841–45, to 750,000 in the next five years. In those same periods, German immigration soared from 105,000 to almost 330,000. The greatest transfer of population the world was ever to experience, the transfer of 35,000,000 people over the course of a century, had begun. Its effect was to change New York permanently.

From 1820 to 1870, 70 percent of over 7,000,000 immigrants to the United States came into this country by way of New York. In part this was due to the revised pattern of trans-Atlantic trade which New York's merchants had created, but it was also due to the undoubted reality that in the "New World" no place represented opportunity and possibilities more than did their City. By 1860, this influx had fundamentally altered the demography of Manhattan; the foreign-born then comprised more than 50 percent of the inhabitants and nearly three of every four New Yorkers would be of foreign stock. These people, brave enough or desperate enough to suffer the agonies of immigration, would provide the human capital for New York's continued expansion and would sometimes reap the benefits of their courage. Regardless of where the immigrants came from, their long Atlantic journey was to remain one of the central experiences of their lives. From start to finish, the newcomers were subjected to all manner of psychological and physical traumas, from disease-ridden ships to charlatans who swindled them of already meager funds; often they arrived in America weak and destitute. The trans-Atlantic journey itself was laden with pain, shortages of food, overcrowding, lack of proper ventilation, and poor sanitation. Sometimes whole boatloads of sick immigrants were dumped on American shores. New York City's hospitals, almshouses, orphanages, and then its prisons were crowded beyond capacity with foreigners. When the newcomers landed at the piers and wharves in New York Harbor, they were met by an unscrupulous army of "immigrant runners," who while sometimes providing them with assistance, often fleeced the hapless greenhorns. In 1846, William Frederick Havemeyer, then Mayor of New York, prohibited the runners from entering the immigrant depots; but they simply waited outside the gates, and the process of exploitation continued. Finally, the state legislature created a Board of Commissioners of Immigration to deal with the situation. While the board was not able to solve the problem of the "immigrant runners," it did designate Castle Garden (1855) near the Battery to act as a central landing spot for all incoming foreigners. Here, relatively honest and reliable ticket brokers, employment agents, and City employees dispensed aid and advice to the newcomers. Homes and jobs were often successfully obtained there by these strangers in New York. In addition, immigrant aid societies established by each nationality group helped their displaced brethren.

The Irish constituted the single largest group of new immigrants. Some 200,000 of them were living in the City by 1860. More than 100,000 German newcomers also settled in Manhattan, while smaller numbers of English, Welsh, Scotch, Scandinavians and Jews were scattered throughout the metropolis. As the foreign-born piled into New York, immigrant enclaves were created. The Irish crowded into rundown housing on the Lower East Side, while the Germans carved out a community farther north, extending from the Bowery to Fourteenth Street, called Kleindeutschland. Similar but smaller foreign sections emerged after later migrations and over the years nineteenth-century New York became an interlocking grid of ethnic neighborhoods.

"Ethnic neighborhood" brings to the mind of the modern reader a picture of bustle, vitality, exotic foreignness, and perhaps even a food festival, but this was not the immigrant reality. Living conditions were abominable, and the "fever nests" greeting most newcomers were already slums. To meet the housing needs of the new arrivals, older buildings had been converted into several apartments which were then further partitioned into still smaller units by unscrupulous landlords. Although immigrants filled these reconstructed houses from cellar to attic, the housing supply could never meet the demand. In 1837, an old brewery was converted into what might be considered the first tenement house; the site rapidly became a horror. One estimate asserts that the brewery was the scene of a murder a night over a three-year period. Even if much exaggerated, bleak conditions which fostered unending violence were everywhere present. Gradually buildings began to be constructed whose purpose was specifically to house immigrants and these were New York's first true tenements. Such buildings were four to five stories high with a narrow hallway opening from a street, courtyard, or alley. On each floor, including the cellar, several apartments opened into the hall and contained windows. But, there were also tiny rooms in the middle of the building containing no windows and whose only ventilation consisted of an airshaft that ran through the center of the structure. In most cases, there was another tenement in the backyard. Such a combination of front and rear buildings on the same lot created a labyrinth of passages and alleys which were dark, dirty, and redolent with odor. The average density per block in these areas was incredible; for example, in the seven wards below Canal Street, the gross density of population per acre rose from 94.5 persons in 1820, to 163.5 in 1850, while the average block density increased from 157.5 to 272.5 in the same period. Rents varied widely, even within the same building, and an apartment with windows could be had for between $3.00 and $13.00 a month. Single rooms in the middle of the building usually went to bachelors and cost $0.75 to $1.25 per week. In 1850, more than 29,000 immigrants lived in dark, dank cellar quarters and paid whatever the landlord could realistically demand. The owner or his agent never thought in terms of tenant welfare, only in terms of profit. The immigrant renter rarely complained, for his landlord held the threat of immediate eviction; someone else was always waiting for the rooms.

The harsh physical conditions of tenement life accentuated the gulf between tenants and landlords. A typical tenement house apartment usually had three rooms; two served as bedrooms, while the other was a kitchen, dining room, and living room combined. Water came from a street pump or well in the backyard, where the toilet was also located. Bathtubs and showers were nonexistent and water for bathing or washing clothes or dishes had to be carried from the street pumps outside to the kitchen sink. Body cleanliness was rare under these circumstances and malodorous immigrants went to public baths or washing establishments built by private philanthropists; the "People's Washing and Bathing Establishment" on Mott Street was the first one erected (1852). However, there is little doubt that many of the immigrants bathed in the rivers and then only during the summer months. Backyard wooden privies, through overuse and improper care, caused a constant health hazard. Their contents, instead of being drained away, often overflowed to the surface and became breeding grounds for disease. A contest to create a better apartment house led to the construction of a "Model Tenement" on Mott Street in 1855, but the model was not emulated by many builders.

Life in the tenements often seemed an endless struggle merely to survive. The high incidence of infectious disease was frightening to City officials, yet in the overcrowded immigrant slums quarantine regulations were impossible to enforce and any communicable disease could become epidemic. Yellow fever, a known factor, had visited the City five times between 1795 and 1822, but in 1832, a new strain of Asiatic cholera swept into New York. The epidemic centered on the warrens where Irish workers lived, and over a third of all cases were reported from the Sixth "Irish" Ward. Unlike the rich, many of whom sailed off on Cornelius Vanderbilt's steamer to Connecticut, the Irish could only die in agony and by the October frost they contributed by far the largest number to the City's 4,000 deaths. Cholera reappeared in 1834, 1849, and again in 1855, while typhoid fever ravaged the immigrants in 1837 and typhus erupted in 1842. All available statistics show that immigrants suffered far more mortality from disease than did the relatively better-off native born; for example, 83.9 percent of Bellevue Hospital's admissions in the decade 1849–59 were foreign born. Moreover, the Annual Report of 1857 showed that 60 percent of cancer deaths occurred among immigrants, and that 656 more aliens than natives died of tuberculosis. Perhaps the most fearful statistic was that two thirds of all New York City deaths in 1857 were the children of foreign-born parents. Nothing so graphically indicates the rigors of slum life than this awesome figure.

The disastrous slum conditions were in part produced by the residents themselves. Neglect, the uncontrolled dumping of garbage into the streets and airshafts, and the haphazard removal of refuse by City workers created a fertile breeding ground for disease. Few health officials had much desire to cater to the welfare of the poor and the City's sewer system for poor areas was nonexistent; indeed services were not provided for well-to-do areas until after 1849. To compound the dilemma of health care, even when immigrants received sound medical advice they often ignored the recommendations. They relied instead on superstition and home remedies to cure every ailment short of broken bones. An army of quacks offered "a pill for every ill" and bottles of patent medicine for a quarter; Dr. Fubarsch's Vegetbliche Lebenspillen, for example, cured "fever, colds, scrofula, worms, carbuncles, hemorrhoids, and all delicate female ailments." Such tonics of course were available to anyone and it would be foolish to believe that the better classes were immune to such remedies. As the population soared, New York was not a healthy environment and disease was no respecter of social status. The ailing public constantly proved receptive to new therapeutic systems which offered the promise of health. During the 1830s, the Botanic System which used herbal remedies was popular, and by the 1840s the "science" of homeopathy swept the City. The appeal of such fads was temporary but did illustrate the general desire for better health care. No additional medical institutions were built in New York during the 1830–50 period, although Bellevue underwent some expansion and several immigrant aid societies began to provide itinerant doctor, dentist, and midwife service. Not until 1855, did a new hospital open its doors, the Jews' Hospital (now Mount Sinai) and in 1858, St. Lukes (incorporated in 1850) also went into operation.

Because of their poverty, alien customs, or simply their inability to speak English, immigrants often clashed with the law. For the most part these were petty offenses such as drunkenness, disorderly conduct, or perhaps robbery. There had been a vast statistical rise in the crime rate as immigration increased, and New York's streets did indeed become more dangerous as the century progressed. As today, however, the victims of such minor criminality were largely found among the immigrant population itself. Both the Irish and German newcomers had a permissive drinking tradition, and this coupled with their assimilation difficuties and familial chaos often led to the local saloon. Frustration and misery could be forgotten there, and "under the influence" all sorts of crimes were possible. Even sober immigrants had difficulties with the native-born police who saw in foreigners a danger to social order and who picked up immigrants for petty misdemeanors. Even after Irishmen began to enter the force, they too repeated the canard that their people were particularly given to violence, and cited as proof the Flour Riot of February 1837, when a mob of hungry Irish laborers sacked warehouses filled with grain. Prostitution also was common among immigrant women, as poverty led many girls to the oldest profession. Immigrant children who survived the rigors of their life usually were helped in doing so because of membership in one of New York's many juvenile gangs. Living amid poverty, lacking familial guidance and educational or recreational opportunities, young men ran with the pack and the gangs of the slums were the result. The

Bowery Boys, the Dead Rabbits, the Kerryonians, and the True Blue Americans all were varieties of the same species, and each adopted "colors" as did youth gangs of a century later. A major difference was that in the 1840s there were no public agencies to deal with such discontents and the public rarely challenged gang domination of the Lower East Side slums. As a result of such gangs, 55 percent of all New York City arrests in 1859 involved Irishmen. Police also estimated that 60 percent of City prostitutes were foreign born.

Yet even as the authorities despaired and elitists lamented the barbarization of their City, another New York was taking shape. Manhatten by 1830 had already achieved supremacy in commercial, industrial, and financial endeavors and in the three decades before 1860 it came to the brink of cultural and artistic dominance as well. The mix of City life was so diverse that the process was to occur simultaneously with the aforesaid barbarization. As the influx of immigrants strained the City environment to the breaking point, another segment of the population brought to New York the cultural distinction it had always longed for yet rarely enjoyed. The pocketbook had usually triumphed over the soul in materialistic Manhattan, and for much of its population this rule remained true. Yet the City's maturation into a great urban center made more New Yorkers believe there was more to life than countinghouse or ledger book. Unparalleled progress was now made in such a varied spectrum of artistic and literary pursuits that Gotham's boosters could claim title as the cultural capital of America even before the Civil War.

One of the most obvious areas of general improvement was in the availability of literature itself. The 1840–60 period saw a large increase in the number of libraries available to adult New Yorkers, although most remained of the subscription society or private variety. The major exception to this rule was also the finest single library in New York, the Astor Library, created by a $400,000 bequest in the will of New York's greatest real estate speculator. Astor died in March 1848, and by April 1849, a board of eleven trustees had approved a site for a public library to be constructed on Lafayette Place. The trustees obtained an act of incorporation from the legislature, and held a competition for design proposals. From thirty submissions, the trustees selected that of Alexander Aelzer and awarded him a prize of $300. A contract for erecting the Astor Library was signed on January 2, 1850, and when the building opened four years later it already enjoyed a national reputation. Its collections would, in the twentieth century, become the nucleus of the New York Public Library.

The libraries of the City served only a small percentage of the population, and for most New Yorkers the most accessible means to cultural advancement was the newspaper. During the Jacksonian era New York City became the center of the nation's journalistic activity and a "newspaper town"; it seemed there was a newspaper for every possible taste. The penny press, which began on September 3, 1833, with the publication of Benjamin Day's *Sun*, offered political and social information within the reach of all, and other editors were not slow to follow this example. James Gordon Bennett founded the New York *Herald* in 1836, and was shortly followed by Horace Greeley's *Tribune* and William Cullen Bryant's New York *Evening Post*. All these papers served up a varied fare of sensationalism, news, essays on science or practical usefulness and gossip. To some extent, the papers also shared a modern, liberal philosophy; Bryant's *Evening Post* soon won a reputation as the most advanced publication in the City. Despite this, almost all readers acknowledged Greeley of the *Tribune* as the best editor of the age, and despite his support for many radical and eccentric causes, Greeley made his newspaper into the most influential in America. Karl Marx contributed incisive articles on European affairs to the *Tribune* and the editor's often-quoted "Go West young man" inspired countless thousands during the age of manifest destiny. The New York *Times*, founded by Henry J. Raymond in 1851, was more sedate in its coverage, but its readership grew and by 1860, it had outstripped all its competitors, including the *Tribune*. A hundred newspapers of a more specialized nature were published during these years and aimed at ethnic readers, religious groups, or laboring men. When one considers that both Herman Melville and Walt Whitman were also writing in New York during these antebellum years, the journalistic and literary quality of the City experience takes on even added luster.

As early as the 1830s periodical writers and artists began to gravitate into the orbit of New York. Nathaniel P. Willis, one of the leaders of Boston and editor of its *American Monthly Magazine* until 1831, moved to the City and explained that, despite Boston's many attractions, "a man who has any taste for cosmopolitanism would very much prefer New York." Manhattan was home to fifty magazines by 1847, including the *Democratic Review*, *Knickerbocker*, and the *New York Monthly*; *Harper's Monthly* was about to begin publishing and would quickly surpass them all. Charles Dickens made the first of several visits to the City in 1842, and was impressed with its commercial bustle and intellectual vigor. Just as New York drew journalists, so too it attracted artistic talent. Portraiture remained the most popular form of painting, but during the antebellum era many other genres made their appearance. Samuel Morse, John Vanderlyn, Thomas Cole, Asher Durand, James Longacre, and Henry Imman were among those who found Manhattan a congenial atmosphere for their art. On a more commonplace level, surely the most successful artistic collaboration of the century was formalized in 1850 when Nathaniel Currier and James M. Ives entered into partnership to produce lithographs which still retain their popularity. Originally sold at prices ranging from a nickel to a dollar, some of these lithographs today are worth over $10,000.00; for almost seventy years the firm's many artists documented a changing nation.

Old World architectural styles were also quickly adopted by New York and in the mid 1830s the Gothic revival was as advanced here as in England. Richard Upjohn was commissioned to build Trinity's third building in that style and when the church was consecrated in 1846 it brought him immediate renown and many private commissions; Trinity's steeple soared 260 feet and was the highest point in the City. Upjohn would soon help create the American Institute of Architects and serve as its first president. Not to be outdone, Archbishop John Hughes, leader of the growing Roman Catholic population, called upon his community to contribute funds to build a suitable cathedral for New York. "Dagger John" had the courage to hire a thirty-two-year old Episcopalian as his architect, and James Renwick began construction of today's St. Patrick's Cathedral in 1853; the cornerstone was set into place five years later, on August 15, 1858. Classicists had had their hour when the United States Customhouse opened in 1842, but the Gothic style was ascendant by 1860. Many other public, private, and even residential buildings bore its distinctive mark before the Civil War began.

Despite a somewhat limited clientele both serious music and

theater became more important in Manhattan during the antebellum years. Although the bulk of the population preferred the simple joys of the saloon or the music hall, wealthier New Yorkers insisted on better music and organized the New York Philharmonic Society; the Philharmonic's first concert was presented on December 7, 1842. The attempt to introduce Italian opera in the 1820s had proven less than successful, but it still remained an annual attraction; the most significant effort to expand that cultural horizon was made by Lorenzo Da Porte, who opened his Italian Opera House in 1832. By the 1850s opera was presented in Castle Garden as well. Attempts to offer "finer" music continued in 1854, when the Academy of Music on Fourteenth Street offered its first series of concerts. Serious music lovers might sniff but the masses still preferred entertainment such as that offered by the Christy Minstrels who first performed in New York in 1846. But high and lowbrow could each appreciate the artistry of the most famous diva yet to perform in New York. In 1850, P. T. Barnum brought Jenny Lind, the "Swedish Nightingale," to America for a series of 200 concerts at the unprecedented fee of $1,000 a performance. She appeared first on September 11 at New York's Castle Garden. Everyone who attended was thrilled, and some even thought the performance was worth the $225 top price ticket that Barnum had charged. The willingness and ability of New York's elite to pay such extortionate prices made it possible for Lind and those who followed her to strike it rich in the land and the City of opportunity. In 1852, singer Adelina Patti filled the Lyceum Theater—she was eight.

The already dominant position of New York in the world of theater was reinforced in the two decades before 1860. The Park remained the most prestigious theater, but the opening of the Broadway and Astor Theaters in 1847 raised several pretenders to its throne. Niblo's Gardens, the National, and the Bowery Theater were also handsome structures, but the Park remained the "fashionable house" which hosted Europe's best performers and Manhattan's best people. Fannie Ellsler, Fannie Kemble, Marcia Maliban, and the brilliant English actor William Macready all played to packed audiences in the Park. Theater could provide the basis for political statements as well as it did in May 1849, when the Astor Place riot erupted as a result of the rivalry between an American actor, Edward Forrest, and Macready. Irishmen who had never seen a play had no doubt who was the better actor, and when their demonstration against Macready got out of hand, troops had to be brought in to quell the riot; over thirty persons died before order was restored. By 1851, Edwin Booth had replaced both men as the matinee idol of the age and he was to remain America's leading actor for a generation. Over all, there was no doubt that in every artistic field New York advanced so rapidly in these years that it achieved a style of cultural life which the rest of the urban nation consciously sought to imitate. The words of the *Broadway Journal* were prophetic. "New York is fast becoming, if she is not already, America . . ."

But if New York was America it was a land deeply divided by an economic and social abyss. What possible connection could there be between the horrors of slum life and the elegance of a merchant's environment? How was it possible for the unlettered drayman and the sophisticated broker to communicate? The answer then, as it is today, was through the medium of political life. The great revolution of this age was in the equality men enjoyed during the voting process. During the 1820s, property barriers for the suffrage and imprisonment for debt had been eliminated in New York, and it had already been shown that Tammany Hall was aware of the potential power of the masses. By the turn of the decade, that organization had made clear its intentions of mobilizing the increasing numbers of Irish voters as its means to power. Tammany was able to naturalize immigrants expeditiously; its local leaders made alliances with the gangs which roamed ward streets; it saw that saloons had no trouble with the police; and it even began to obtain City jobs for Irishmen as lamplighters, fire wardens, meat inspectors and policemen. Slowly the power of Tammany grew and, though its leadership remained old-line merchant, its electoral strength was increasingly the product of the masses it cultivated. Everyone recognized that as newcomers to New York the Irish tended to be clannish, and took their enjoyment from the local saloon and the Roman Catholic Church. Tammany threatened neither of these outlets and offered a way of advancement. The Irish became the rank and file of an organization still dominated by New Yorkers of native birth; in time they would move into major positions where they would exert control. That process would take several generations but it was inevitable; the course of ethnic succession still manifests itself in the ethnic and racial politics which dominate our American scene today.

Moreover, the process of bringing immigrants into the political system seemed in conformity with the temper of the times. Across America the spirit of Jacksonian democracy was operative; the common man was taking power. In New York, where the City had been "the child" of state government since Colonial times, the Jacksonian spirit stimulated the citizens' desire to control their own affairs. This was especially true in regard to the office of Mayor, which continued to be a gubernatorial appointment. Excellent mayors had often resulted from this selection process; DeWitt Clinton had been succeeded by leaders such as Philip Hone, William Paulding, and Gideon Lee, but New Yorkers now clamored for the right of choosing their own chief magistrate. Not until 1834 did they achieve that privilege. In that year, popular election made Cornelius Lawrence, the Democratic candidate, Mayor for the first of his three terms; his tenure indicated the new reality of City politics. Lawrence was of course well-to-do, but in the words of aristocratic Philip Hone, his role had changed from that of a "respectable functionary," to being "the Mayor of a party." Hone seemed perversely pleased that "the rabble" of the Democratic party, during 1837's traditional New Year's Day greeting in the Mayor's home, actually took over the premises. They turned it into "a Five Points tavern" until Lawrence was forced to summon policemen to clear his rooms. By that time, the workingmen of New York "looked like men who knew they were free" and it seemed clear that their allegiance would go to the party or organization which served them best.

But Tammany in the 1830s was not the mythical, finely tuned, highly organized political machine described in the works of some political scientists. It was a coalition of factions deeply divided over questions of leadership and national issues such as banking, westward expansion, and abolitionism. These issues split the Democratic party in the City into radical and conservative wings. In 1835, the radical faction of Tammany Hall, calling itself the Equal Rights party, attempted to gain control of the club from the more conservative members representing the banking interests in the City. Leaders such as the agrarian reformer George Henry Evans, William Legget, editor of the New York *Evening Post*, Alexander Ming, Jr., John W. Vethake, and many others, met at

Tammany Hall on the evening of October 29, 1835, to decide on a course of future action for the Democracy. During the meeting, the conservatives plunged the hall into darkness by turning off the gas lights. This was an old tactic used in Tammany decision-making, but this time the radicals had come prepared. Producing candles from their vest pockets, they immediately lit them with a new type of wooden matches known as locofocos. The meeting of the rebels continued, and by the next morning all New York was chuckling at the new name of the radical wing of the Democratic party—Locofocos. What they stood for, however, was not so humorous. They professed above all to oppose monopoly in any form. They were disillusioned with the Tammany organization because they found it too elitist; its democratic promises were seldom matched by real accomplishments. Because they hoped to "democratize democracy," the Locofocos drew support from segments of society ranging from laborers to the professions. As hard money men, they distrusted the paper money of the banks. Banks themselves were despised as agencies of oppression and corruption, and corporations were opposed as inequitable and dangerous. They also opposed as unconstitutional, imprisonment for debt. In short, they sought to free American democracy from any taint of privilege and to purge it of inequities.

Such beliefs seemed sacrilegious to the merchant aristocracy which for so long had dominated both the economic and political life of New York. Locofoco radicalism led many Democrats to defect to the opposition Whigs and intensified the growing class and ethnic divisions of local politics. Immigration from Ireland and Germany continued to grow in the late 1830s and the Whigs, who futilely opposed Jacksonian democracy nationally, now feared that control of City life was about to be taken from them as well. The newcomers, who seemed determined to give their political fidelity to the Democrats, represented not only a new class but also a new religion. Whigs were both elitist and Protestant, and they saw in the emerging Democratic power bloc a threat to their hegemony and to the traditional separation of Church and State. Conservatives predicted meddling by the Catholic Church in politics, and feared for the purity of American, or rather Protestant, institutions. The Church's identification with Europe and its despotic monarchies made some New Yorkers even suspect the existence of a far-ranging papist plan to subvert the free government of the United States. In 1834, for example, the artist and inventor Samuel F. B. Morse wrote a series of letters to the New York *Observer* in which he argued that a papal conquest of America was already afoot. Whigs emphasized as well the economic competition that clannish, uncouth, criminal foreigners offered to honest, stalwart American workers. Thus, nativism and prejudice made their joint appearance in the politics of the City.

Whigs benefited immensely from their economic argument because of the "disappointed hopes and dwindling opportunities" which accompanied the national Panic of 1837. Early in that year the high cost of simple bread had fostered the "flour riot" outside the warehouses of Eli Hart, and by April there had already been 98 reported business failures in Manhattan. On May 8–9, a run on all City banks occurred and by May 10 all but three had suspended specie payments. In this chaotic situation, most voters turned again to Whig competence and they elected Aaron Clark, a rabid nativist, to serve as Mayor. That their new executive was bigoted didn't concern the workers in this year of national ruin; those workers fortunate enough to keep their jobs gratefully accepted shinplasters for their wages and ignored politics altogether. There were over 6,000 unemployed men in the construction trades alone, and despite Clark's attitude, a phenomenal 70 percent of all City relief went to the Irish. Shortly the storm passed. By August 1838, specie payments were resumed and by mid-1839, Democratic strength had recovered sufficiently to regain City Hall. Once again jobs became available and by the end of the decade New York, its work force, and Tammany Hall seemed poised to enter a new era.

For much of the 1840s the Democratic party controlled New York City politics but its domination was never secure because the Whig opposition constantly resorted to bigotry and economic discrimination to win votes. Nativists believed that foreigners were subverting the economic and moral foundations of the nation by causing the Panic, depressing wages, causing the decline of the apprentice system, and blindly voting en masse for unqualified candidates. As a result, signs reading No Irish Need Apply appeared in New York shop windows and a mounting harvest of anti-Catholic literature and oratory became a staple of political discourse. In 1841, artist-inventor Samuel F. B. Morse openly ran for Mayor as a nativist; though he lost, he established the mean spirit of the decade. In 1842, when the City inspected slum areas, reports ascribed the housing crisis to the immigrants and to their habits. Reform-minded gentlemen might organize an Association for Improving the Condition of the Poor (1843), but more of that wealthy class were apt to vote their prejudices; in 1844, James Harper, the publisher, won election as both a nativist and a reformer. Politically overt appeals to base instincts made sense to many of the middle-class artisans of the City, and the struggle for their allegiance became a vicious battleground during the rest of the decade. As the forties went on, a new reality became clear. In the age of democratic suffrage, the voters would select those men who not only promised, but also delivered, services that would prove useful to all citizens. In the confused politics of the decade, the obligation to upgrade the environment of the City to the benefit of all became the one unchallenged goal. The result of this harsh party competition would be a more modern New York.

The first and most essential City need was to develop an adequate and pure water supply, both for disease control and fire protection. When Mayor Cornelius Lawrence was elected in 1834, the City drew its water from only five sources—the Manhattan Company, public pumps, the famed Tea Water Pump, Knapp's Spring, and imported casks. The quality of New York water was so bad that many believed it to be the prime explanation for the increase in public drunkenness, and since 1818 those few who could afford it had purchased carbonated "soda water" as a substitute. Brewing was a major New York industry, but companies were threatened with extinction because the water used to make beer was so unpalatable. Doctors warned that disease would constantly recur unless substantial improvement in the water supply was effected. All these factors led the City Council to endorse in April 1835 construction of an aqueduct and reservoir system to be built with public money. Whether the project would have been pushed to rapid completion is questionable, but fate now took a hand and forced City action. Since the age of New Amsterdam, fire had been the most terrifying of all urban problems, and serious damage was caused each year by its ravages. The only existent mechanism to fight City blazes were poorly organized volunteer fire companies using outmoded, inefficient equipment; firemen were more interested in social and political activities than with the dangers of fire fighting. Rarely could such companies do more than confine blazes to already burning buildings. But on the morning of December 16, 1835, in zero degree temperatures, and with a virtual gale blowing, a fire in the warehouse district had suddenly blazed out of control. Many companies responded to the call but discovered that water outlets had frozen solid. Fire fighters were forced to watch as the seventeen-block area below Wall Street, over 700 structures, was consumed. The blaze was visible in Philadelphia and did not burn itself out for three days. There would be other giant conflagrations; one in 1845 burned for five days, and in 1858 a blaze consumed part of City Hall, but the "Great Fire" of 1835 was surely the worst in City history. Losses were estimated at $18–20 million and several insurance companies were driven into bankruptcy; several investors later cited the fire as a fundamental cause of the Panic of 1837. By 1839, however, reconstruction of the burned district was earnestly begun. So extensive were the changes that Philip Hone, ever the observant critic, remarked that New York is a difficult city to love since it is "rebuilt once every ten years." The fire, terrible though it was in its effect, contributed much to New York's future since it forced a revision of building codes upon a once reluctant merchant community. Even more important, it encouraged and made easier the task of those who were demanding a more certain water supply for the metropolis.

Until the fire, property owners had rejected all entreaties that they accept the taxes that a public water system would cost. Then in 1836, with the tragedy still fresh in mind, voters agreed to finance the Croton Aqueduct System. Charles King planned the project, thousands of construction jobs were filled by immigrant laborers supplied by Tammany, and the tunnels and dams necessary for the undertaking slowly took shape over the next few years. Among the special projects which were built as part of the system were the High Bridge across the Harlem River, the world's largest earth dam in Westchester, and an Egyptian-style reservoir on the site of present-day Bryant Park—for which 100,000 bodies had to be disinterred. Finally, in the summer of 1842, two reservoirs were filled and on October 14, a City-wide celebration marked the completion of a project almost as noteworthy as the Erie Canal. The daily flow of water was measured at 35,000,000 gallons and by 1852, each City resident was using up to 90 gallons of that most precious commodity daily. Health conditions soon showed dramatic improvement, the danger from fire was decreased, and property owners smiled at increased real estate values and a decline in insurance rates. New York's Croton System was the most modern in the United States and, with various extensions made over the decades, served as a model for the construction of other municipal waterworks. Croton also fostered a public demand for sewers which began to be fulfilled after 1849. Perhaps the only area which showed little improvement was the volunteer fire fighter system. Members of those companies adamantly opposed any innovation in an arrangement which guaranteed them income and importance. Since most companies were pillars of strength within the Democratic organization, Tammany successfully opposed all suggestions to create a metropolitan fire department. Not until 1865 was a paid, professional fire department created by the legislature, even then over the loud protests of the vested interests. New Yorkers had to be temporarily satisfied with a few new fire engines, the installation of more efficient firebell warning stations, and greater cooperation among the numerous volunteer companies.

Even before Croton was completed the next controversy involving public service had erupted, one made even more complex because of its relationship to the nativist issue. In 1840, Governor William Seward had suggested that public money should be made available to support Roman Catholic public education in New York, an idea that caught the immediate fancy of Bishop Hughes. On September 21, Hughes requested funds from New York's City Council and was informed that the Protestant-dominated Public School Society, a legacy of DeWitt Clinton, opposed the grants (as they had opposed grants to Protestant schools) as improper and probably unconstitutional. Hughes argued that the entire atmosphere and temper of the education available to Catholics attending public school was permeated with Protestant tenets, but his appeal was denied. Thus for Catholics, the few schools which parish donations had built were their only real alternative to a public education built on Protestant thinking. Hughes' plea for funds was rejected 15–1; in retaliation he organized a predominantly Catholic municipal ticket (the Carroll Hall slate) which proved to the Democrats that they could not win in

New York if they lacked Catholic support. The alliance between the Catholic Irish and Tammany thus became solidified after 1841, just as were the fears of City nativists. As a result of Catholic pressure, a law was enacted which, while it did not give money to Catholic schools, did appoint a Public Board of Education to administer the City school system; it was tacitly understood that instruction was to become less overtly Protestant. The first ward school opened in 1843, and Catholics felt that they had won a significant victory even though they had not won public financing of their separate schools.

During the years before the Civil War the average schoolchild in New York City rarely progressed beyond grade school, where he received an education based upon the traditional three Rs. Yet if quantity can be viewed as a mark of progress, the public school system by 1860 did enroll ninety percent of those children actually attending schools. There was, moreover, increasing demand that free instruction be offered at the secondary level, and in May 1846 the state legislature permitted the City Board of Education to establish a Free Academy; its first classes did not meet until 1849, but they were the precursors of a free City University system. The board also opened schools designed for artisan instruction and for tradesmen specializing in practical subjects; the first free evening school was also established in 1849. The next decade saw the creation of several public high schools and, although their physical conditions and teaching standards were poor, these did present the first real alternative to private secondary education anywhere in urban America. As for higher education, only a tiny fraction of City residents attended college and usually did so outside of New York. Still a few institutions of higher learning were founded; New York University was incorporated in 1831 as a nondenominational rival to Columbia's conservatism and Episcopal haughtiness. Union Theological Seminary (1837) was established by "New School" Presbyterians as an alternative to the Episcopalian General Theological School (1842), and the Jesuit Order founded St. Johns College at Rose Hill in the Bronx (1841), a school today known as Fordham University. These new schools had long paths of development before them and, with the exception of Columbia, New York higher education remained undistinguished until the late nineteenth century.

Thus, regardless of which party elected New York's Mayor, or whatever that executive's personal attitudes might be, all of the candidates discovered that the demands of the public for more efficient municipal government had to be met. The best example of this new political reality was the Nativist movement which had formally organized a political party in 1842, and in 1844, succeeded in electing James Harper as Mayor. Against all expectations, Harper could spend little of his time excoriating the Irish or lamenting the cuisine of Kleindeutscheland. Instead, his major preoccupation proved to be the creation of a municipal police force. Until Harper's administration residents of Manhattan were inadequately protected by an archaic police system which had evolved over two centuries. Among the defenders of public order were a night watch, 100 appointed City marshals, 31 constables, 16 daytime policemen, and an additional 35 men elected to serve as ward police. Although a legendary cop such as High Constable Jacob Hays might himself constitute a "one-man force," there was no doubt that a City of over 320,000 people needed a more effective system of maintaining order, especially given the rise in public awareness of crime. Some three years before Harper's election, the Common Council had authorized the industrialist Peter Cooper to investigate the expediency of creating a corps of 1,200 policemen. Little came of Cooper's proposals until May 7, 1844, when the state legislature gave its final statutory approval to a municipal police system; the law abolished the night watch and gave Mayor Harper the right to appoint 200 men to police the City. Because the legislation removed a time-honored source of local patronage and enhanced the Mayor's power, the aldermen of New York rejected the statute and substituted an ordinance which established three separate forces, each to be named by different levels of government. While the wrangling went on, the Mayor selected his first 200 men and they immediately won approval as "Harper's police." George W. Matsell, a bookseller turned police magistrate, was named first superintendent and the blue-clad police began to patrol the streets. Because uniforms set them apart from ordinary citizens, the new officers found they often became the target for unprovoked attacks and soon they demanded the right to work in plain clothes. Exactly how Harper intended to resolve the issues of police protection remains unclear, for in April 1845, he and his nativist allies were rejected by the voters. Democrat William Havemeyer took office and on May 13, 1845, a reorganization of the entire police system was enacted, and a force of 800 men was authorized. Uniforms were temporarily abandoned and stationhouses were established where patrolmen could be found and criminals detained. The City was divided into three districts, each of which had a court, magistrates, and clerks. The Mayor appointed the chief of police and all captains with the advice of the council, but the selection of policemen became a right of political leaders on the ward level. The NYPD had been born and although its professionalization was still far in the future, there was at last reason to hope that the streets might be safe for the public.

But though the streets might belong to the people, there could be no doubt that they were filthy. One of Havemeyer's major tasks was to overcome New York's well-deserved reputation for squalor, a reputation it maintained despite innumerable regulations dating back to Colonial days. Horses remained a prime mode of transportation, pigs still scavenged in the streets, and cattle on their way to slaughterhouses contributed to the piles of manure which fouled already dirty streets. Led by Havemeyer, the Common Council in 1845 enacted a comprehensive sanitation law which provided for the cleaning of the streets by means of mechanical devices, and appointed an adequate staff of street and sanitation inspectors who would work conscientiously at their jobs. For a few years, the law was obeyed and real improvement was apparent. Garbage was collected and taken away in small carts; fines were levied on private citizens who did not clean their portion of the curbsides; and health inspectors began to see to the proper cleaning, draining, and maintenance of privies and cesspools. Unfortunately, the political influence of private contractors who collected the garbage and refuse prevented the formation of a publicly owned and operated sanitation department until 1866. During this twenty-year-period the mayors who succeeded Havemeyer allowed the regulations to fall into a state of neglect. All during the 1850s, however, City-financed sewer construction and the systematic paving of Manhattan's streets generally added to the improving appearance of a modern Gotham.

Such a basic amenity as paving was very important because the City's growing population constantly filled the streets. New arrivals had totally saturated the housing supply and the lower part of

Manhattan Island was filled from river to river. Immigrants settled as close to the existing job market as they could, and most business enterprise was clustered in the dock and warehouse area at the southern end of the island. Repelled by the hordes of laborers walking to work or seeking jobs, the owners of homes and businesses downtown began to relocate their families to the relative quiet of uptown addresses. Since real estate values were rapidly increasing, row housing replaced the traditional single lot residence of earlier New York. The Washington Parade Ground was a preferred area for the new construction, and Gramercy Park was already an exclusive residential enclave. The turmoil of New York's traditional moving day—May 1—thus saw the uprooting of the old and the influx of the new as Manhattan's population groups rearranged themselves on their common island home.

Wherever their hegira took the rich, they agreed that a better transportation system would be necessary in order to provide them quick access to their place of business. The small six-passenger stages which once ruled New York's streets and made its traffic jams nationally famous were replaced by omnibuses in the 1830s, and by streetcars in the 1850s. Despite the larger capacity of those conveyances, traffic conditions continued to deteriorate. Moreover, railroads such as the New York and Harlem actually ran on rails laid flush with City streets until such traffic was banned in 1839. By 1858, the streetcar lines serving Manhattan carried 35,000,000 passengers annually, a ridership drawn from workers and from the wealthier classes. Ordinary New Yorkers still walked to work, but as the century progressed the age of mass public transport systems would transform the City and create both straphangers and commuters. In any case, it was evident that a growing transportation system demanded paved thoroughfares, and by the time of the Civil War half the island had been so improved.

As New York built northward, it eliminated forever the rural quality which had once been evident in the metropolis. By the mid 1840s the ravages of the Great Fire had been eliminated, but tenements filled with immigrants had replaced the warehouses of the Lower East Side. In that area of the City, grass and trees were virtually nonexistent. Although Bryant Park near the Croton Reservoir was enclosed in 1846, and Madison Square opened in 1847, both were small in area; it became suddenly apparent that no real public parklands graced the teeming Manhattan landscape. Many considered the salvaging of green space to be a private rather than public responsibility, but as the population (515,547 in 1850) continued to soar, popular demand for park facilities increased. Mayors Ambrose Kingsland and Jacob Westervelt both favored such an initiative, and in 1853, the state legislature approved the construction of a park of 760 acres on the wasteland "goose pasture" located north of present-day Fifty-ninth Street. In 1857, a national contest to design a Central Park for Manhattan was won by Frederick Law Olmsted and Calvert Vaux. Andrew Green was appointed president of the Park Commission and work quickly began on what today is universally considered one of New York's unique treasures. Much was accomplished in the first year of construction since thousands of jobs were given to men unemployed because of the Panic of 1857, but during the Civil War years work virtually halted. Not for twenty years would the vast project be completed, but the grandeur of its design and the integrity of its implementation have made Central Park America's model for urban green space.

The reality of New York life in these active decades was that whichever party held power, its primary concern had to be the creation of a suitable urban environment for the people of an important world metropolis. Whether a Mayor won office as a Locofoco, Whig, Hunker, or Nativist, he found that his popularity and his future depended on his ability to bring water, sanitation services, police protection, or parks to City residents. The voters proved to be stern critics and few mayors were granted more than a single reelection during these decades when New York became modern. Progress was not only a matter of municipal or mayoral initiative. In 1837, after eight years of experimentation, Samuel Morse had exhibited the first successful electric telegraph; five years later he supervised the laying of a submarine cable between Governor's Island and Manhattan. By 1846, a telegraph line to Philadelphia opened for public use. The nation had suddenly become much smaller and that shrinking was also obvious as rail connections knit Manhattan to the nation. Perhaps a dozen railroads depended on the commerce of New York and in 1853, Commodore Cornelius Vanderbilt, whose first fortune grew out of steamships, began to consolidate many of them into the Grand Central System. But the sea remained the key to New York's trade and in 1840, a fifth of all American shipping was owned by New Yorkers. The 113 docks on the East and Hudson rivers provided thousands of jobs for both artisans and unskilled immigrants. Steam packet service with Europe had been established in 1838, and *Cunard* Lines moved to New York from Boston a year later because its lucrative trans-Atlantic business now centered on the port. But despite the many smokestacks in the bay, the most envied workers on the docks were those artisans and sailors who labored on the famed clipper ships. Constructed and launched along the East River, these vessels were perhaps the loveliest of man-made commercial ships. The clipper age was short in duration (1843–60), but immensely profitable for a few. Spurred by the repeal of Britain's Corn Laws (1846), and by the discovery of gold in California (1848), fleet vessels such as the *Rainbow* could earn a 200-percent return on a single voyage, while the *Flying Cloud* set speed records that caused men to shake their heads in wonder. Across the globe the most famed City area was South Street, that "forest of masts" which illustrated as nothing else the commercial supremacy of New York. It is interesting to note that modern Manhattan is attempting to recapture some of the glory of that age with its renovated and expanded South Street Seaport Museum which opened in July 1983.

Beyond its municipal growth, its economic development, and its cosmopolitanism, New York participated as well in the "democratic ferment" that marked Jacksonian America. Reform in virtually all areas of social life made the age one of ferment and change, and some City residents joined wholeheartedly in crusades against the evils of society. In New York the temperance movement probably aroused the most passion. Alcohol was identified with immigrants and condemned by reformers as the major cause of poverty, ruined health, and criminal behavior. Throughout the City, unlicensed establishments sold liquor to anyone with the price of a drink while "hole in the wall" saloons operated openly in defiance of statewide laws which prohibited the sale of liquor without licenses. During the 1840s, excessive drinking became commonplace among all classes and the temperance movement grew accordingly, especially among Protestants. In an inevitable counterstroke, it was Tammany leader Isaiah Rynders who organized legitimate liquor dealers into a Protective Union to oppose ordinances against drink; the Union successfully opposed any statutory action by the City Fathers. The influx of whiskey-drinking Irishmen and beer-loving Germans made distilling and brewing big business, and hundreds of New York hotels, board-inghouses, and restaurants relied on spirits to turn a profit. Liquor sales were critical to successful business, and the connection between dealers, hosteleries, and City Hall, was close. Meetings might be held and temperance rallies might evoke enthusiastic responses among the committed, but by the 1850s liquor interests were able to mobilize the foreign-born voters into a strong antitemperance bloc. Over 5,000 City establishments sold liquor, and many grogshop owners were ward heelers within political organizations. Thus, despite the hopes of those reformers who hoped to banish "Demon Rum" and eliminate forever the "face on the barroom floor," no action was taken by New York to prohibit drink.

New Yorkers also, for the most part, remained aloof from the abolitionist movement. Although Manhattan was home to Arthur and Lewis Tappan, men who contributed prodigious amounts of time, effort, and money to national abolition efforts after 1831, the average citizen did not rally to the antislavery crusade. Only in the 1840s, as the controversy became more heated due to territorial expansion, did more New Yorkers embrace this particular reform. Within the Democratic party a deep cleavage developed after the Mexican War (1846) and a radical group called Barn-burners arose within Tammany Hall. Barnburners were hostile to banks and to increases in the state debt, and were especially opposed to the extension of slavery into free territories. As their name implied, if they could not control the Democratic barn they would willingly burn it down and their principled split from the more pragmatic Hunkers shook the very foundations of Tammany Hall. The party's division over abolitionism paved the way for the election of the Whig candidate for Mayor in 1847, and ushered in a period of Democratic decline. Irish voters were largely unsympathetic toward abolitionism—they already competed for jobs with free blacks—while German immigrants seemed more favorable to the cause; many of the latter in time left the Democratic party and became Republicans. Thus the slavery issue, while peripheral to the daily concerns of the City and to the vast majority of its citizens, nonetheless had a major impact on New York because it led to the rupture and remodeling of the Tammany organization.

Temperance and abolitionism aroused the greatest interest but they were far from being the only causes championed by progressive New York in the antebellum years. Many specific reforms derived from the sympathy of the "better classes" for the plight of recently arrived immigrants; for example, in 1836, John McDowell organized the New York Magdalen Society to help Manhattan's prostitutes, and six years later, Thomas Eddy and John Griscom founded the New York House of Refuge, the first juvenile reformatory in this country. In 1843, the Association for Improving the Condition of the Poor was established, and in 1848, the New York Ladies' Home Missionary Society of the Methodist Episcopal Church made plans for the reformation of the notorious "Five Points" section. From their work, the "Five Points" Mission and the "Five Points" House of Industry were created to serve the Irish. Socially aware New Yorkers established in 1853 the New York Juvenile Asylum to cope with the problem of vagrant children. In the same year, the Children's Aid Society was founded by Charles Loring Brace. Pauperism, relief for the poor, care of the insane, improvement of prisons and local jails, and equal rights for women, all raised the urgent concern of some dedicated Manhattanites. Though the reformers did not always achieve their goals they, nevertheless, won some significant victories. Their personal commitment and public accomplishments were of lasting value to the development of a social consciousness in New York.

* * * * *

By the mid 1850s, New York had taken its place as the greatest City in the nation. In the generation since the opening of the Erie Canal, its population had soared beyond 700,000 and the influx of immigrants still showed no signs of abating. Phenomenal growth, continued economic strength, and cultural maturity were the hallmarks of the age. New York had been transformed from a cohesive geographical and economic unit into a sprawling, untidy giant. The diverse economic, ethnic, and racial groups which made up its large population had little in common except that they all were New Yorkers and somehow had to learn to coexist. The municipal government, a product of eighteenth-century philosophy, suddenly was forced to cope with problems created by growth, technological change, and the need to acculturate thousands of new citizens. With a few notable exceptions, the public officials of New York were undistinguished leaders forced to deal with unprecedented issues of crime, disease, poverty, and development. That they managed as well as they did and made significant progress in providing essential services to all New Yorkers is amazing. The City had not been mastered, but at least there was hope that it might yet be controlled.

What seemed most urgently needed was the development of greater political and social coordination through effective leadership. Leaders must be found who could respond positively and effectively to the changing economic and social conditions of the City. No longer could municipal offices be staffed by one-dimensional, if public-minded, merchants or aristocrats. New York's leaders would now have to be men with a different view of municipal government, professional politicians who viewed public service as a legitimate career. Since these new leaders held no particular interests other than power and personal aggrandizement, they might well be able to centralize government and offer programs to unite the varying economic, political, and social interests of New York's vast, heterogeneous population. Beginning in 1854, with the rise to political prominence of Fernando Wood, the City would receive this new kind of leadership. New York's "Bosses" had a greater effect upon the society and government of the metropolis than any men of their time.

BRIEF BIBLIOGRAPHY

Barrett, Walter. *Old Merchants of New York, 1863–1866.* 5 vols. New York.

Dolan, Jay P. *The Immigrant Church: New York: Irish and German Catholics, 1815–1865.* Baltimore, 1975.

Ernst, Robert. *Immigrant Life in New York City, 1825–1863.* New York, 1949.

Furer, Howard B. *William Frederick Havemeyer: A Political Biography.* New York, 1965.

Gibson, Florence E. *The Attitudes of the New York Irish Toward State and National Affairs, 1848–1892.* New York, 1951.

Grinstein, Hyman B. *The Rise of the Jewish Community of New York, 1654–1860.* New York, 1945.

Hansen, Marcus L. *The Atlantic Migration, 1607–1860.* New York, 1940.*

Hugins, Walter. *Jacksonian Democracy and the Working Class: A Study of the New York Workingman's Movement, 1829–1839.* Palo Alto, 1960.

Nevins, Allan, ed. *The Diary of Philip Hone.* 2 vols. New York, 1927.

———, and Thomas, Milton H., eds. *The Diary of George Templeton Strong.* 4 vols. New York, 1952.

Rosenberg, Charles E. *The Cholera Years: The United States in 1832, 1849 and 1866.* Chicago, 1962.*

Spann, Edward. *The New Metropolis: New York City, 1840–1857.* New York, 1981.

*Paperback

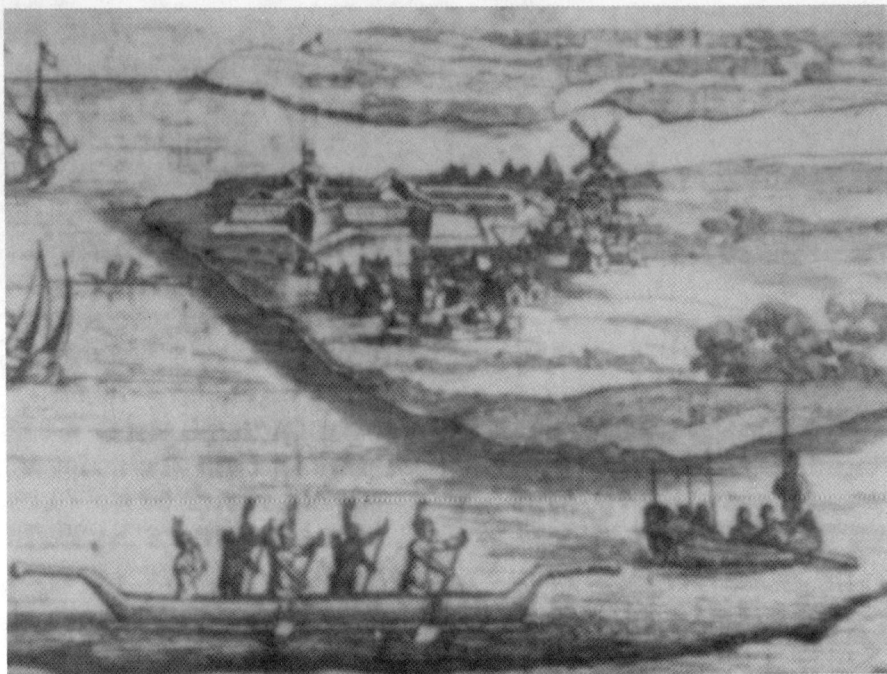

Earliest View of New Amsterdam, 1620s

J. Clarence Davies Collection,
Museum of the City of New York

New Amsterdam on the Eve of Incorporation, 1652

Museum of the City of New York

Peter Stuyvesant
New York Historical Society

Federal Hall, 1789
*Edward W.C. Arnold Collection,
Museum of the City of New York*

New York from Governor's Island, 1774   *Museum of the City of New York*

Broad Street in New York City, 1797

I.N. Phelps Stokes Collection
New York Public Library
Astor, Lenox and Tilden Foundations

Government House, 1797
New York Historical Society

Tontine Coffee House, 1798
New York Historical Society

Broadway and City Hall Park, 1820s

*J. Clarence Davies Collection,
Museum of the City of New York*

South Street's "Forest of Masts," 1830s

*Edward W.C. Arnold Collection,
Museum of the City of New York*

Trinity Church and Wall Street, 1829   *New York Historical Society*

St. Paul's Church and Broadway Stages, 1831   *Edward W.C. Arnold Collection,*
Museum of the City of New York

The Great Fire, December, 1835

New York Historical Society

The Life of a Fireman — The Race, 1854

*J. Clarence Davies Collection,
Museum of the City of New York*

New York from the Steeple of St. Paul's, 1848

Eno Collection,
New York Public Library
Astor, Lenox and Tilden Foundations

The Seventh Regiment in Washington Square, 1851

Museum of the City of New York

The Crystal Palace and Manhattan, 1856 *New York Historical Society*

Printing House Square, 1864 *Edward W.C. Arnold Collection, Museum of the City of New York*

"Model Mayor" Fernando Wood

William Marcy "Boss" Tweed
Culver Service

"Honest" John Kelly
Brown Brothers

Richard Croker, "Master of
Manhattan"

The Tammany Tiger Loose "What Are You Going To Do About It?"

To the Victor Belong the Spoils (In center) Thomas Nast's cartoons chronicled the awesome power and the sudden decline of the Tweed Ring in *Harper's Weekly*, November, 1871.

The Seventh Regiment Parades on Broadway, 1862   *Harper's Weekly*

A Panorama of New York and its Wharves, 1876   *New York Historical Society*

The William K. Vanderbilt Mansion

New York Historical Society

Bandits' Roost, 1880s
*The Jacob A. Riis Collection,
Museum of the City of New York*

Tenements on Roosevelt Street
*The Jacob A. Riis Collection,
Museum of the City of New York*

Union Square, 1882   *Museum of the City of New York*

New York and the Brooklyn Bridge, 1889   *J. Clarence Davies Collection,*
                                                Museum of the City of New York

Mayor Seth Low

Mayor William Gaynor
Courtesy of Harris & Gifford

Mayor John Mitchel

Mayor John Hylan
Underwood and Underwood

Judge Seabury confronts Jimmy Walker, 1932   *Brown Brothers*

Fiorello LaGuardia and Robert Moses, the Great Collaborators, 1935
Collection of the Municipal Archives
of the City of New York

Rockefeller Center's First Christmas Tree, 1931   *Courtesy of Rockefeller Center*

Rockefeller Center, the "City within a City," 1981 *Courtesy of Rockefeller Center*

The George Washington Bridge to New Jersey
Courtesy of the Port Authority of New York

Mayor Vincent Impellitteri
Wide World Photos

Mayor William O'Dwyer
*Collection of the Municipal Archives
of the City of New York*

Lower Manhattan and the East River Crossings
Courtesy of the Port Authority of New York

The United Nations Complex and Midtown Manhattan
Courtesy of the United Nations

Mayors John V. Lindsay, Edward I. Koch, Abraham Beame and Robert F. Wagner
Photo by Holland Wemple

New York Harbor, 1982

Courtesy of the Port Authority of New York

V

THE AGE OF THE BOSSES

FROM 1830 TO 1860, THE City of New York quadrupled in size to become both America's metropolis and a major factor in the pattern of world trade. It accomplished this growth with a ramshackle type of government and little effective administration. The City obtained the right to select its own Mayor in 1834, but that official was not even granted a two-year term until the charter revision of 1849. Yet somehow Manhattan incorporated hundreds of thousands of immigrants, drew the commerce of the nation and the world toward its bustling harbor, and provided its citizens with a better quality of life than any astute observer would have thought possible. To a large extent the growth of the City resulted from the ambition of its individual members; the larger corporate body proved far harder to prod into activity. This chapter will examine the careers of several New Yorkers who learned to manipulate and move the government so effectively that they were labeled "Bosses." The political careers of Fernando Wood, William Marcy Tweed, and "Honest" John Kelly dominated the political life of the City for thirty years and gave it a reputation for municipal corruption and political chicanery which would long endure. These Bosses were opportunists, political pragmatists, and implacable enemies to those who opposed them, but each was more than simply a plunderer of the public. It is necessary to understand the complex role of the Boss before one can appreciate the nature of nineteenth-century urban politics.

137

Although there were many factors causing Bossism, the increasing public demand for urban services was perhaps the most crucial factor behind its emergence. To provide such innovations as sewers, pure water, transportation systems, and police and sanitation departments cost vast amounts of public money. In the twentieth century we have become accustomed to "special interest" politics and to "iron triangles" of bureaucratic/business/governmental influence. Similarly, it is hardly surprising that mid-century America created alliances between City officials who awarded construction contracts, and the utility franchises and businessmen who sought those lucrative plums. Bribery emerged as a fixed cost of business enterprise in Manhattan, and law enforcement officers closed their eyes to corruption and crime; it was not only profitable for them to do so, but also sometimes necessary. New York's Bosses found their most loyal support among immigrant voters. In return for votes, Bosses provided new citizens with municipal functions not usually performed by agencies of government. In recent times, films, plays, and novels have all had a tendency to overromanticize municipal machines and their great Bosses, yet the system which they operated arose from necessity and often did perform nobly. In 1837, for example, the food baskets distributed by Tammany Hall—at a time when no Boss ruled—kept hundreds from destitution. Charity and comradeship were as essential to the Boss and his machine as were contracts and commissions. Democracy had transformed politics into a mass participation sport, and the Bosses understood this before anyone else; they would remain in charge as long as they met the demands of the public. Because of their usefulness and insight, Bosses were to dominate New York politics for a century.

*   *   *   *   *

The years of the 1850s were a time of political chaos and sectional animosity which culminated in the Civil War. New York was hardly immune to such epic concerns, and the disorder of national politics had a major impact on City life. As the decade began, the Congress agreed upon the Compromise of 1850, the last great attempt to settle the slavery and territorial issues dividing the nation. The national Democratic party endorsed the compromise but many New Yorkers found the legislation unacceptable. Dissidents from the national consensus included not only abolitionists, but also Democratic Barnburners and "conscience" Whigs. Conversely, it was the conservative, mercantile Whigs of New York, whose prosperity and future depended on continued Southern trade, who took the initiative of supporting the compromise; in October 1850, they sponsored a mass meeting of commercial New York. A committee report urged that the entire business community, regardless of political affiliation, endorse the provisions of the compromise as good for the City. After hurried consultations, a Union electoral ticket was agreed upon, won the endorsement of ten thousand merchants and firms, and swept to a massive victory on November 5, 1850. The theme of the merchants' campaign was Save the Union, and the appeal won City-wide support because New Yorkers were deeply frightened by the divisiveness of the slavery controversy. The Union ticket, led by Mayor Ambrose Kingsland, restored calm to the City and initiated a period of four years of business domination.

New York had always been a "City of Commerce" and it was somehow natural that businessmen should seek and obtain a temporary lull from conflict. But the larger reality of the early 1850s was that party lines across America were disintegrating under the pressures that were beginning to convulse the nation. As the moral issue of slavery and unending discussions about the nature of the Union dominated the atmosphere, opinions and ideas shifted and the ties of party loyalty snapped. By the end of the decade only the Democratic party would remain as a national political organization, and its influence alone would not be sufficient to prevent Civil War. A fragmented party structure became apparent in New York's coalition election of 1850, and continued to operate for the rest of the decade. But unlike the national scene, where weak figures such as Franklin Pierce and James Buchanan came to power, in New York the breakdown of party structure offered opportunities to stronger leaders. It was an unfocused, disordered, and confused age, one made for the independent and self-centered operator. Mayor Kingsland himself proved to be less committed to Whigery than he was to personal gain, and he shortly entered into an alliance with Democratic members of the Board of Aldermen which enriched them and their associates at public expense. So blatant did the overcharges become that by 1852 the administration had been baptized "The

Forty Thieves." Compared to future depradations, the corruption of the Kingsland regime was of secondary stature and its padding of City accounts by thousands of dollars was minor. But so intense was the public reaction that Kingsland was forced into retirement after only one term, and a Citizen's Committee led by Peter Cooper saw that many of the Democratic aldermen were involuntarily retired. A revision of the municipal Charter in 1853 removed franchise-granting powers from the City Council and restricted the appointment power of the aldermen. Perhaps the most inventive of those ousted officials, a young Tammany partisan named Bill Tweed, landed on his feet and spent a term in Congress from 1853 to 1855. He there discovered that his taste ran to municipal rather than national politics, and he returned to Manhattan where he set his sights on higher realms of power than that available to a simple alderman.

Temporarily, however, the purity of reform ruled in Manhattan and the metropolis could bask in both rectitude and continued growth. The 1853 edition of the *Stranger's Handbook* for New York listed 272 churches, 8 marketplaces, 25 Broadway hotels, and 7 theaters to service the tourist or businessman. A visitor could visit Castle Garden, Franconi's newly opened Hippodrome, Barnum's world famous museum, or even have the thrill of ascending the 350-foot tower of the Latting Observatory. Built of timber and braced with iron, the observatory was the tallest structure yet built in America, and perhaps qualifies as New York's first skyscraper. At its base, the observatory was filled with expensive shops, and a steam elevator provided visitors with access to upper landings where telescopes were installed for public use. Yet with all its tourist appeal, the Latting Observatory was only an adjunct to the major attraction of 1853, the first American World's Fair. This vast exhibition had been opened by President Franklin Pierce on July 14, in a vast, unique structure on Forty-second Street, the Crystal Palace. The fair had over 6,000 exhibits from the United States, Canada, the West Indies, and most of the nations of Europe. It ran for 16 months, and after it closed the palace was used for concerts, balls, banquets, and local fairs. Sadly, both of these spectacular structures were victims of fiery disaster. In 1856, the observatory burned down, and on October 5, 1858, a blaze consumed the supposedly fireproof

Crystal Palace; in less than 20 minutes the pride of Manhattan became an "incandescent ruin."

In 1854, the disintegrating process which had been apparent in municipal politics for several years was completed. The precipitating factor once again was national affairs, specifically the introduction into Congress of Stephen A. Douglas' Kansas-Nebraska Act. Since this measure virtually nullified the Missouri Compromise of 1820 and reopened all slavery discussions, its condemnation by the majority of New York merchants is not difficult to understand. Manhattan's business community led anti-Nebraska opinion in America, but despite all its arguments and efforts Douglas' measure became law on May 30. Politically, the legislation shattered the remnant of the Whigs, led to the formation of the Republican party, and forced the remaining Barnburner Democrats to leave their party. The chaos that resulted in both nation and City demanded strong leadership and authoritative action, and it provided the background out of which New York's first Boss would emerge. His name was Fernando Wood and, in November 1854 he was the mayoral candidate of Tammany Hall, the club which remained one of the few enduring realities of City politics. National crisis or party structures might come and go, but the Hall's desire to elect the Mayor of New York was a constant upon which everyone could rely.

Fernando Wood was one of the most charming rogues ever to serve as Mayor of New York. In his later years, he adopted a debonair and elegant bearing, but that pose was far removed from his origins and character. Wood was the son of a cigarmaker who successively had his own cigar shop, ran a dockside tavern, owned and operated a fleet of sailing vessels; he managed to amass a fortune before the age of forty. He served a term in Congress as a loyal follower of Tammany, and in 1850—as an adventurer returned from San Francisco and the gold rush—he had run for Mayor only to lose to the Whig coalition. His rather unsavory reputation did not help his cause then and diarist Philip Hone wrote that "the incumbent of this office should be at least an honest man. Fernando Wood, instead of occupying the Mayor's seat, ought to be on the rolls of the State prison." By 1854, however, Wood had somewhat overcome the odor of his past adventures and was acting as conciliator to bring together all the diverse groups within the Democratic spectrum. Although his loyalty to Tammany was certain, in this year of reaction against corruption he spoke the language of reform. Historically, it was one of Tammany Hall's most endearing traits that it periodically demanded a purging of the system, a cleansing which only it could apply; in 1854, Wood's campaign promised to restore lost honor to City politics. He promised also to obtain greater home rule for the City from Albany, limit both prostitution and gambling, and get animals off the City streets. On November 7, he was elected because the Irish Sixth Ward cast 400 more votes for him than it had registered voters. The first of New York's several Bosses had come to power in a fashion soon to become all too typical and familiar.

Despite the fears of patricians who knew his reputation and perhaps even in the face of Tammany expectations, Wood's first term proved exceptionally beneficial to New York. The new Mayor used the Charter reforms of 1853 to justify further consolidation of executive authority, and actually did prohibit the archaic practice of driving cattle through the streets of the City. Moreover, Wood effectively championed the cause of Central Park, established a "Complaint Book" for citizen gripes, ordered that prostitutes spend at least one night in jail if arrested, and put the municipal police into uniforms so that it became more difficult for them to leave the scene of a crime without acting. The Mayor made speeches endorsing temperance and thus won German support, but he did not enforce saloon closings because he believed—correctly—that the law was unconstitutional. His inaction therefore garnered him Irish votes. He made additional City land available to the diocese of New York so that construction of St. Patrick's could smoothly proceed, and so obtained Catholic support for his next campaign. He made the better classes very happy when he moved to prevent the immigration of paupers and criminals into the City and, in 1855, his administration witnessed the transformation of Castle Garden into an immigrant-receiving station physically separated from the City itself. On August 3, the first shiploads of new arrivals were processed there, and over the next thirty-seven years Castle Garden was to be the reception area across which almost 8,000,000 people entered the United States. In all, the dire apprehensions that had attended Wood's election seemed unfounded as he acted the part of a

"Model Mayor." He had enhanced executive power and authority, but his efficient administration had won wide support.

The first Wood administration brought contentment and order to Manhattan but there was no such respite in sectional tensions. The pro-Southern attitude of the Mayor was well-known, for he and Tammany Hall both recognized the importance of Southern cotton and credit requirements to City prosperity. Yet after the passage of the Kansas-Nebraska Act, more New Yorkers than ever seemed to regard the South, its aristocratic leaders, and its "peculiar institution" as a national curse. Raising funds to "save" Kansas and oppose slavery became relatively easy in New York after 1854, and some City residents went so far as to actively support Eli Thayer's Emigrant Aid Society (which provided Kansas' settlers with guns called Beecher's Bibles), and participate in the clandestine operations of the Underground Railroad. Henry Ward Beecher of Brooklyn was perhaps the most outspoken of area clergymen in his condemnation of slavery, but equally influential was the editorial support for slavery's limitation provided by Greeley of the *Tribune*, Bryant of the *Evening Post*, and Raymond of the *Times*. The Republican party grew in strength as ex-Whigs, Free Soilers, Democrats, and moralists joined its ranks and, after open fighting erupted in Kansas late in 1855, its appeal became even broader. A metropolitan campaign to raise funds for "the suffering free men of Kansas" was successful in the summer of 1856, though it won little support from any major political figure. Yet, despite these changed attitudes, City voters in the presidential election of 1856 cast their ballots for James Buchanan, the Democratic candidate. While there might be increasing distaste for slavery, the City at large did not wish Republicans to occupy the White House, where their presence and platform would menace both the Union and New York's trade. In fact, half of Wood's annual message of 1856 dealt with the dangerous national situation and with New York City's commitment to "free trade."

After Wood's successful first term, it seemed certain that he would run once again but his very achievements caused a falling-out between himself and Tammany. The Mayor complained that his commissioners—originally all drawn from Tammany—were too independent and were unconcerned with efficiency. Whether Wood himself was unsure of his direction cannot be known, but in May 1856, after his candidate for Grand Sachem of Tammany Hall lost, he allowed his supporters to publicly ask if "the Sachems or the people" should rule in New York. Vicious infighting took place within Tammany that fall as Wood struggled with Sachems who opposed him; he discovered as well that a strong Know-Nothing candidate would enter the contest against him. The mayoral race became one of the most complex in Gotham's history as five candidates and their supporters literally fought for control of the City government. When the battles ended, Wood had won reelection but his position within Tammany was shattered. An outcast from his parent organization, Wood now radically changed his attitude toward government. He adopted the accounting methods of the Forty Thieves and the organizational techniques of Tammany Hall. His second term thus featured the open sale of offices and contracts, the blatant padding of bills, and use of the executive power to benefit the bank accounts of the Mayor and his family. In addition to graft, Wood's tenure in 1857 would be marked by controversy, riot, and economic disaster.

One crucial factor in Wood's transformation from Model Mayor to spoilsman, was the decision by Republican Governor John King to assert state control over New York City. King sought to reduce the home rule which Manhattan had gained in the Charter of 1853 and decided to focus his attention on creating a new police system, one that "the legislature will hesitate to entrust" to Wood. Municipal reformers in New York, most of whom now were Republicans, did believe there had been an increase in police corruption in Wood's uniformed force and thus supported the Governor's plan. On April 14, the legislature abolished the municipal police and created a Metropolitan Police run by five commissioners appointed by the Governor with the consent of the state senate. In effect, the City lost control of its own police force and the opportunities for patronage it provided. The legislature went even further and decreed that a special mayoral election would be held in December, thus arbitrarily cutting Wood's term in half. On the grounds that all this constituted an unwarranted attack on metropolitan home rule, Wood, with the support of many concerned New Yorkers, decided to resist. Though the new law became effective on May 25, he refused to surrender any police stations or to order the disbanding of the "municipals." When King's newly appointed officials attempted to take control of the force, they were expelled from City Hall by Wood's loyal municipals under Chief George Matsell. Matters came to a head in June when the "Battle of the Ms," Metropolitans versus Municipals, took place in City Hall Park; peace was restored only by the intervention of the Seventh Regiment. For a time "criminals ruled the streets," and there were gang battles in the Bowery while two police forces did their best to avoid action against anyone except the opposing faction. Not until the Court of Appeals rendered a decision in July did Wood disband his force. Although the Metropolitans won a belated civil judgment against Wood, the Mayor turned the bill over to the City taxpayers who paid for his mistaken show of independence. It is interesting to note, however, that five of the six judges who upheld Governor King's action were Democrats. Wood's independence and greed had totally separated him from the Tammany organization by the summer of 1857.

And the summer of that year brought more unexpected trouble to the regime of the once Model Mayor. In the decade since the end of the Mexican War, America had experienced a speculative boom in railroad construction, wheat acreage expansion, and state banking institutions. The opening of the California gold fields and the nationwide growth in manufacturing capacity had only intensified that fever for quick wealth. New Yorkers had particularly plunged into manufacturing expansion and extensive clipper ship construction. Then in August the far too liberal credit policies which had fueled the boom suddenly came to an end after the unexpected failure of the Ohio Insurance Company. The collapse of that Cincinnati concern had a ripple effect throughout the East and fostered a series of business failures which soon numbered about a thousand in Manhattan alone. City banks had to suspend specie payments and there was widespread want and discontent. One estimate stated that a seventh of the City was receiving charity. Several thousand unemployed artisans marched through the streets demanding bread and that construction jobs in Central Park be made available to them. The militia had to be mobilized several times to reinforce the metropolitan police and not until December 12, when banks resumed specie payments, did the disturbances end.

The third and perhaps greatest of Wood's woes was his rejection by Tammany Hall. The Mayor had taken full advantage of his right to name the heads of executive agencies and by 1857 he had filled them with men loyal to him and not to the Tammany society. In the process, scores of offices had been virtually auctioned off to the highest bidder, with an unmentioned but understood clause that the buyer could recoup his investment at the expense of the City. Fraudulent street-cleaning contracts and dozens of unsavory real estate transactions provided lucrative returns but only for Wood adherents, not for Tammany Hall politicians. Though Wood controlled the official Democratic nomination, Tammany Hall and its rising young leader William Marcy Tweed decided that he had to be stopped. In a stunning reversal of the club's traditional party loyalty, Tammany decided to oppose the "regular" Democratic ticket with their own nominee, an alderman named Daniel Tiemann. Thus Wood had to fight the influence of the Governor, the effects of the Panic, and the combined opposition of Tammany's Sachems in the special election of December 1857. Tiemann was presented as a reform candidate and obtained some Know Nothing and even Republican support; even more important was the fact that Tweed mobilized the Bowery B'hoys and other Irish gangs against Wood. In a bitter and violent election, Wood was defeated by 2,300 votes. After Tiemann took office in April, the "Model Mayor" announced his withdrawal from Tammany and the creation of a personal political organization he called Mozart Hall. By that summer's Democratic Convention he could exclaim, "I am henceforth and forever against Tammany . . . now let them beware."

Nothing is sweeter to Tammany Hall than the opportunity to run for office in the cloak of reform, but a problem they had not anticipated was that Tiemann, a rather well-to-do man, actually believed the rhetoric. Although personally honest, the new Mayor quickly proved himself to be a political incompetent who was incapable of either reducing Wood's high tax burden or carrying out reforms within the administration. While Tiemann was floundering about and feuding with the Tammany organization, Wood created a meticulously constructed rival machine. Tiemann was embarrassed when a fireworks display in August 1858, set off to celebrate the completion of the Atlantic Cable, also succeeded in igniting the cupola, dome, and roof of the City Hall. His discomfiture was increased by a Court decree which auctioned off the remnants of City Hall in October to pay a debt that had been contracted by the Wood administration. Although Tiemann personally purchased the structure for $228,000, a sum for which the City later reimbursed him, the incident brought him little honor and much ridicule. He naturally was refused the Tammany Hall Democratic nomination in 1859.

The election of 1859 offered Wood a chance to return to power as a man who understood and cared for the citizens of New York. By a strange quirk, he actually was the poorest man in the race, for the Republicans nominated millionaire clothier George Opdyke while the Tammany ticket, still eager to flaunt the label of reform, was headed by sugar millionaire William Havemeyer. As a result, Wood was the candidate with the most appeal to ordinary people, and there is no doubt that the voters remembered his relatively effective public assistance programs in the bleak fall of 1857. In any event the "Model Mayor," who now bossed Mozart Hall, won the support of most of the Irish and by a margin of 3,000 votes became Mayor of New York City for the third time. When he took office on January 1, 1860, his executive departments were led by Tiemann holdovers, and those jobs were secure since the Board of Aldermen was still ruled by Tammany men. Thus factional politics continued and government as a whole remained inefficient, venal, and corrupt. The City now had 814,000 citizens, but Wood claimed he had been reduced to a "functionary" in their service; he nonetheless continued to make deals which added to his wealth. There is no evidence that he displayed any reaction to Abraham Lincoln's "House Divided" speech which was delivered at Cooper Union on February 21, 1860. Although he was Mayor as the nation moved toward the horror of Civil War, the judgment of his critics was that Wood was only concerned with himself and that "his patriotism never seemed to reach beyond the limits of Manhattan Island."

During the presidential race of 1860, both Wood and the Tammany organization agreed that abolitionism rather than slavery was the cause of America's difficulties. Wood, in good demagogic fashion, denounced the Republican party as a "fiend which stalks within the narrow barrier of its Northern cage," and contrasted this with the nationwide support enjoyed by Democratic candidates. Both Wood and Tammany did their best to elect Stephen A. Douglas in 1860, and the "Little Giant" received twice as many votes in Manhattan as did Lincoln—although the Republicans carried New York State. Wood sincerely believed that much of New

York's prosperity depended on its Southern connections, and that an accommodation with the planter aristocracy was in the City's best interest. After Lincoln's election, indeed after secession was a fact, this belief led to an extraordinary mayoral message to the Common Council on January 7, 1861. The Mayor suggested that Manhattan, in combination with Staten Island and Long Island, secede from the United States and create a free and independent City-state. The financial basis of this new entity would be secure because of its trade dominance and the vast tariff duties it was certain to collect. Most people ridiculed the idea but it did not become "outrageous" until war erupted in the spring and interred the plan. When the South fired upon Fort Sumter, Wood proved capable of reversing himself. He ordered Mozart Hall to organize a volunteer regiment and waved the flag of patriotism as fervently as anyone. However, he never really seemed to favor active prosecution of the war and the conflict marked the end of his career as Manhattan's leading political figure. His ambivalence toward the Union tainted Mozart Hall with treason, and when the Mayor sought reelection in December 1861, he finished third; his only accomplishment was to cost Tammany Hall the election by splitting the Democratic vote. In time-honored fashion, Wood now made a deal with the organization he had so long fought. Tammany Hall agreed to satisfy Wood's campaign debts and to provide him with a congressional nomination in 1862, if he would remove himself from City politics. Once elected to Congress, Wood became a leader of the nation's "Peace Democrats" for the duration of the War. He ultimately served a total of eight terms in Congress and was very influential as an expert in currency and tariff policy.

The Tammany Sachem who negotiated Wood's departure was William M. Tweed, a leader who would soon be the first Tammany man to be publicaly acknowledged as "Boss." E. L. Godkin later wrote in The Nation that "If Wood was the Ring's Caesar, Tweed was its Augustus," yet, as with the Model Mayor, there was little in his early career that set Bill Tweed apart from the other roughnecks who did the hard, political labor for Tammany Hall. Tweed was born on April 3, 1823, on Cherry Street, the youngest of six children born to Scotch parents. Young Bill was bored by school, yet as an apprentice in his father's chair-making concern he also had difficulty with hard work. His attempt to establish his own firm collapsed, in part because of his brother's drinking and in part because Bill was far more interested in the operation of the local fire brigade than he was with his own company. It was as the leader of the "Big Six" Americus Engine Company that the 270-pound Tweed found happiness. He had the knack of getting to the water supply first and worked harder at quenching fires than he ever did on a chair. His fire brigade prospered and bluff, gregarious Bill Tweed was soon contemplating a political career. It was traditional that fire companies, compact units of men with lots of relatives and similar attitudes, provided candidates for Tammany Hall slates and this road to glory was followed by Tweed. In 1851, he was an alderman, and by most reporters was given credit for orchestrating the activities of the Forty Thieves. Later, as Boss, Tweed was to recall fondly for the New York *Herald,* that "There never was a time when you couldn't buy the Board of Aldermen." As noted, Tweed's single term in Congress provided him with a dislike of Washington; he wanted only to manage New York. In 1855, he served on the Board of Education and discovered the money to be made from textbook contracts and teacher bribes. As a supervisor of public works from 1857 to 1870, his eyes were opened to magnificent vistas of unending payoffs. Tweed thus organized the Tammany Hall faction which opposed the Wood regime and it was clear that his purpose was not good government, but rather the replacement of one Boss by another. He made alliances with men such as Peter Sweeny, Richard Connolly, A. Oakey Hall, and Judge George C. Barnard, and by 1861 the coalition successfully expelled Wood from New York. The cost was minor, only a congressional nomination and two years of Republican rule, and the prize was New York City. While the nation fought its Civil War, Tweed's fight had already ended in victory. The age of the Ring, "a hard band in which there is gold all around," was about to begin.

In politics the word Boss is not to be considered an insult, and the title was being applied to Tweed even before the final exiling of Wood. He had been made chairman of the Democratic Central Committee of New York County in 1860, and set about the task of making that group synonymous with Tammany Hall itself; it was the completion of this campaign that made him the Boss. By astute political dealing, Tweed and "Brains" Sweeny won control of Tammany's General Committee, and so obtained dictatorial power over party nominations as well as appointments to judicial posts. In 1862, A. Oakey Hall became New York district attorney and thus assured the Ring's legal invulnerability. On January 1, 1863, Tweed was made permanent chairman of the Executive Committee of the Tammany Society; all the other Sachems who were elected were his allies. Finally in July—the same month that riots against conscription convulsed New York—Tweed became the Grand Sachem of Tammany Hall. The structure of the Ring was thus in place even though Tammany itself was out of power. In December, the mayoral campaign resulted in selection of a Democratic Mayor, C. Godfrey Gunther, who was neither a spoilsman nor a good politician. He was only the necessary front for the Ring and would be replaced in the next election.

The Tweed Ring is instantly identified in the minds of Americans as the epitome of municipal corruption, but no one knows how much money was stolen and almost everyone agrees that substantial contributions were made to City life during the Ring years. Graft of its nature is never a one-way street. It is true that Tweed and his cohorts were greedy for money, but reputable companies and citizens had to pay them and willingly did so. What sets Tweed's Ring apart from the corruption that has characterized municipal affairs since Sumerian times was the order and coherence that this Boss brought to the payoff process. He succeeded in extending graft to virtually every corner of the system and saw that the benefits of criminal activity were widely dispersed. If everyone did it, how could there be guilt? If in the long run the citizenry paid, New York was a very rich town and could afford such a tax! Tweed's genius was to regularize and bureaucratize an empire of graft, an empire which for a brief time was virtually all-encompassing.

In 1863, in addition to his Tammany duties and his place on the Board of Supervisors, Tweed assumed the post of deputy street commissioner as well. Each of these positions gave him the opportunity to name legions of workers, and the system of job-related payoffs now began to mount. In his latter post, for example, there were not only street-cleaning contracts to let, but also substantial revenues to be gained in "fees" related to street openings; as the City expanded even farther northward these charges were lucrative indeed. The Ring elected its first Mayor, John T. Hoffman, in December 1865, and its control of municipal finance was assured when "Brains" Sweeny became City chamberlain and

"Slippery Dick" Connally advanced to the comptroller's office. Contractors to the City soon understood that a 10-percent kickback must be added to any bid they made. In time that percentage rose to 15, 50, 60, and in some contracts to an astronomic 85-percent level. The existence of the payoffs was virtually an open secret yet initially produced as little outrage as the well-publicized Department of Defense "cost overruns" do in modern America. By 1867, Tweed was already a millionaire. The system of Ring levies was well established, yet within the organization there was a tacit division of labor: Sweeny was in charge of judicial nominations, Connally took care of financial accounts, and Hall advised the group on legislation and legal matters. Tweed presided over all with the calm of a field marshal and the largess of a potentate. When he was asked in 1870 to contribute Christmas baskets for the Seventh Ward, he gladly wrote out a check for $5,000, only to be begged for "another nought." Without a blink, Tweed added another zero and the Seventh had quite a Christmas. The Boss was lavish, fun loving, and generous and many persons in the City he ruled shared in the benefits.

Between 1865 and 1871 the Tweed Ring enjoyed virtually complete control of the financial life of New York City. All contracts were padded, and the face amount was paid by City Auditor James Watson to the contractor, who then repaid 10–85 percent of it in cash. Watson, who acted as Ring's paymaster, then distributed specific shares of the stolen money to the various members of the inner circle. Probably the most notorious example of this system was provided by one of the Ring's favorite henchmen, Andrew J. Garvey, who did much of the plastering work for the City of New York. His bills were so high that it was said that he could have plastered all of Europe at the same price and still made a profit. In two years' time, Garvey charged the City almost $3,000,000 for plastering work, nearly 60 percent of which was kicked back to the Tweed Ring. No wonder the New York *Times* called him the "Prince of Plasterers." But colossal frauds were also carried out in connection with stationery supplies, where bills for two years ran $2,280,000. Tweed personally profited from all the printing done for the City for he owned the printing company that performed the work.

The most infamous example of Ring plundering took place in the construction and furnishing of the New York Courthouse, which still stands at the northern edge of City Hall Park. John Kellum had designed a three-story structure to cost $350,000 and work began on the project in 1862. The advent of the Ring changed the function of the building into a conduit by which public funds could be transferred to Tweed and his associates; before the building opened, its total costs approached $13,000,000. Thermometers cost $7,500 each, brooms were a steal at $41,190.95, and carpeting costs could have covered the entire expanse of City Hall Park several times over. Bills were paid on Sunday to men such as I. C. Cash, and at least five dead men were on the janitorial staff. Before its completion the Courthouse cost New York almost four times as much as the House of Parliament cost Great Britain.

The larceny and fraud which characterized Ring operations was possible only because of its total control of the electoral process. The decades-old alliance between Tammany and the immigrant, particularly the Irish, was now irreducible. The machine added to its vote totals each year by effecting mass naturalizations, a process made simple because of Ring control of the courts. New York had always experienced rowdy elections, but in the heyday of the Ring ballots were stolen, boxes of votes were lost or deposited in the rivers, "repeaters" were imported, violence kept opponents from the polls, and several wards regularly exceeded their total of registered voters. Tweed had himself named to the state senate in 1867, made Hoffman Governor in 1868, saw Hall become Mayor in 1869, and smiled all the time. Despite charges of gross electoral fraud nothing could be proven, and by 1869 the Ring controlled not only New York City, but also both houses of the state legislature. In 1870, when Hoffman was reelected, the Republicans reclaimed the legislature but even this loss proved to be only a minor setback. Tweed believed that everyone had his price and suitcases full of cash were soon on their way to Albany to purchase Ring domination. The municipal debt soared, as did taxes, but there was little demand for change or reform in these years of truimphant Ring hegemony.

How did Tweed get away with such blatant fraud? A good part of the answer seems to be that the Ring and its masters could "point with pride" to substantial improvements in the municipal government. In 1865, the old system of volunteer fire companies was abolished and a Metropolitan Fire District (Manhattan and

Brooklyn) was created to be served by uniformed, salaried, professional fire fighters. Early in 1866, the City became part of the Metropolitan Sanitary District and a Board of Health was created to deal with the centuries-old issue of communicable disease. City money was made available to subsidize both Mt. Sinai Hospital and Catholic education; in fact, Protestant Tweed provided over $1.4 million for Catholic schools over a three-year period. As senator, Tweed introduced bills which incorporated the Metropolitan Museum of Art, the New York Stock Exchange, and the Lenox Library. As supervisor he saw that Broadway was widened, removed the fences from around public parks, established public bathhouses, authorized Riverside Park and Drive, and participated in the early planning of the Brooklyn Bridge. It was true that problems of poorly maintained wharves and streets, insufficient housing, ineffective public transit, and inadequate sewers continued, but these were problems that predated Tweed and would outlast his Ring. Citizens could boast of the new clubs, the first elevated train, the extraordinary new Tammany Hall, and the Museum of Natural History as continued proof of their City's dominance. Inertia and the desire for calm and stability after the agony of the Civil War also played their role in the rather overwhelming acceptance that the Ring enjoyed in its brief heyday.

On April 5, 1870, the Ring won its greatest legislative triumph when Albany approved a new frame of government for the City, the so-called Tweed Charter. This "reform" measure had been secured only by massive bribes to Republicans, but it boasted virtually unanimous support from New York City because of its home rule guarantees. The charter increased the authority of the Mayor, who now could name his comptroller and his department heads, consolidated many offices, abolished the old Board of Supervisors and replaced it with a Board of Audit. By abolishing the metropolitan police force which had existed since 1857, the charter restored to the City control of its own streets; authority to complete Central Park was granted to Manhattan as well. Although Tweed lost his supervisor's post, he was immediately named commissioner of public works (which made him a member of the Board of Audit) and his control over jobs and the City payroll continued without interruption. In fact, a good portion of Ring strength came from its ability to provide employment for friends, relatives, and political allies. Few appointees complained that "kickbacks" of salary were extorted. In May, elections were held under the charter and, as expected, Tammany swept the City by over 60,000 votes, electing 5 judges, all 15 aldermen, and their 22 assistants. The circle of Ring authority was now complete.

In 1871, Boss Tweed was at the peak of his power and prestige. He lived in a palatial mansion on West Thirty-sixth Street, served on the boards of a dozen corporations, and freely indulged his taste for fine food and fast horses. Millionaires partook of his lavish hospitality, while dockworkers and ward heelers competed for his favorable glance. An investigation of City finances conducted by John Jacob Astor III asserted that there was no substance to charges that financial manipulation had occurred in the past. And an incipient revolt within Tammany, the "Young Democracy" led by Jimmy "The Famous" O'Brien, had been crushed so that Tweed still reigned as Grand Sachem. The Boss had more than enough time to concentrate on the marriage of his daughter, Mary Amelia, and spent $700,000 to arrange the social event of 1871. One effort to please the Boss was a campaign to erect a statue of him in New York Harbor, a campaign which Tweed himself had to halt because he was afraid he would appear ridiculous. The privately subscribed money was returned, but the Boss retained a list of those who had contributed and he was certain to remember those who had—and had not—shown their affection. Perhaps the only troubling cloud was that for over a year *Harper's Weekly*, and its brilliant caricaturist Thomas Nast, had been running a series of cartoons highlighting the greed, arrogance, and plundering operations of the Ring. Far more than the unproven charges of newspaper critics Tweed feared Nast's pen. "I don't care what people write, for my people can't read, but they have eyes and can see as well as other folks." Yet even cartoons could be ignored as long as public apathy made Tweed invulnerable.

But as so often happens, a falling-out among thieves proved the Achilles' heel of the Tweed Ring. In the spring of 1871, Tweed and his associates made a serious mistake. They made an enemy of the sheriff of New York, Jimmy O'Brien, when they refused to honor his claim for a quarter million dollars needed to carry out the "extra" functions of his office. O'Brien then threatened that unless his bill was paid, he would disclose and have published all of the machinations of the Ring. O'Brien had obtained the facts and figures from William Copeland, a friend of the sheriff, who worked in the comptroller's office, and who had made a duplicate set of all bills, vouchers, records, and transcripts. The Ring paymaster, James Watson, had recently died in an accident and the copies had been secretly made. Faced with extortion by one of their own, the Ring refused to pay and, after his ploy collapsed, O'Brien turned the evidence over to George Jones, editor of the *Times.* The Ring, which had tried to buy off Nast with a half a million dollars, now offered Jones $5,000,000 not to publish these proofs. Jones refused the offer, and in July 1871, began publishing the transcripts. By the end of the month, every intelligent citizen knew that the Ring had stolen at least $6,000,000, and subsequent estimates by historians have ranged in amount from $30 to $200 million. Mayor Hall protested his innocence, Tweed kept a brazen silence, and Sweeny and Connolly vacillated between courage and cowardice. The political response, however, was predictable. Indignant public gatherings were held, a Council of Political Reform was organized, a mass meeting at Cooper Union called for action, and Samuel J. Tilden, the state chairman of the Democratic party, openly broke with the Ring. In September, a Committee of Seventy civic leaders was formed to look into the operations of the Tweed Ring, whose members for the first time were now thoroughly frightened.

Attacks on the Tweed Ring grew more intense as the *Times,* belatedly joined by other newspapers, kept up an editorial cannonade. During the next few months, the Committee of Seventy, headed by ex-Mayor Havemeyer along with Samuel J. Tilden, Joseph Choate and others, uncovered additional masses of evidence against Tweed and his Ring. Nevertheless, Tweed won reelection to the state senate in November and hoped still to ride out the storm. That dream faded when a grand jury returned an indictment of 120 counts against him and he was arrested on December 16, 1871; he was also replaced as Grand Sachem of Tammany Hall and would have to face the law by himself. When asked his occupation by the prison attendant, Tweed replied, "statesman." The Boss removed, his Ring scattered as quickly as it had been forged. Sweeny resigned as parks commissioner and left on a visit to Canada which turned into a "vacation" in Europe. "Slippery Dick" Connolly also hurriedly crossed the Atlantic and found refuge there. The Ring judges either resigned from office or were impeached. A. Oakey Hall was still the Mayor but after being indicted by a grand jury he conducted his own defense and was acquitted by a hung jury. After some foreign travel, Hall would return to become city editor of the New York *World*. The elections of November 1872, resulted in a repudiation of the Ring when William Havemeyer, twice reform Democratic Mayor in the 1840s, was elected for the third time to serve as chief magistrate of the City. Reform was in power and the Boss now must pay for his crimes.

The trial of William Tweed began over a year after his arrest, on January 7, 1873, before Judge Noah Davis. Despite all the alleged thievery of the Ring, Tweed was not accused of any felony but rather of the technical misdemeanor of failing to adequately perform his auditing responsibilities. Although the legal case was quite flimsy, the verdict was foreordained because an example had to be made. On November 19, 1873, Tweed was found guilty, sentenced to jail for 12 years, and fined $12,500. The former Boss served 12 months both in the Tombs Prison and on Blackwell Island, but won release when the Court of Appeals threw out the trial decision on technical grounds. His legal adventures were not over, however, because a civil suit for $6,000,000 had been started against him, and he was arrested and confined to the Ludlow Street Jail. There he was treated with a great deal of consideration by his jailers. He was permitted to drive out in a carriage in the custody of deputy sheriffs, and to dine with his family. On the morning of December 5, 1875, the City was startled to read in the newspapers that Tweed had escaped from prison during one of his frequent carriage rides. After a variety of adventures, the Boss made his way to Spain only to be imprisoned upon his arrival in that country. The Spanish government shortly thereafter returned Tweed to New York where he was once again imprisoned in the Ludlow Street Jail. The stories that Tweed told while in jail were never fully published; many were "lost" because of the embarrassment that they represented for still prominent leaders. He never was tried again and died in prison on April 12, 1878. In various proceedings New York City recovered $876,241 of the many millions stolen by the Ring, but with the death of the Boss public outrage was ended. Justice had been vindicated and civic morality restored.

A Boss had fallen but Tammany Hall remained and within its

confines the ideal of Boss rule persisted. Augustus Schell, the Sachem who replaced Tweed in December 1871, was a former collector of the port and a leading businessman, but he was old and hardly inclined to seize the fallen Tweed's mantle. He presided over a lost mayoral race in 1872, and tried his best to restore Tammany's public image by dealing for positions with Havemeyer, who after all was a Democrat. Although the organization had been hurt by loss of patronage and factional disputes, Schell managed to restore a semblance of order. The Havemeyer regime was in the process of reforming Manhattan—garbage was picked up twice daily, the market system was rebuilt, police pay was increased, the City *Record* was founded, and the public debt reduced—so Tammany could call for no less. A new City Charter replaced the Tweed Charter and within Tammany a man had to be found to undertake the ambitious job of making the machine acceptable once more. The leader who accomplished this improbable task was certain to become the new Boss; his name was John Kelly.

Kelly, the first Irish Catholic Boss, was born in 1822 and came to his position only after many years of service to Tammany. The son of immigrants, young Kelly worked at a variety of jobs including office boy at the New York *Herald*, grate setter and stone cutter. Like Tweed, he served in the volunteer fire company of his ward and built up a political following. He was an alderman in 1853 after the expulsion of the Forty Thieves, a congressman for two terms, and sheriff of New York County for three. In the 1850s, he had opposed Wood and allied himself with Tweed before the Ring had been created. As sheriff, an office which entitled the occupant to fees but no salary, he grew rich and won for himself a prefix for his name; he became "Honest" John Kelly. Relatively well off and devastated by familial deaths, Kelly had left his office and during the excitement of the Tweed exposures he was in Europe, insulated from scandal and rumored to be entering a monastery. It was only the solicitations of "hundreds of leading men" which convinced Kelly to return to New York and attempt to pick up the pieces for Tammany. His rise to leadership was merited, but was also due to the fact that he was one of the few Tammany leaders not tainted by the Tweed debacle.

Kelly's genius was organization, and his epitaph might well read that "He found Tammany a horde, and left it an army." One of his first moves was to restore probity to Tammany's image by convincing men of impeccable reputation to serve as Sachems. Schell was already Grand Sachem but leaders such as Samuel J. Tilden, Horatio Seymour, August Belmont, and Abram S. Hewitt also agreed to become chiefs; the new regime was hailed as "a congregation of the City's honest men." Mayor Havemeyer was not convinced, however, and in a letter of 1874, accused Kelly of being a thief. "I think you were worse than Tweed, except that he was a larger operator." Havemeyer believed that the City should be run as a business enterprise, much as he had managed his American Sugar Refining Corporation, but Kelly held that the municipality must be more concerned with the welfare of its ordinary citizens and its jobholders. In 1874, he and the Mayor had a series of patronage disputes over election inspectors, representatives to the Police Board, and the appointment of magistrates which only added to their personal bickerings. Kelly finally decided to sue the irascible Havemeyer for libel but on the day that the trial was to begin, November 30, 1874, the 80-year-old Mayor died suddenly of apoplexy in his office.

The fireworks of a libel trial would surely have been entertaining, but Kelly had already won his battle to control New York. Ever the "inventive mechanic" of party building, Kelly had already elected a new Mayor of New York by appointing thirty-three district leaders who had delivered the vote of their areas to the regular Tammany candidate in 1874. Even before Havemeyer's death he had been replaced by William Wickham in the election of November 3. A pliant servant of the new Boss, Wickham named Kelly as City comptroller and over the next five years the debt of New York was reduced by over $12,000,000. Kelly's organization now was in control; his major difficulties in City politics for the next decade occurred only when district leaders forgot how they had received their posts and attempted to rebel. Wickham was succeeded as Mayor in 1876 by Smith Ely, the smoothly running Tammany organization providing a sufficiency of votes. Under Kelly, really for the first time, a party machine had been organized.

Kelly believed that Tweed's avarice had been outrageous, and that both money and power could be obtained with safety by collecting only "honest graft." There would always be some bribes, kickbacks, and "gifts" within an organization, but these were for the most part unnecessary as long as there was real estate to be sold, franchises to be awarded, and contracts to be let. Legitimate money could be made from all these transactions, for the age was hardly troubled by scruples over "insider" knowledge. The machine also controlled two New York newspapers, the *Star* and the *Evening Express,* and these kept up a drumbeat of praise for the Boss; Tammany also employed "spouters" on other papers who could be relied upon to place events in the proper light. Yet Kelly as Boss was never unopposed and his imperious orders were often ignored by Democrats in the districts. Secessionists formed the Irving Hall Democracy in 1878 and actually elected Edward Cooper Mayor over aged Augustus Schell, but in general Kelly's will prevailed. He was intelligent enough to compromise with his enemies and share patronage, and thus maintained mastery of City politics until his death. In 1880, he elected William R. Grace as Mayor, the first Catholic to lead the City since Dongan had served as Governor almost 200 years earlier. Reformers might lament that Manhattan, "without a steady body of civic opinion," was ill managed by ward politicians but it still prospered. Herbert Spencer, visiting in 1882, asserted that "New York—like the Italian republic of the Middle Ages—was losing the substance, if not the forms, of freedom," but Kelly carried on. Without scandal he accumulated a personal fortune yet maintained his reputation as an honest man. Tammany also thrived and avoided implication in major scandals. In general, therefore, Kelly's reign as Boss was considered eminently successful by the machine, by the City, and by himself.

Only when Kelly's ambitions moved beyond New York City's border did he almost invariably fail. During his first years as Boss, Kelly had clashed with Samuel J. Tilden for control of the state party organization and had been defeated. Later, Kelly became so incensed by the shabby treatment that state Democrats accorded the jailed Tweed, that he launched an independent gubernatorial race in 1879 which cost Democrats the state house. Almost read out of the party, he returned to the City only to discover that his mayoral candidate—William Grace—was not willing to mindlessly dole out patronage jobs to Tammany. The Boss called it treason! Grace called his actions independence. Grace was defeated for reelection. In 1883, Kelly decided to oppose Democratic Governor Grover Cleveland, who had also displayed an independence in regard to patronage which Tammany's Boss considered sinful. As a result of the clash, Kelly refused to support Cleveland for the presidency and openly predicted his defeat. He concentrated instead on the mayoral race in the City where Grace was attempting a comeback. When both Cleveland and Grace won, something vital died in the Boss. He became ill, lost his decision-making ability, and could not sleep without the aid of drugs. In 1885, he left Tammany Hall and spent the rest of his days sitting in his home on West Sixty-ninth Street, visited regularly by his protégé Richard Croker, wondering what went wrong. The broken Boss died on June 1, 1886; the mass in St. Patrick's Cathedral was crowded with simple workers and City officials who came to bid farewell to a man who had been a benevolent Boss.

* * * * *

By the time of Kelly's passing Bossism had become an accepted part of the New York political scene. The heritage of Wood, Tweed, and Kelly made it a simple matter for Croker to inherit the mantle. Nothing was said about his right of succession for unobtrusively the leadership had been passed on even before Kelly's death. The leadership of Tammany had become "a growth and not an appointment" and the leader to whom the scepter had been given was to bring the City renewed corruption. As "Master of Manhattan" Croker was the culmination of a long process; he combined the flexibility of a Wood, the avarice of Tweed, and the organizational know-how of Kelly. His reign would bring about a totally different New York. It is important to recognize that the urban Bossism represented by these leaders was by no means a phenomenan that can be simply categorized. Tammany Hall cut across all the economic, social, and political aspects of City life and its leaders were far more than personifications of evil. Each Boss used the system to enrich himself, some more so than others, but each also claimed to speak and act on behalf of the people. Certainly each further centralized government administration and provided increasingly efficient municipal services. The cost was high, perhaps exorbitant, but as a result Tammany became the spokesman for New York and provided urban America with a new vision of itself. Immigrants of every continent achieved their first identification with American society through the Tammany ward heelers in every section of the metropolis. Bossism provided them with jobs, food, friendship, and advice, and they in return became doggedly loyal to the machine. They gave their votes unhesitatingly in exchange for these services. The wealthier classes, too, supported Tammany Bosses, for the legitimate profits to be made in fulfilling rich City contracts and franchises seemed boundless. Municipal government, likewise benefited because Tammany's machine proved adept at cutting through the red tape of bureaucratic administration. In short, whether operating on a state, local, or even sometimes on a national level, Tammany and its leaders got things done. Sporadic and unsuccessful attempts at reform were made, but what could the reformers offer in the face of Boss expertise? While New York's Bosses may not have functioned on an exalted moral or ethical plain, there is no doubt that they governed the mushrooming metropolis with an efficiency that had been sorely lacking in earlier times.

BRIEF BIBLIOGRAPHY

Asbury, Herbert, *The Gangs of New York: An Informal History of the Underworld.* New York, 1927.*

Callow, Alexander B. *The Tweed Ring.* New York, 1966.*

Foner, Philip S. *Business and Slavery: The New York Merchants and the Irrepressible Conflict.* Chapel Hill, 1941.

Lee, Basil. *Discontent in New York City. 1861–1865.* New York, 1944.

Lynch, Dennis T. *Boss Tweed. The Story of a Grim Generation.* New York, 1927.

Mandelbaum, Seymour. *Boss Tweed's New York.* New York, 1965.*

Mushkat, Jerome. *Tammany: The Evolution of a Political Machine. 1789–1865.* Syracuse, 1971.

Myers, Gustavus. *History of Tammany Hall.* New York, 1917.

Peel, Roy V. *The Political Clubs of New York City.* New York, 1935.

Pleasants, Samuel A. *Fernando Wood of New York.* New York, 1948.

Shaw, Frederick. *History of the New York City Legislature.* New York, 1954.

Werner, Morris R. *Tammany Hall.* New York, 1928.

*Paperback

VI

The American Metropolis

ON THE EVE of the Civil War New York was indisputably the leading City of the American nation. Despite the dogged, inventive, and sometimes frantic efforts of its competitor cities, New York steadily widened the lead in commerce and finance that its businessmen had achieved since the opening of the Erie Canal (1825). Goods carried along the "Big Ditch" had increased each year since its opening and by 1860 the total stood at 4,650,000 tons. Internal traffic was more than matched by the domination New York Port held over the foreign commerce of the nation; by 1860 the City handled two thirds of all American imports and a full third of our export trade. The City ranked first nationally in all but seven articles of exported goods, while the combined imports of Boston, Philadelphia, and Baltimore amounted to less than New York's imports in textiles alone. City merchants held a virtual monopoly over the marketing of English woolens, Irish linens, and French lace.

In emerging transportation areas and in the crucial field of banking the City also held sway. Both the New York Central and Erie Railroad systems had begun to drive into the interior of the state but both maintained terminals and their headquarters in the metropolitan area. Despite the anger of the farming community, railroad service had also been instituted on Long Island. Thriving shipyards along the East River, producers of the "Flying

Clipper," continued to build the finest and fastest wooden ships ever constructed and meant employment for over 2,000 men. During the first winter of the war, Brooklyn's Navy Yard would use New York City's accumulated expertise and produce America's first ironclad warship, John Ericsson's *Monitor*. The banking fraternity of lower Manhattan, freed in the 1830s from the restrictions imposed by the Bank of the United States, had attained substantial control of American finance. Wealth from the cotton trade, extension of credit to inland jobbers, and a willingness to invest in manufacturing enterprise all solidified that position. In the 1850s alone the capital resources of the City doubled.

Foreshadowing the future, the New York of 1860 had in an almost unnoticed fashion become a leader of American business enterprise. The census of 1850 indicated that the state led the nation in the value of its manufactures, and this surprising fact was due in large part to smaller businesses clustered within the City. Immigrants such as Henry E. Steinway and Duncan Phyfe created their masterworks in New York as it became the center of the furniture industry. That the metropolis ranked first in printing and publishing was not surprising for it was the center of American journalism, but that New York dominated, among other industries, both sugar refining and jewelry making seemed less probable. Its 162 cigar makers alone produced over a million dollars worth of smoke. In 1860, the total value produced by the 4,375 City manufacturing establishments, factories which employed 90,204 workers, was $159,107,369. New York, boasting a population of 813,669, was by its size, its productive capacity, and its enterprising spirit the leader of America's economic life. In the decades from 1860 to 1900 New York outstripped its already fantastic achievements and became the foremost City not only in America but also of the world.

* * * * *

It is one of the minor ironies of history that when the cannon fire at Fort Sumter announced the beginning of the American Civil War, the very loyalty of America's greatest City was much in doubt. On January 7, 1861, Mayor Fernando Wood had proposed that New York, in order to protect its commercial predominance and its excellent trading relationship with the Southern states, should withdraw from the Union and declare itself a "free City." He believed that continued prosperity depended on thriving Southern plantations. Moreover, Wood argued, his City was victimized by a state legislature insensitive to urban problems. Was not a war on behalf of the inferior black man absurd? The Mayor believed that the City could generate enormous revenues by simply imposing a modest import tariff. His position seemed strengthened when the state Democratic party, at its convention in late January, issued a call for peaceful secession. A massive petition to Congress drawn up by City merchants went so far as to suggest giving half of all U.S. territories to the South. Beyond Wood and the merchants, the incoming Lincoln administration also had to be troubled by the fact that New York City had 386,345 foreign-born residents. Would they be willing to fight for something called The Union? Why should New York's despised and oppressed Irishmen, estimated at 204,000, be loyal to America?

With the fact of war, however, such proposals and fears quickly were proven to be illusions. Manhattan rallied to the Union cause as ardently as did the rest of the nation, and Wood reversed himself in good political fashion to lead the chorus of "Union forever." On April 20, 1861 over 100,000 New Yorkers gathered in Union Square to pledge money and soldiers to the cause. The Seventh Regiment marched out to "save" Washington, D.C. and after July, when the Union Army reeled back from its defeat at Bull Run, the support of New York's population was assured. Indeed, at Bull Run the New York City Garibaldi Guards and its Tammany regiment were greatly mauled; one third of the Union losses in that first battle came from New York State. Mayor Wood himself proved surprisingly loyal to the Union and led a campaign which raised a million dollars for the war effort. But too many voters had been alienated by Wood's excesses, and despite his rediscovered patriotism Wood lost his reelection attempt to Republican George Opdyke. In January 1863, Opdyke asserted that the City had already supplied over 80,000 volunteers for the war, an unprecendented showing. Many recruits were foreign-born residents of the City who proved their American loyalty by flocking to the colors. The *Irish American* editorialized that immigrants could never "countenance the destruction of the government which naturalized, enfranchised, and protected them." Horace Greeley, editor of the *Tribune* and advocate of "On to

Richmond," was frankly amazed at the number who volunteered to serve in City regiments. Psychologically and morally, the wartime sacrifices of the New York immigrant population helped to integrate immigrants into American society by giving them a vested interest in the national destiny and helping to overcome prejudice against them. In the final analysis, no American City contributed as much to the Union cause as did New York, which supplied over 150,000 enlistments and countless millions of dollars to help save the Union. Though her clipper ships were driven from the seas and thousands died, there is no doubt that the war confirmed New York's already dominant economic power.

While the magnitude of New York's wartime effort is recognized, it is all too often negated by historical emphasis on the one major disruption identified with the City during the war, the bloody Draft Riots of July 1863. Until the spring of 1863 the war, at least in the East, had seemingly resolved itself into a long series of lost, or at best drawn, battles with the armies of Robert E. Lee. Moreover, with the Emancipation Proclamation the focus of the war had shifted from saving the Union to freeing the blacks. When Congress enacted the Draft Law of March 1863, the New York laboring population was faced not only with conscription, which threatened their lives, but also with emancipation, which would make freed blacks into economic competitors. Since under the terms of the Draft Law a rich man could purchase exemption for $300, the conflict suddenly became a war fought by the poor and of benefit only to the rich. The cost of living in New York had doubled since 1861 but wages had lagged far behind. Irish dock-workers were particularly incensed that black scabs had been used to end their attempt to win decent wages. Nerves were on edge due to Lee's advance northward in June of 1863 and thus, when the draft was instituted on July 11, trouble of some sort should have been expected. Almost all troops had been stripped away from the metropolis and a heat wave was searing the streets. In addition, the invincible Lee was now in full retreat from Gettysburg and news had arrived that Grant had captured Vicksburg. How important Confederate agitators were in provoking the crisis will probably never be known, but from July 13 to July 16 vast mobs of unhappy men roamed the City and clashed with the Invalid Corps militia and the 2,300 men of the Police Department. Forgotten were the huge Union rallies of July 1862 and

April 1863; now the cries were that the war was ending, the draft was unneccessary, and no white man should die for black freedom. For two full days random atrocities were committed, largely against blacks, and pitched battles were fought along both the East and Hudson Rivers. The mobs were Irish dominated, of that there is little doubt, not the least evidence being the reluctance of Archbishop John Hughes to address the rioters until the violence was largely spent. Extraordinary police bravery and the return of regiments from Pennsylvania battlefields ended the carnage, and the draft resumed in August without further incident. Between 1,000 and 2,000 persons died in the worst riots ever experienced by an American City, more casualties than the U.S. Army suffered during the entire war against Mexico. Millions of dollars in property damage resulted; the nineteen rioters who were ultimately convicted served an average of five years' imprisonment. Men love drama in their history and so perhaps inevitably they concentrate upon the riots while ignoring the City's contributions to four years of war. Yet a mature reflection upon the war years must honor New York. Although the City remained staunchly Democratic—in 1864 it voted 6 to 1 against Lincoln's reelection—its services to the Union were unmatched. A true mark of its loyalty was the five-mile cortege of April 25, 1865 which escorted the body of the assassinated President during its sad journey through the New York City streets.

It was not with a feeling of triumph, therefore, that New York returned to the routine of peace. Nevertheless, it was a wartime financial measure which greatly aided her accelerating development in the postwar era. The National Banking Act of 1863 was passed after a short-lived financial panic in 1860–61 and the March 1862 creation of legal tender greenbacks as a method of paying for the war. The cost of saving the Union was enormous, and the nation's financial structure groaned under the strain—a strain made even more serious by the unsound practices of many state-chartered and private banks. When Congress approved national bank charters in the legislation of 1863, bankers across America almost automatically turned to New York's national banks as institutions where their own reserves might be secure. Since 1853, New York had offered a national clearinghouse for checks. Now under the terms of this new law, local banks might count as reserves any deposits they had in New York banks. Thus their money would be safe, easily managed, and close to the most active financial market in the nation. By 1866, New York had 58 chartered national banks and was the national marketplace for bankers acceptances, call money loans, commercial paper, and government securities, as well as stocks, foreign trade, and insurance. Moreover, since national banks paid interest rates of 6 percent, over 100,000 new depositors were gained by City institutions.

The end of the war thus found New York financially supreme, economically thriving, and still anxious to expand its influence. Physically, the City had expanded to Thirty-fourth Street and now the thrust of settlement continued northward along the bank of the East River. In 1874 the first additions to New York since the Montgomerie Charter of 1731 were made. Portions of lower Westchester County (Morrisania, Kingsbridge, and Fordham) almost doubled the area of the City and added over 30,000 people to the population. War had temporarily reduced the total population of Manhattan, but with the coming of peace demobilized soldiers returned. More importantly, new immigrants once again filled the Castle Garden reception center. Thus the City had vast reservoirs of labor, mostly unskilled, and it was soon able to extend its lead both in the value of its manufacturing output and in the diversity of its production. The census of 1870 reported that the population had risen to 942,292 and that 7,624 factories were producing goods valued at $332,951,520, more than twice the level of 1860. That profits depended on cheap labor costs cannot be doubted; it is estimated that in 1867 at least 30,000 women in the City worked twelve to fifteen hours daily for only thirty cents. Nevertheless, the growth in wealth and services characteristic of New York's past was apparently stronger than ever. The value of City property doubled between 1860 and 1870 and no less than nine ferries tied New York to Brooklyn, America's third largest City. An expanding urban population demanded greater services and the City responded by authorizing a municipal Fire Department in 1865 and enacting the first Tenement House Law in 1867. America's first true apartment house, "The Stuyvesant," was constructed in 1869. Merchants interested in foreign trade were able to take advantage of the completed Atlantic Cable (1866) which guaranteed them access to the European marketplace; domestic traders were equally active as the New York Stock Exchange swelled beyond 1,060 members. Frederick Law Olmstead added a touch of sylvan beauty when he returned from England to complete the vistas of Central Park and to win the landscape architect's contract of the Prospect Park being planned for Brooklyn. Nothing seemed impossible for New York. In 1871, its port handled 71 percent of the total value of all United States imports and exports combined, an all time high point. A third widening of the Erie Canal from 1872 to 1876 guaranteed the continued flow of midwestern produce to its wharves. Until the 1930s, the region would increase more rapidly in proportionate size than the rest of the nation.

The years after the war were notable not only because of New York's economic strength but also as the heyday of the Tweed Ring. The "Boss" controlled the City, he dominated Albany in alliance with his "Black Horse Cavalry," and in 1868 he dared to reach out toward Washington itself. In that year, the magnificent new Tammany headquarters on East Fourteenth Street was the scene of the National Democratic Convention. The Tiger went all out to impress the delegates and even an experimental elevated train going fifteen miles an hour was opened for their pleasure. Nevertheless, Democratic stalwarts complained that New York had "ill-regulated, badly paved, filthy streets crowded with vehicles." They also ignored Tweed and after twenty-two ballots named former New York Governor Horatio Seymour to run against and lose to General Ulysses S. Grant. Tweed learned much, however, and was convinced that he and Tammany would be able to win at the next convention. Before he had the opportunity to test his theories, however, his Ring would collapse. In fact, history seems to prove that the peculiar New York style of politics does not translate well to either the state or national scene. Tweed would soon fall from power, yet Tammany's power in the City continued unbroken for another two decades. Amid crime and misgovernment both Tammany and the City thrived. No Republican would hold the mayoralty from Opdyke's wartime tenure until William L. Strong was elected as a reform candidate in 1894. The New York democracy invariably had far more difficulty with disaffection within its own ranks than with the Republican opposition. It is indisputable that during the age of economic revolution in which New York became the world's metropolis, the City was almost always ruled by Tammany bosses.

Within Tammany an ethnic revolution was also taking place. In the 1870s the Irish, heirs of the destitute immigrants of the forties, finally attained political power in New York. George W. Plunkett, a Tammany ward boss who managed in 1871 to simultaneously collect three public salaries, put it very simply. "The Irish was born to rule and they're the honestest people in the world." The long-repressed fears of aristocratic leaders like Phillip Hone were now realized; his elite class recoiled in horror as they recognized that political power now resided in the docile wards controlled by Tammany's leaders. Hibernians were given a major voice in 1871 when the *Irish World,* today the oldest weekly in New York, began publication. It was also in this decade that Protestant attacks on Catholic Irish functions came to an end; Orangemen were simply overwhelmed by numbers. Indeed those numbers would soon help elect a Catholic Mayor. An Irish-Tammany axis was being forged, and fundamental to its strength was the machine's unparalleled ability to provide concern and services to immigrants already in New York and those who would arrive over the next fifty years. Newcomers to America must be familiarized with the new land, have their wants heard, and be given personal assistance. A later Boss, Richard Croker, argued that Tammany alone performed all of these functions; it took "hold of the untrained, friendless man and converted him into a citizen." All it asked in exchange was his vote. The system Tammany evolved worked well and, as experience was to prove, it could service Italians, Jews, and Poles as well as Irishmen.

The pace of immigration to the United States had slowed substantially after 1857. A decade later, with the return of peace and prosperity, the traffic once again increased. By 1873 a new peak of immigration was attained when almost 400,000 aliens landed in New York. The bulk of these new arrivals were typical of the "old immigration" in that they were people from England, Ireland, Germany, and Scandinavia who arrived here determined to improve their economic status. Over 2,700,000 newcomers arrived in the United States in the 1870s—the last great influx of Irish came after a minor famine in 1879—and northern Europeans dominated immigration statistics until the early 1880s. Their numbers continued to swell and in 1882, despite passage by Congress of a fifty-cent "head tax," over 788,000 immigrants arrived in the United States, most by way of New York. At Castle

Garden they met "steerers" who led them to licensed boar-
dinghouses or gave information on ship and train schedules.
Many chose to remain in New York and provided the indispensa-
ble labor that solidified the City's manufacturing base. The poorest of necessity settled in the already warrenlike rooms of the
Lower East Side. The teeming slums expanded to accept the
newcomers and there, often with the help of family members or
Tammany Hall block-captains, they began to become Americans.
Reporters from the *Times* who ventured into the Fifth, Thir-
teenth, and Fifteenth wards dutifully reported on atrocious conditions within the "human hives" and on the "pestiferous atmosphere," but for these latest New Yorkers it was "home."

The physical and territorial expansion of the underclass horrified the merchant entrepreneurs and bankers who dominated the
New York economy. The City had expanded into the Forty-second-
Street area, but the fertility as well as the proximity of the lower
classes was feared. Suddenly life in the suburbs—Long Island or
the Bronx—became an attractive alternative for many upper-class
New Yorkers. If a man chose not to leave the City, he could live in
the far precincts of Harlem without inconvenience, due to the fine
rail system that served Manhattan. Urban transportation was
facilitated even further when three new elevated lines began to
operate in 1878. For many, suburban Brooklyn would have offered the greatest attraction had it not been for the inconvenience
of the ferry transit.

Thus it was with a personal interest that many upper-class New
Yorkers carefully watched as the Brooklyn Bridge project, first
proposed in 1857 by John Roebling and later constructed by his
son, Washington, slowly moved toward completion. After involved
political maneuverings, construction had actually begun in January 1870 and the great span grew daily in size and beauty. No one
before the Roeblings had thought it feasible to span a 1,600-foot
wide river where the bottom was questionable. But in May 1883—
after 13 years of effort, at least 26 lives and his own incapacitating
case of the bends—Washington Roebling was about to complete
the job. On the twenty-fourth of May, President Chester Arthur,
Governor Grover Cleveland, and Mayor Franklin Edson dedicated
the bridge. Since by chance it also was Queen Victoria's birthday,
a riot by the Irish population was only narrowly averted. The
greatest engineering project since the Erie Canal, the bridge not

only provided a convenient outlet to the fields of Brooklyn, but also probably made the creation of Greater New York inevitable! For the fee of a single penny one could walk across the bridge that connected the first and third largest cities in America. Despite the Decoration Day tragedy of 1883—12 persons died of injuries when crowds panicked—the bridge soon became a symbol of metropolitan New York City.

Although Brooklyn had sponsored two thirds of the project, the Brooklyn Bridge became Manhattan's glory and remains so to the present day. Even Steve Brody, who supposedly leaped from the span in 1886, was a Manhattan saloon-keeper. In any case, the bridge offered an outlet to those who decided to leave the City in the face of its progressive barbarization. Not surprisingly, Irish and Germans followed in the latter 1880s when Manhattan became the target for new and greater waves of immigration from southern and eastern Europe.

For those well-to-do New Yorkers who decided to leave the City, the decision must have been difficult and not only in a business sense. They fled a metropolis which offered more of the amenities of civilized life than any other in the nation. The Museums of Natural History and of Art had recently opened and a Symphony Orchestra led by Leopold Damrosch was created in 1878, the same year that Gilbert and Sullivan's *Pinafore* was first performed here. Telephone service was now available and the incandescent lamp of Thomas Edison first illuminated New York streets in September 1882. The $2,000,000 Metropolitan Opera House opened with a glorious *Faust* on October 22, 1883 and immediately replaced August Belmont's Academy of Music as the standard of artistic greatness. In pre-Civil War years, Manhattan had ruefully accepted second position behind Boston as "the Athens of America," but in the glamorous decades after 1865 the City seized a primary position in music and the arts that it maintains to this day. There might be danger for the unwary in its attractions—in Barnum's Museum signs directed eager viewers to the Egress—but the metropolis never again would accept second place in cultural affairs.

In architecture as in everything else the colossus on the Hudson seemed determined to overwhelm its competition with the variety and quality of its output. For ordinary citizens the brownstone façade still sufficed but on Fifth Avenue the homes of the elite adopted a "château" style. Wealthy New Yorkers had originally made lower Fifth Avenue their habitat, but in May of 1879, when America's first Cardinal, John McCloskey dedicated St. Patrick's Cathedral, he signaled the start of another in the northward surges which had become common in the growth of the metropolis. The cathedral, along with St. Thomas' Episcopal Church (1883) became a kind of magnet drawing the rich northward for a new round of conspicuous consumption. Astors, Whitneys, Vanderbilts, Goulds, and Huntingtons had to build mansions at addresses on upper Fifth Avenue, where their wealth and good taste would be visible to all. But in addition to private housing, hotels like the Waldorf seemed to be springing up everywhere. And even more impressive was the development of the skyscraper. It seems clear that Chicago was the first home of the steel-structured building, but once the principles were established New York asserted its claim. The Washington Building, even though it rose twelve floors in 1882, was entirely constructed of masonry but the Tower Building of 1886 used steel. It was only the first of hundreds of skyscrapers which would be anchored into the solid bedrock of Manhattan. Electric elevators were soon perfected and made possible the construction of taller structures such as the Manhattan Life Insurance Building (1893), new headquarter structures for Standard Oil and American Surety, and, perhaps most impressively, the twenty-five-floor Flatiron Building (1902). All were forerunners of the distinctive skyline today's world immediately identifies as New York.

Of all the alterations in the cityscape, none was of greater importance or more symbolic of New York's future than was the City acceptance of a gift from the people of France. In 1865, a French admirer of American greatness, Edouard René Lefebvre de Laboulaye had decided to give the United States a monument and had employed Frédéric Bartholdi as architect. In 1871, while sailing into New York Harbor, Bartholdi was inspired with the vision of a gigantic welcoming statue that would represent "liberty." Over 180 French cities raised a quarter of a million dollars so that Bartholdi could design and construct, around an iron frame created by Alexandre Eiffel, the most massive statue in the world. One hundred fifty-two feet high, with a svelte 35-foot waist, a 3-foot mouth, and a 13-inch fingernail, the woman named "Liberty" slowly took form. At the 1876 Centennial celebrations in

Philadelphia over 9,000,000 visitors saw her right arm and torch. The French asked only that America provide a fitting pedestal for this gift. Typically the federal and state authorities did not act, although in February 1877, President Grant did approve a site on Bedloe's Island. It took fully nine years of effort, and a final whirlwind campaign led by Joseph Pultizer's New York *World*, before New Yorkers contributed the cash to complete the pedestal. The project was finally completed, however, and when the Statue of Liberty was assembled it towered 305 feet over its harbor site. Its dedication, on October 26, 1886, was attended by President Cleveland and thousands of the ordinary New Yorkers whose pennies had made completion of the project possible. Some in the crowd were angered by the implied slight of Emma Lazarus' words of poetry for not all newcomers to American shores were "tired . . . poor . . . huddled masses." But that mattered little. The City now possessed a more enduring symbol than finance, manufacturing, or architectural innovation. New York meant liberty, opportunity, and hope. "Miss Liberty" presiding over the harbor was to become the single most lasting memory for the millions of oppressed immigrants who, in the later years of the nineteenth century, arrived in the United States. The strength of that first view of the statue was to profoundly influence their lives. Its enduring power can be gauged even today by listening to the comments of the tourists who daily sail from the Battery to visit the one monument which continues to remain symbolic of both New York and the nation.

Before 1883 about 85 percent of all immigrants came to America from the countries of northern Europe. That year, however, marked so decisive a change in the lands of origin of new arrivals that historians have consistently labeled the phenomenon "new immigration." The focus of immigration now shifted to southern and eastern Europe—Italy, Russia, and the Balkans—and the number of arrivals became greater than ever before; in the 1880s alone the figure was twice that of any previous decade. The highest peak, however, was not to be reached until 1907. For the first time, vast numbers of the immigrants were Russian Jews, for Tsar Alexander II had begun a program of religious persecution in 1881. In the years that followed, each persecution brought a flood of Jewish immigrants to New York and in thirty years over 1,562,000 East European Jews, a third of Europe's Jewish population, were to arrive in the City; the census of 1910 reported that New York had 1,252,000 Jews. The influx of these poor, persecuted, yet young and intensely ambitious people was to affect the future of the City fundamentally.

Even more impressive than the Jewish arrivals was the influx of southern Italians, a migration that has been labeled the "greatest and most sustained" population movement from one country to another. In 1880, most of the City's 20,000 residents of Italian heritage came from northern Italy. The arrivals of the eighties were largely agricultural workers from southern Italy. During the 1870s Italians were already held in low estimation in New York because of their religion, their customs, and their willingness to act as strike breakers. The newcomers therefore met less than an enthusiastic welcome. As with most migrations, the first arrivals were largely males, many of them "birds of passage" intending to return to their homeland. Obviously liable to exploitation, they were often used to break labor unions early in the decade. Congress reacted to the problem by passing the Foran Act (February 1885) which made it unlawful for anyone to import laborers specifically for use as strikebreakers. The statute aimed at the *padrone* system which enabled resident leaders to contract out the labor and arrange the lives of Italian immigrants. The *padrone* held social as well as economic power in his community, but his influence soon waned under pressure from the law and the ministrations of Tammany Hall block-captains. As early as 1885 the New York Bureau of Labor reported that Italian immigrants who first worked for almost any wage, had become "sufficiently Americanized" to themselves join and lead strikes for higher wages. One of the first and most successful Italian labor leaders was Salvatore Ninfo who organized more than 4,000 Italians who helped construct the New York subway some years later.

It was normal for new immigrants to settle near compatriots who had also surmounted the traumatizing immigrant experience. For both Italian and Jewish newcomers, this meant that they inevitably gravitated toward the low-rent, rundown areas of the Lower East Side. Their arrival encouraged Irish and German residents to leave, and, within only a few years new languages, foods, and customs dominated the area. The Italians carried their clannishness to such a degree that certain streets of the Fifth

Ward were not only Italian, but Neapolitan (Mulberry Street), Genoese (Baxter Street), or Sicilian (Elizabeth Street). The old North Italian community itself migrated to the Eighth or Fifteenth Ward streets west of Broadway. Naturally not all Italians stayed in the City, substreams were going out toward Brooklyn, Jersey City, Newark, and the rest of the nation, but the census of 1900 reported that New York included 145,433 residents of Italian descent and the even greater migrations of the early twentieth century were yet to arrive. By 1908, New York held over 500,000 Italians, more than the population of Rome itself. Today Italians comprise the single largest ethnic group in a City which remains the most polyglot amalgam in America. The Italians and the Jews, as the Irish and Germans before them, and so many others to follow, saw New York as a "promised City." They had great dreams and occasionally a talented individual could transform his poverty into a life of wealth and plenty. More often, the lot of the newcomer was harsh poverty and a precarious existence. Yet each new arrival made an impact on his new home.

Already in the 1870s it had become obvious that the social fabric of the City was under severe strain. The tenements that housed newcomers were denounced as "the nursery of increasing vice" as early as 1857, and organized churchgoers saw Tammany-dominated New York as Sodom on the Hudson; in 1866 Bishop Matthew Simpson ruefully admitted that New York had "more prostitutes than Methodists." Thousands of unlicensed saloons, the number varied but surely no one lacked for a drink, catered to the city-folk. It took the inspired leadership of Anthony Comstock and an extended campaign during 1872–73 to even temporarily halt the proliferation of obscene literature. Seemingly beyond effective help was the problem caused by thousands of homeless children. The New York Home of Refuge had been established as early as 1825 and its efforts were abetted by the Catholic Protectory (1863), but the true pioneer in the field of juvenile care was Charles Loring Brace, secretary of the Children's Aid Society from 1853. Brace believed that children would develop most successfully in rural, more godly, environments and began the policy of placing homeless juveniles into that better situation. He also created a Newsboy's Lodging Home (1853), a Girl's Lodging Home (1862), and a system of vocational training schools that numbered 33 in 1893. Brace's work was helped when the Child Care

Act (1875) forbade the City to place children from two to sixteen in almshouses; his lifetime of work ultimately relocated about 100,000 children. The plague of juvenile crime which had existed for decades finally began to be faced when Juvenile Court was established in 1901. Yet the problems of the immigrants, adult and child, were so enormous that the harassed organized charitable societies of the City finally attempted to form a single society. In 1882 Josephine Shaw Lowell established the Charity Organization Society which tried to give overall direction to the allocation of relief services. No state, federal, or City agency existed then to care for newcomers and whatever services were provided for them came out of philanthropic motives. The sole alternative to private benefaction was, as already noted, the largess of Tammany Hall and its coterie of ward captains.

But relief and juvenile crime were almost minor issues compared with the perennial New York problem of finding adequate housing. There were no Fifth Avenue mansions available for these newcomers; housing meant taking up residence in one of the "dumbbell" tenements of New York. These five-or six-story structures, airless, virtually windowless, and with only the most minimal toilet facilites, were the standard housing of the Lower East Side. There, seventy-five cents a week obtained a room some twelve feet square where a man could live after a fashion. As early as 1857, a legislative investigation had expressed horror at the conditions of New York's slums, but nothing had changed. Already deteriorated housing simply could not cope with the overwhelming demand, and despite a code revision in 1887 which mandated plumbing improvements and fire escpes, the congested tenements remained abominations. To the *Times,* they were not homes but schools for vice and crime. Yet in those crowded rooms entire families worked to make clothing, cigars, artificial flowers, and many other products. In 1890, over a million New Yorkers resided in 37,316 tenement houses and some estimates are that by 1893 half of New York lived in tenements. Political and philanthropic reaction to this continued scandal was inevitable and it was in 1890 that Jacob Riis, himself an immigrant from Denmark, published his searing account of *How the Other Half Lives.* A reporter for the *Evening Sun,* Riis analyzed conditions from "Jewtown," to "The Bend" of Mulberry Street, and into the Tenth or "Typhus" Ward. He concluded that the East Side "is not fit for

Christian men and women" and his writing inspired a generation of reformers from Theodore Roosevelt to Frances Perkins. Riis not only wrote but also took a series of classic photographs of the Gothic conditions he described. In sum, the contrasting extremes of wealth and poverty characteristic of New York were rarely so profound as in the concluding years of the nineteenth century.

But whether New Yorkers were rich or poor, the services provided by the metropolis constantly had to be expanded to meet their growing demands. The efficient horsecar system, which carried 35,000,000 passengers yearly even in 1858, simply could not be expanded rapidly enough to service passenger demand in the 1880s; additionally, there was the sanitation problem of horse-droppings. In 1892, in an effort to rationalize and improve elevated service, the Manhattan Railway Company was permitted to merge the four existing lines into a single system. Increased passenger loads were immediately evident and the company was able to reward its investors with dividend payments. In 1892, the growing City proudly opened the taps on the newly completed Croton Reservoir System which guaranteed 300,000,000 gallons of pure water each day; the next year New York became the first City to treat water with chlorine to safeguard the health of residents. A fire-alarm system, first used in 1876, was improved and garbage incineration began at a plant constructed on Governor's Island. Commissioner George Waring's "white wing" sanitation men provided the City with extraordinary service during the 1890s, a contrast to recent years when New York suffered through several garbage strikes. Completion of the Williamsburg Bridge in 1896 offered an alternative route out of the East Side ghetto, while those located in Manhattan's northern precincts could cross the Washington Bridge (1889) into the rural Bronx.

City educational efforts were at least matched by the continuing efforts of individuals. Settlement houses such as the Neighborhood Guild, the College Settlement, and the Henry Street House were established in the 1890s. Organized by progressive social reformers, settlements offered individual attention and some education aid to Manhattan's immigrants. Their efforts were supplemented when the City school system, which already provided textbooks (1877) and kindergartens (1888), was expanded in 1895 to offer both free medical examinations and a high school education. The Board of Education's evening lecture series for slum dwellers, inaugurated in 1888, was increasingly popular. Fittingly, it was in 1898 that the Charity Organization Society offered its first courses in "social work." Many churches also actively attempted to help the immigrant. William S. Rainsford, author of *Christianity and the Social Crisis* and rector of St. George's Episcopal Church, organized both a community center and a boy's military company. Grace Church sponsored a "Boy's Choir School." Yet delinquency, both adult and youthful, remained a pressing social concern; in 1888, the Penal Hospital on Blackwell's Island alone examined 2,000 prostitutes, 1,238 of them recent immigrants. By far the largest number of girls were Irish (706) while the fewest came from Italy (17). In reality, despite the stereotyped view of Italian immigrants as criminal or wastrel, the records of New York in 1901 show that group as having the fewest admittees to the Almshouse, the Incurable Hospital, and the Blind Asylum. This surprising reality is partly explained by the work of Mother Francesca Cabrini's Sisters of the Sacred Heart, by the strong Italian family tradition, by the aid of Gino Speranza's Society of Italian Immigrants, and by the many Mutual Aid societies—258 in 1912 by actual count—which ministered to that community. The nineteenth-century Italian influx provided New York with a hard-working and almost autonomous community which even today looks primarily to its own resources rather than those of the City.

In 1890, with a population of 1,515,301 New York was a fundamentally different City than the one which had gone to war in 1860. It had almost doubled in population and the ever-increasing streams of European immigration gave it an unfinished, exciting quality which it still retains. In the 1880s elevated lines were built on both sides of Manhattan Island to facilitate transportation for the masses and to provide access to the thousands of small business establishments which had transformed the City into America's prime manufacturing center. In 1890 in New York there were 25,399 factories dealing with 299 industrial products and producing goods valued at $777,000,000. Manhattan so totally dominated both the men and women's clothing trade that regional manufacturers found it necessary to establish themselves there in order to take advantage of both its expertise and its markets. The relocation of the Duke Tobacco distribution center to Manhattan (1884) soon enabled that company to flood the nation with its product and ultimately led to the formation of the American Tobacco Company (1890). By 1900, New York was headquarters for 69 of America's 100 largest corporations; it became the arena in which the vertical organization of business enterprise was perfected. Manufacturers slowly accepted sales, bookkeeping, and credit-extension obligations and looked to mergers and consolidations to enhance their market position. New York's banking and legal communities proved quite capable of creating new forms of business organization. Bankers such as Morgan, Lehman, Sage, Ryan, and Whitney were consolidators, architects of complex financial mergers. They never lost their heads in a crisis and it was their expertise which enabled New York to withstand the Panic of 1893 and insured the City's financial primacy into the twentieth century.

In the mercantile field, the new generation of retailers led important sales innovations. The thirty-year reign of A. T. Stewart as proprietor of the best store in Manhattan ended with his death in 1876. By 1896 his famed "marble palace" was the domain of John Wanamaker, who pioneered advertising campaigns which soon filled New York newspapers with announcements of sales, spectacular bargains, unprecedented savings! But Wanamaker's old-fashioned reluctance to advertise in the Sunday editions of newspapers was soon to cost him his leadership position. Sunday advertising quickly became essential to mercantile success; New York City was thus again first with an initiative which was to become America's norm. Whether it was due to advertising or the variety of goods they offered, the new style department stores appealed to shoppers. R. H. Macy, a dry goods emporium which opened in 1858, was thinking of moving its retailing operations uptown to give easier access to a richer clientele. Under the leadership of Oscar Strauss, the "world's greatest store" soon began to rise on Thirty-fourth Street; Benjamin Altman, not to be outdone by a competitor, began to put together a building site two blocks east. Both stores opened early in the new century and others, such as Gimbels and Bloomingdales, followed them north.

Manhattan proved at least equally adaptable in catering to the entertainment demands of its varied population. The heart of the legitimate theater had been located between the "Rialto" of Fourteenth Street and Madison Square, where Edwin Booth opened his theater in 1869. But late in the century theater companies began to slowly move uptown. Vaudeville, once a source of shocked disapproval or embarrassed apologies, was "purified" by Tony Pastor in the 1870s and emerged as the most popular of entertainments. The concentration of music halls, coneys, and gambling establishments in the West Twenties soon obtained for that area a dubious reputation. When a police captain, elated at the transfer which would enable him to become rich from graft, labeled the section the "Tenderloin" he added a unique phrase to the language. In the "gay nineties" entrepreneurs of the legitimate theater, led by Oscar Hammerstein, decided to leap beyond the Tenderloin to the Longacre (Times) Square area and so relocated the theater industry. But no matter where its theaters were located, New York remained a magnet for the great performers of the world. The Lind and Dickens tours of pre-Civil War days were succeeded by visits from Mme. Helena Modjeska, the "Divine" Sara Bernhardt, Eleanora Duse, and Ellen Terry. Home-nurtured talent such as Ada Rehan, John Drew, Mary Anderson, and George M. Cohan also lit up the footlights. Perhaps the greatest of all entertainment phenomena was Lillian Russell, who first became a star at the New York Casino. When she appeared at Weber and Field's Music Hall in 1898 she commanded a salary of $1,250 a week. For the cultural elite, Monday night at the Metropolitan Opera was socially obligatory and the opera repaid their patronage by bringing Giulio Gatti-Cassazza, Enrico Caruso, and Arturo Toscanini to New York. "Diamond Jim" Brady, Lillian Langtry, and Police Chief William Devery added their larger-than-life personalities to the glitter of the New York night. The City dazzled the nation with the wealth and variety of its cultural display, a rainbow of offerings available to rich and poor alike.

In the face of ceaseless excitements, perhaps the most fundamental challenge which New York had to meet each day was the continued influx of European immigrants. After January 1, 1892, all newcomers entered New York through the federal reception center located on Ellis Island in the mid-harbor. Before it closed in 1954, Ellis Island received over 12,000,000 immigrants—all of whom must have gazed in wonder at the great City only a mile away. Although the number of Italian immigrants continued to rise, there was in this last decade of the century a perceptible shift toward an increase in migrants from Eastern

Europe. In Russia yet another great pogrom encouraged the flight of 81,000 Jews to New York in 1892; the even fiercer persecutions of 1905-06 caused the arrival of 258,000 Russian immigrants in 1907. Many historians have recounted the saga of their successful accommodation to urban life while the latest analyses indicate that even in the first generation, Jews were intensely upwardly mobile. Within a few years they came to dominate the ready-made clothing industry and became involved in real estate development. Although the unique cultural contribution of these new immigrants was yet to be made, everyone understood that a dynamic new element was being added to America's most important City.

For Jewish immigrants of the nineties, life was a constant struggle to win their daily bread in an alien land, yet the vitality of their spirit almost immediately fostered adverse reaction. Nativism, whether in the jeremiads of Josiah Strong or in the fulminations of the American Protective Association, was predictably strong and even the august New York *Times* noted the Jews' "utter disregard for law" and saw their "clothing reeking with vermin"; the paper concluded that "they cannot be lifted to a higher plane because they do not want to be" (1895). More dangerous than lamentations of the elite, however, was ethnic conflict with Irish or Italian groups already resident in New York. Still the City accepted the Jewish influx as it had so many previous immigrants, though the social order was strained as never before. Tenements on the Lower East Side became more crowded and loathsome than ever while the incidence of tuberculosis soared. From 1896 to 1897, the Foundling Hospital on Randall's Island recorded a death rate of 97 percent among its 366 foundlings, with only 12 surviving the year. In 1900, the population density of the Jewish East Side ghetto reached 640,000 persons in a square mile, the highest such figure in world history.

Chaos was averted due to the efforts, uncoordinated for the most part, of social reformers, settlement houses, and City agencies. Perhaps the most pressing concern was the need to rectify the medieval housing conditions of the ghetto. In 1879 a mass meeting at a Cooper Union resulted in the formation of the Improved Dwelling Association but, despite all efforts, by 1897 seven eighths of New York's population still lived in slums south of Fourteenth Street. A Commission chaired by James Watson

Gilder had documented the conditions and abuses of tenement life and Riis had taken photographs. Nevertheless, Housing Code reform was aborted in 1896 by Tammany Hall and landlord interests. Only a recent CCNY graduate refused to give up the fight. Lawrence Veiller believed that men have a "God-given right to light and air" and he was able to build a coalition which effected change. In 1901 a New Tenement House Law was enacted which became a model for cities throughout the nation. The law ordered that windows be cut in 350,000 previously airless rooms and mandated minimum sanitary standards for all new construction. Since New York was primarily a renters' City with only 12 percent of its residents owning their own homes in 1900, the legislation was designed to improve conditions for the majority. However, 86,000 "old law" structures remained common housing stock in 1901 and the "new law" mandate for yearly inspections was soon shown to be a farce; the first full inspection of "old law" buildings was not completed until 1908. The lot of the newcomer to Manhattan was to remain difficult, and in 1910 reports indicated that New York's tenements housed 3,000,000 people at twice the average density of 1880. And by 1931, when 3,000,000 New Yorker's lived in "new law" housing, the slums were worse than ever. In 1965 43,000 "old law" tenements were still occupied by New York's then current wave of immigrants.

The historian can only marvel at the changes in architecture, the arts, life, and population which characterized New York in the last decades of the century. Yet with all the ferment one institution remained rock-stable and constant—Tammany Hall. Since Mayor Opdyke's brief wartime tenure no Replibican had served in City Hall, although reform Democrats such as Havemeyer, William Grace, and Abram Hewitt had briefly held sway. The title "Boss" had since 1886 belonged to Richard Croker, a man whose career was often cited as proving that talent and ambition could find a reward in New York. Croker had matured in typical Tammany fashion, from a vicious street fighter to leader of the Fourth Avenue Tunnel Gang, from volunteer fireman to ward captain, from courtroom bailiff to alderman. When John Kelly took power, Croker had allied himself with the Boss and had been rewarded with the post of coroner, an office worth $15,000 a year in fees. As leader of the Eighteenth District, he regularly delivered to the Tammany machine one of the strongest Democratic votes in

Manhattan. When "Honest John" died, Croker had stepped behind the Boss's desk without serious opposition.

In the election of 1886, Croker's first as leader of Tammany, the Hall had somewhat reluctantly backed the candidacy of Abram S. Hewitt as Mayor, a decision the new Boss came to regret. A rich, opinionated, and difficult man, Hewitt proved far too independent and in 1888 the Democrats turned away from him. Croker gave the regular nomination to his old friend Hugh J. Grant and, although Hewitt mounted a rival campaign, the machine vote of Tammany Hall elected Grant by a sizable majority. Patronage and lucrative contracts flowed toward the faithful and Croker, as the dispenser of City largess, became a rich man. Since the most essential element in Tammany's effective control was the police force, special care was taken to ensure its loyalty. The organization controlled fully 85 percent of all appointments to the force and the police commissioner made transfers or promotions only after consultation with the local district leaders. Policemen who received their positions through political influence felt no qualms about kicking back money to individual leaders and to the Clubhouse on Fourteenth Street. They in turn collected what graft they could from the prostitutes, saloons, gamblers, and merchants of their neighborhood. The genius of Croker's "wide open town" was its latitude; personal graft was permissible as long as Tammany received some of the loot. "Contributions" were expected from both the collectors of graft and from the legitimate merchants. So well understood were the requirements of the system that Tammany's Finance Committee never kept books yet never lacked for funds. From the Tenderloin to the Gas House District, from the village to the Bowery "everybody was happy" except possibly for the people.

If no enterprise was too small to escape the eye of some patrolman, no corporation was too large to be immune from Tammany's system. Payoffs were simply a necessary part of business overhead. An entrepreneur such as Charles W. Morse, who wished the exclusive right to land ice at the City's docks, found it expedient to give stock to high-up Tammany men. His "Ice Trust" then was able to announce that in the future only hundred-pound blocks of the precious summertime commodity would be sold. A $200,000,000 stock fraud by the Ramapo Water Company was averted, much to Tammany's chagrin, when engineers discovered that the system of pipelines which were supposed to supply New York could never work. The contract had to be rescinded. On other occasions, officials willingly hampered the development of new business enterprises if they had no share in the profits. For years Croker effectively blocked the construction of a subway because his associates felt that it would interfere with the elevated railroads in which they held stock. Whenever Croker was asked about the possibilities of a subway in New York, he ridiculed the idea and called it a hole in the ground. Croker and Tammany also caused the Third Avenue Railroad Company to go into the hands of a receiver in bankruptcy. The main cause of the bankruptcy was a city mandate that the company shift to electric power by contracting with Naughton and Company, a firm with which Daniel F. MacMahon, head of the executive committee of Tammany Hall was associated. The previous contractor employed by the Third Avenue Railroad Company had offered to do the work for $7\frac{1}{2}$ percent of the labor payroll and no commission on material, but he was removed from the job. The work was then given to Naughton and Company which demanded 15 percent on the labor payroll and 10 percent commission on the cost of material. The men working on the job loafed, the job went on interminably, and the company ultimately filed for bankruptcy.

It seemed that each generation of New Yorkers had to discover for itself the crimes of Tammany and so it was with New York in the nineties. It mattered not a particle if the Mayor's name was Hugh Grant or Thomas Gilroy; the mark of the Tiger's paw was upon him. The open alliance between the underworld, business, and the Hall was the operative City reality. However, in 1894 the partisan enmity of Thomas C. Platt, the Republican Boss of New York State, combined with the moral outrage of Reverend Charles H. Parkhurst to upset Tammany's system. An investigation conducted by State Senator Clarence Lexow disclosed the extravagant corruption of Tammany's rule to the roused populace. As the information developed by Reverend Parkhurst and Lexow poured forth, a convenient "illness" struck Richard Croker and he sadly informed the Executive Committee of Tammany Hall that his health demanded full attention. He retired to splendid exile at Wantage, his Irish estate, and thus effectively removed himself from the scene as reformers girded to battle the machine in the fall of 1894. Fusionists made a conscious effort to reenact the drama of Tweed Ring exposures so a Committee of Seventy was chosen; it briefly toyed with the idea of nominating for Mayor John Goff, who had conducted the Lexow Committee investigations. Ultimately, the reform coalition chose William L. Strong, a banker of solid reputation, whose character and rectitude gave just the right tone to reform's successful election campaign. Tammany was defeated and reform "came to town."

The Strong administration represented a Republican opportunity to provide New York with good government conducted on a businesslike basis. The Mayor appointed a series of excellent commissioners and succeeded in improving a highway system sadly in need of repairs. Undoubtedly his most flamboyant appointee was young Theodore Roosevelt, who led the Board of Police Commissioners and was given the task of trying to close down illegal drinking and gambling establishments. Roosevelt's spectacular nocturnal forays into the streets to personally test the rectitude of his patrolmen became part of the legend of the man the world would soon know as "T.R." Incidentally, Roosevelt remains even today the only President of the United States to have been born in New York City. But more important than any commissioner, was the plot hatched by Republican leader Thomas Platt to wrest control of New York from Tammany Hall. Platt believed that he could use the temporary weakness of Tammany, the incumbency of Strong, and the Republican tendencies of three suburban areas around Manhattan to obtain political control of an expanded New York. Thus it was that the most important development of Strong's regime was not its achievement of better government, but rather that it prepared the way for the creation of the Greater City.

The dream of an expanded City was an old one for a proposal to unite Manhattan with its surrounding counties had been raised by Andrew Haskell Green thirty years earlier. Moreover, a nonpartisan report of 1890, which Green had written, had again proposed consolidation of Kings, Queens, and Richmond counties with New York while cogently summarizing the arguments for unification. Such proposals had always been wrecked by the opposition of the state Republican party but in the elections of November 6, 1894—while New Yorkers elected Strong—a consolidation plan won substantial approval by Manhattan while losing by only 277 votes in Brooklyn. New York clearly wanted to grow—it annexed the Westchester towns of Eastchester, Pelham, Wakefield, and Williamsbridge in 1895—and Platt made his decision to gamble that he could win control of a greater metropolis. In March 1896 both Republicans and Democrats in Albany agreed to establish a commission of fifteen members, chaired by the ubiquitous A. H. Green, to create a Consolidation Act. Many Manhattan residents now had second thoughts; would not the acquisition of rural districts raise their taxes? Opposition to the proposed Charter was in fact led by the Republican mayors of New York and Brooklyn, both of whom vetoed early editions of the commissions's work in defiance of Boss Platt. Nevertheless and probably inevitably, Platt and his Democratic allies were able to work the measure past legislative pitfalls and it was approved on May 4, 1897. New York's pride played some role in overcoming last-ditch opposition. Proponents of consolidation cited enormous population gains by the upstart city of Chicago and argued that expansion was necessary if New York was to retain its primacy.

Thus, by the summer of 1897, it was recognized that a 600-page charter creating Greater New York would soon go into effect. The new Mayor to be elected in November would not only have greater municipal responsibilities than ever before but also dispense three times the patronage of any preceding administration. Perhaps only an opportunity such as this could have lured Croker back from his castle. Perhaps it was the special visit by William C. Whitney and Hugh Grant which convinced him to return. Whatever the reason, Croker "returned from exile" in September, reasserted his control of Tammany by October, and brought forward a magnificently acquiescent mayoral candidate. Robert Van Wyck, a judge of the City Court since 1889, was the "leader" necessary for Greater New York. Certainly Croker had faith in him, for Van Wyck immediately accepted the condition that Tammany would control City patronage. Republicans, on the other hand, were obviously disconcerted at the thought of actually competing with Croker for control of New York. Platt insisted on running his own candidate, former Secretary of the Navy Benjamin Tracy, while municipal reformers at first preferred Mayor Strong, who labeled consolidation a "funeral service" for New York. Such a stance was hardly useful, however, and the Fusionist movement finally compromised on the candidacy of Brooklyn's Seth Low. A fourth candidate, Henry George, mounted an independent campaign on his old tax-reform platform. George's exertions cost him his life only five days before the election. Faced with such a plethora of opponents, the united Democracy had no difficulty in regaining the mayoral chair on November 2, 1897. Van Wyck was sworn in on January 1, 1898 amid a citywide celebration. In the background, the party faithful could be heard happily chanting "to hell with reform."

Under the new charter, City government was greatly centralized, with the Mayor being granted extensive authority. Each borough of the City was to elect a president with local authority who would also sit on the municipal council. The Mayor was given veto power over council actions as well as vast appointive power. Van Wyck proved to be an incompetent administrator who, since he had conceded control over 40,000 patronage jobs to Boss Croker, had little actual influence. Though real power centered on City Hall, it was wielded by the Boss, not by the Mayor. New York now stretched seventeen miles north from the world's best harbor and its population of 3,393,000 was twice that of Chicago. It was big, wealthy, exciting, and arrogant and all of it belonged to Richard Croker. The once "master of Manhattan" now ruled Greater New York.

* * * * *

In the last forty years of the nineteenth century, New York had taken a quantum leap forward and became not only America's greatest City but also the largest, most economically powerful metropolis in the world. Its longtime commercial supremacy was maintained but was now joined with manufacturing strength to create a diversified economy. The gross value of City manufacturing surpassed the billion-dollar mark in 1901, with its factory workers making $110 more yearly than did the average farm laborer. The City ranked first nationally in number of factories, their capital valuation, the gross value of their product, and total employees. The Port of New York dominated both American export and import trade, the City's banking institutions held 30 percent of all national monetary resources, and the value of City land had quadrupled since 1860. By any standard of measurement, New York was indisputably a prime national resource.

Yet, despite statistics proving fantastic growth, perhaps the real saga of these decades was the polyglot excitement of New York life. The City remained a beacon of hope and opportunity to the oppressed and ambitious of a dozen nations; the "refuse of foreign shores" continued to arrive there in ever-expanding numbers. New York demonstrated again its ability to integrate and acculturate the refugees who arrived, to house them after a fashion, to educate, employ, and challenge them all. With all the tragedies of tenement life, the cruelties of the urban environment, and the sufferings of a laboring underclass, the decade 1890–1900 saw the population of New York rise an incredible 126.8 percent. Over half of New York's residents in 1900 had been born on foreign shores; some 173,000 of them could not speak a word of English while another 7 percent were illiterate in any language. The task of education and Americanization seemed beyond anyone's ability, yet New York almost blithely assumed that the impossible would happen. Despite all hazards and in the face of incredible suffering, the metropolis was optimistic and forward looking. City newcomers proved ambitious and hardworking while established groups were undaunted by the difficulties they saw and experienced daily. New York had passed in four decades through an expansion that quadrupled its population and gave it unprecedented territorial size. Why should there be any limits at all to its growth, its population, its power? Greater New York thus entered the twentieth century calmly acceptant of its multiple roles; it was the arbiter of taste, the nation's workshop, a commercial emporium, a port unequaled, a melting pot. It seemed to be both the fulfillment and the promise of the American dream.

BRIEF BIBLIOGRAPHY

Andrews, Wayne. *Architecture in New York: A Photographic History.* New York, 1973.

Barlow, Elizabeth, and Alex, William. *Frederick Law Olmstead's New York.* New York, 1972.

Birmingham, Stephen. *Our Crowd: The Great Jewish Families of New York.* New York, 1967.*

Hammack, David C. *Power and Society: Greater New York at the Turn of the Century.* New York, 1982.

Hirsch, Mark D. *William C. Whitney: Modern Warwick.* New York, 1948.

Huxtable, Ada Louise. *Classic New York.* New York, 1964.

Marcuse, Maxwell. *This Was New York: A Nostalgic Picture of Gotham in the Gaslight Era.* New York, 1965.

McCullough, David. *The Great Bridge: The Epic Story of the Brooklyn Bridge.* New York, 1972.*

Nevins, Allan. *Abram S. Hewitt with Some Account of Peter Cooper.* New York, 1935.

Pitkin, Thomas M. *Keepers of the Gate: A History of Ellis Island.* New York, 1975.

Riis, Jacob. *How the Other Half Lives.* New York, 1957.*

Stoddard, Lothrop. *Master of Manhattan: The Life of Richard Croker.* New York, 1931.

*Paperback

VII

Tammany Against Reform

In 1897, New York City was the most populous City in the nation surpassing Chicago by some 400,000 people. It also was America's greatest economic force. The harbor facilities along the bay shipped forty percent of all American exports. The teeming streets, peopled with immigrants from scores of countries, provided the labor essential to the manufacturing enterprise; indeed, the economic prowess of the City was based on its small businessmen whose unceasing competition created an atmosphere of entrepreneurial vitality. In addition, Manhattan served as headquarters for 69 of the 100 largest firms in the land. And for sheer elegance—for theater, opera, music, or shopping—as well as native terrain for the inhabitants of "millionaires' row" above Fiftieth Street, New York was unsurpassed.

Yet despite the abundant evidence of prosperity, some New Yorkers remained apprehensive that Chicago's enormous recent growth rate and its undoubted economic strengths might someday enable that inland metropolis to challenge or outstrip New York's primacy. It was the Consolidation of 1898 that forever ended those fears and permanently made Chicago into America's "second City," a position it holds to the present day. In 1874 Manhattan had annexed three Westchester towns and added most of the Bronx in 1895. The key to future growth, however, was whether or not Brooklyn would join New York. Brooklyn had been an independent City since 1834 and its population of 850,000 made it the nation's fourth largest City. It was only by the narrowest of margins that Brooklyn agreed to go "from great to greater", and so made Consolidation a fact. On January 1, 1898, the City of Greater New York came into existence, Brooklyn's last Mayor deposited $10,000,000 into the new common treasury, and New York became an awesome new set of statistics. The City encompassed 359 square miles, had 578 miles of waterfront, was financed by a budget of $90,000,000, and boasted a population—3,437,202 in 1900—larger than all but six states. Consolidation meant also that the City would soon handle 67 percent of all American imports. By the stroke of a pen, it had become the world's greatest City.

Not the least ironic result of the Consolidation was the total destruction of "Boss" Platt's dream that the more conservative voters of Brooklyn and Queens would change New York into a Republican bastion. The easy triumph of Robert Van Wyck in the first mayoral contest disproved that expectation. New York was a Democratic town and seemed likely to remain so always. Only when Tammany's yoke was unskillfully placed could temporary alliances between reformers and Republicans threaten Democratic domination. Much of the City's twentieth-century political history revolves about the unloving but inescapable relationships between these three groups. The advantage Tammany would always enjoy in the conflict was the inability of its foes to cooperate. Even in 1897, with the first administration of the City as the prize, the Republicans and reformers could not agree on a common candidate; their combined total was 55 percent of the vote yet Richard Croker's candidate easily won. Tammany followers chanted "to hell with reform" as Van Wyck took office, where he loyally served as Croker's man. For the most part he used his extensive patronage powers to reward clubhouse hacks and nurture the organization. Although New York was the greatest ornament of American society, it was at best indifferently governed. The metropolis desperately needed political leadership that could match its economic strength. The search for such leadership continued, with only intermittent success, for the next three decades.

* * * * *

The City of Greater New York hailed its birth with a daylong gala party on New Year's Day 1898. A hundred guns boomed Consolidation while celebrations, sponsored by various civic groups and individuals such as William Randolph Hearst, took place all over the metropolis. That the largess of a mogul such as Hearst should dominate the municipal festivities seemed somehow fitting. The owner of the *Journal* was representative of the wealth and power that a man might gain in New York; indeed some New Yorkers outstripped in importance and prestige the men who served as Mayor. New York responded more readily to a Richard Croker, a J. P. Morgan, an Andrew Green, or a Hearst than it did to a weak reed such as Robert Van Wyck. The former men were the arbiters of metropolitan life and they could oftentimes move the nation. In 1898, for example, a clash between two of New York's greatest individualists would help maneuver America into a needless but nevertheless "splendid little war."

Newspapermen such as John Peter Zenger, William Cullen Bryant, Horace Greeley, and Henry Raymond had often prodded New York to greatness. If events seemed more sensational, more visceral, and more exciting here than elsewhere, it was perhaps due to their editorial skills. Yet never before 1898 had newsmen's concern for circulation helped create a war. In that year, the City's dominant publisher was Joseph Pulitzer of the *World*, a New Yorker only since 1882. His was a democratic newspaper which spoke for the masses against the "interests" and crusaded for public causes like the Statue of Liberty; the paper also provided jobs for 1,300 New Yorkers. Pulitzer had created a comprehensive, illustrated, and extremely profitable paper that in Frank Cobb's phrase was "unmuzzled, undaunted, and unterrorized." Yet newcomer William R. Hearst dared to challenge the *World!* In 1895, driven by ambition and financed by his mother, Hearst had purchased the *Morning Journal*, a scandal sheet called the chambermaid's delight. Soon he was ready to challenge Pulitzer. Both men admired Napoleon and, like him, sought to expand their empires. Hearst as the newcomer was the aggressor and launched raids upon the *World's* stable of reporters. He hired away Arthur Brisbane and made him his editor. Hearst reduced the price of the *Journal* to only a cent, demanded sensational headlines, and opened his pages to the cartoon adventures of the "Yellow Kid." But it was all for nothing, as Pulitzer kept the *World* safely in front of the *Journal's* circulation and far ahead in advertising lines.

To men such as Pulitzer and Hearst, the increasing tension between the United States and Spain over the insurrection in Cuba was merely another round in their heavyweight battle. That the Commander of the *Maine*, which exploded in Havana harbor on February 15, 1898, happened to be a New Yorker only added to the fervor of their editorials. Both papers, joined also by the *Herald* and the *Times*, established Caribbean news syndicates to supply a stream of often spurious stories to arouse the public and sell more newspapers. So was born "yellow journalism." A single newspaper would publish up to 40 editions daily, and prices rose to two cents to finance the publishing madness. Yet the press succeeded in its goals, for public outrage moved the nation ever closer to conflict. It was on April 25, 1898 that Hearst triumphantly asked New York, "How do you like the *Journal's* War?" Some 300 correspondents descended on Cuba and Hearst himself sailed off in his yacht to join the *Journal's* fleet of 10 dispatch boats which were providing rapid delivery of the latest news. Hearst's exertions drew his paper abreast of the *World's* circulation at 1,125,000 daily copies, but the end of the brief war soon reestablished Pulitzer's primacy; it also saved both newspapers from bankruptcy. After the war Hearst decided to return the price of his paper to a penny. The far less flamboyant *Times*, published by Adolph Ochs, matched the price cut in October and in self-defense 15 other dailies followed suit. New Yorkers certainly got their money's worth of news.

The Spanish-American War dominated the news during 1898, but almost anything would have overshadowed Mayor Van Wyck. Totally ruled by Tammany Boss Croker, the pliant Van Wyck dispersed patronage as directed and turned his back as the police allowed vice to flourish. In return, Croker agreed to run his brother for Governor. Augustus Van Wyck probably would have won the state house—the possible gains for New York City from brotherly love are mind-boggling—had not his opponent been Theodore Roosevelt. Roosevelt refought the battle of San Juan Hill on speaker's platforms across the state and triumphed every time. He became Governor much to the chagrin of Croker who thus had to be satisfied with control only of the City. Nevertheless, at Croker's appearance the Metropolitan Opera's orchestra routinely played "Hail to the Chief" in recognition of the Boss's supremacy.

No area of City government suffered more substantially under Van Wyck as did law enforcement. As Deputy Police Commissioner Croker had decreed the appointment of William Devery, reputedly the overlord of Manhattan's midtown vice. Devery's Bowery counterpart was "Big Tim" Sullivan who had no aspirations toward law enforcement, but whose name is forever honored with the municipality's gun control law. The Sullivan Law was enacted so that "Big Tim's police cohorts might easily dispose of his opponents by planting guns on them and then hauling them off to jail. Decorum and order became the rule in Sullivan's saloon empire; men were known to sew up their pockets in order to prevent arrest. In Greater New York, a tacit understanding between business, politics, and vice was arrived at—each partner understood the greed, the necessities, and the ruthlessness of the other. An honest official like Chief John McCullagh inevitably was replaced by the vice boss of the Tenderloin; a district attorney led a chorus of the ever popular "to hell with reform"; and business leaders supervised Croker's speculations on Wall Street. When the Lexow Committee had investigated the Police Department in 1894 they found it "an established caste" dedicated only to "the cohesion of public plunder." Despite reform's brief fling under Mayor Strong, the Van Wyck administration had restored that old-time reality.

Once again, however, maladministration of the City led to state action. In the summer of 1899, an investigative commission led by Senator Ferdinand Mazet was able to document the revival of "dirty graft," organized vice, and police corruption in New York City. Mazet's report, issued in January 1900, also charged that the American Ice Company, a City-granted monopoly which refused to sell ice in less than sixty-cent blocks, had enriched such Tammany Hall luminaries as Croker, Van Wyck, and Docks Commissioner Charles Murphy. The depredations were startling only because they were made at the expense of the lower-class voter that Tammany claimed to represent. The impact of artificially high ice prices was understood by even the most ignorant slum-dweller. Croker's delicate political antennae picked up the popular anger. Rather than take on the demand for charter revision fostered by the Mazet revelations, Croker surprised everyone by retiring. After almost sixteen years as Boss, Croker withdrew to Wantage, where he happily bred horses—including the Derby winner of 1907—for the rest of his long life.

Croker left New York for Ireland in February 1901, amid signs that it would be a bad year for Tammany. The Episcopal bishop, Henry Potter, had issued an open letter condemning the Van Wyck administration and, in one of his last acts as Governor, Vice-President-Elect Roosevelt removed District Attorney Asa "To Hell with Reform" Gardiner. The party organization itself was divided by territorial and patronage disputes. Indeed, the intraparty investigation carried out by Louis Nixon, Croker's nominal successor, was so damning that a public report could not be issued. Ambitious ward leaders now asserted "Croker ain't the whole thing" and struggled to safeguard their fiefdoms against the rising tide of reform. Special Session Court Justice William Travers Jerome began systematically to question police captains about protection of vice; he soon launched a series of "John Doe" raids that won popular acclaim and catapulted him to the post of Manhattan District Attorney. Most ominous of all was the slow minuet toward political accommodation between the good government forces of Robert Fulton Cutting's Citizens' Union and the Republican followers of Thomas Platt. If that coalition could be achieved, and the experience of 1897 proved it must be achieved in order to defeat Tammany, then reform might once again visit New York. On September 5, 1901, the *Nation* editorialized that reform's cause was "not electing a Mayor, but saving a city" and on September 10 the Citizens' Union called for a Fusion Ticket (Republicans-Reformers) to oppose Tammany.

The demand for Fusion threw the political spotlight on the patrician figure of Seth Low, President of Columbia University, who had unsuccessfully carried the banner of reform in 1897. A successful businessman and the formidable Mayor of Brooklyn from 1881 to 1885, Low had dedicated his life to public service. His personality was cold, however, and his capacities failed to include the wiles of the professional politician. Even in his career as President of Columbia, Low would allow his successor to claim the credit for valuable academic reforms. Yet despite his lack of concern with recognition, Low was identified with the ideal of the Greater City. He had served on the Charter Commission of 1896 and had long promoted Consolidation. Although Platt found Low personally obnoxious, he could not ignore the possibility of victory that Low's candidacy presented; he gave his grudging approval to a Fusion ticket headed by Low and Judge Jerome.

Tammany countered with its own expedient reformer, Edward Shepard, but a united opposition, the public's revulsion against vice, Low's competence, and Jerome's demagogic rhetoric doomed the Democratic effort. Low proved a dull campaigner who trailed the Fusion ticket, but he nevertheless defeated Shepard and in January 1902 took office as New York's ninety-second Mayor.

The single greatest irony of the Mazet investigation was that reform cost New York City two years of honest and efficient government. Senator Mazet had recommended and the legislature had enacted into law a charter revision which reduced the term of Mayor by half and reorganized the City into five "boroughs." Hence, Low entered office with only two years in which to reform the administration and impose his will on the bureaucracy, business, and the politicians. Given decades of gross Tammany misrule, two years was simply not enough time to show results. Low's rigorous honesty offended many vested interests which managed to coexist with Tammany, while his reform backers began to lose their enthusiasm. The reform impulse in New York has historically been of brief duration and notoriously fickle.

Yet in his brief tenure, Low achieved much. City franchises were renegotiated to raise income and the dead wood of Tammany was ruthlessly pruned from the payroll. The entire City was reassessed and the tax rate thereby reduced, but business hardly enjoyed paying more in taxes. Low began a vast school construction program, authorized contracts for the Manhattan bridge, and also accelerated work on the subway system. He opened the first public baths on the East Side and sponsored Tenement House reform. Yet despite his efforts, tenement dwellers were to increase by 500,000 from 1900 to 1910, surpassing the 400,000-rise of the previous decade. Low worked hard to expand a program under which indigent New Yorkers received treatment in voluntary hospitals with their bills paid by the City—he thus initiated the humanitarian concern that has led New York to build the world's greatest municipal hospital system. In all, it was an extremely progressive two-year term.

Given Low's substantial accomplishments, it was unbelievable that the major public issue of his tenure was the peripheral one of Sunday liquor sales. District Attorney Jerome's attempt to enforce closing laws ended in a failure which alienated the WASP and clerical adherents of Fusion. Even more importantly, when

Police Commissioner Francis Greene continued that ineffective campaign into 1903, Low sacrificed lower-class voter support. Moreover, rigid police enforcement of the archaic peddler license requirements cost Low dearly in the increasingly powerful Jewish vote. The Fusion administration rapidly moved toward political tragedy. Low had successfully launched a series of long-term innovations (for which he received no credit) but his short-term expedients had alienated powerful blocs of voters. An uninspired speaker, Low could not articulate his concern for the common man but was increasingly perceived as a traitor by his own class. Perhaps a four-year administration could have made both achievements and concerns obvious, but Low was mandated to stand for reelection in two years because of the very success of the reform movement he represented. When Boss Platt, who received little patronage from the righteous Low, defected from the coalition, it became obvious that 1903 presented an opportunity for one of Tammany's periodic rebirths.

The organizer of a new Democratic coalition was Charles Francis Murphy, a former baseball catcher turned saloon-keeper who presided over the Gas House District and ministered to the needs of his people from a lamppost on Second Avenue. Murphy, probably Tammany's greatest twentieth-century figure, had by 1902 displaced Louis Nixon as leader; he now evolved a strategy to restore respectability to the Democrats. Clearly, if they were to challenge Low, they were in need of a man of equal probity. Murphy found his man in George B. McClellan, Jr., a son of the Civil War general and, at thirty-eight, a veteran of both Tammany politics and the House of Representatives. A victorious McClellan campaign would also allow Murphy to crush his opponents (led by Bill Devery) within Tammany and solidify the organization. To that end, Murphy was even willing to endorse Fusion candidates for the posts of Comptroller and President of the Board of Aldermen. McClellan was honest, but even better, he entertained hopes of running for national office. He was thus certain to attract independent voters, keep his eye off details and, according to the *Herald*, "take orders and he doesn't look it." The campaign of 1903 was a clean campaign between two gentlemen, one seeking to maximize the organizational vote and the other seeking to reconstruct a factionalized reform coalition. In the end, reform was rejected because it and Low appeared far too puritanical while McClellan offered enlightened government and the right to drink freely. Murphy's "artful raising of the partisan cry" was quite enough to win, and the organization had no need to even think of stuffing ballot boxes. McClellan swamped Low by 314,782 to 252,086 and reform's epitaph was pronounced by Platt. Low "came and went," said the Easy Boss, "and New York City is still the same old town."

McClellan's election in November 1903, signaled the start of two decades of Murphy rule in Tammany Hall. But despite the expectations of some Democrats, it did not mean "The lid is off." McClellan provided vast patronage to the machine, but he would not accept incompetents in high posts. He insisted, for example, on appointing his own men to the crucial posts of police, health, and street-cleaning commissioners. Nevertheless, Jacob Riis called McClellan "the best organization Mayor" New York ever had. Not only did he refurbish the machine but also he appointed a City Improvement Commission to revitalize the Greater City. A comprehensive traffic plan was adopted and Police Commissioner William G. McAdoo saw that traffic ordinances were obeyed. A unified park scheme for the five boroughs was enacted and approval was granted for the widening of streets, public utilization of waterfront acreage, and the modernization of piers; from 1902 to 1907, the City spent $15,000,000 to construct nine Hudson River berths. In all, McClellan presided over accomplishments that not even Seth Low could fault.

Yet all improvements paled before the grand achievement of McClellan's first administration; the opening of the subway system under construction since 1900. Indeed, the Mayor was even to drive the first train. Ever since the incorporation of New York's first elevated line in 1866, citizens had been offended by the noise and filth they created. As early as February 1870, the Beach Pneumatic Transit Company had dug a block long subway beneath Broadway. Alfred Beach was far ahead of his time—his stations included frescoed waiting rooms that featured a grand piano and fountains—and his initiative failed due to technological and political problems. One aspect of Beach's genius that survived was a pneumatic mail system that for decades sped letters beneath the streets of Manhattan until it was replaced by modern, if much slower, mail delivery. The dream of underground travel persisted, however, and ground had been broken for a subway system on March 24, 1900. Under the leadership of John McDonald and August Belmont II work proceeded all during the Low administration. Some 12,000 laborers worked long and hazardous 10-hour days at the magnificent wage of 20 cents an hour to build the underground tubes; the excavated earth was used to enlarge Governor's Island. Finally, on October 27, 1904, Mayor McClellan gingerly took the controls of an 8-car train and made a 9-mile, 26-minute trip beneath Manhattan Island. The subway, then the focus of many City hopes and today the City's despair, was operative. On the first day 110,000 citizens bought passage and the first subway crimes were reported. By October 29, daily ridership reached 350,000 yet even that host represented only the vanguard of the billions of fares to follow. New York still has the world's most extensive and perhaps most efficient mass transit system.

Boss Murphy benignly watched the success of his protégé. Perhaps the most astute leader in Tammany's long history, Murphy was honest and limited himself to the "honest graft" to which his eminence entitled him. Modern investigators have discovered that his contracting firms performed jobs valued at $15,000,000 for the City, and the work seems to have been well done. The Boss lived in style but without ostentation; he never failed to serve his constituents. Murphy shared Tim Sullivan's credo, "There is no crime so mean as ingratitude in politics," and he lived by this in 1905. McClellan deserved renomination and, since the state had approved a revised mayoral term, he fully expected to serve another four years. But William Randolph Hearst, whose money had already won him a congressional seat, attempted to wrest the Democratic nomination from McClellan. When Murphy's control of the party denied Hearst the prize, the outraged publisher launched an independent candidacy. McClellan was all but ignored in the brawl that followed. The contest was a battle between "Moiphy voises Hoist," a campaign of bitter words and foul deeds on both sides. Murphy labeled Hearst a Socialist who proposed municipal ownership of the expanding yet efficiently run subway system. Hearst counterattacked with personal libels; "Everybody works but Moiphy, he only rakes in the dough." When the carnage was over, the organization had triumphed although some observers maintained that certain ballot boxes had found a watery

Hudson River grave. The Mayor won by a mere 3,500 votes as Murphy fulfilled his obligations of loyalty. Yet McClellan was appalled by the activities carried out in his name and a rupture soon occurred in the relationship between the gentleman Mayor and Murphy. When new appointments were announced on December 30, only two Tammany leaders were among them and both were men personally committed to the Mayor. Murphy's vendetta against Hearst had sentenced his party to a term in the political wilderness. When the Boss cynically forced the Democrats to nominate Hearst for Governor in 1906, the breach widened. Even though Hearst lost, McClellan was angered and allowed John Purroy Mitchel to conduct an investigation of Tammany corruption. As a result of Mitchel's findings, a Republican Governor removed three Democratic borough presidents from their positions. McClellan ignored both Murphy and the machine for the rest of his term.

From 1906 to 1909, McClellan pursued his independent course and effectively administered a thriving City. Business remained good even though the tobacco industry had begun to leave for the sunnier climes of the South. New York was the brewing center of the East and had more breweries than Chicago, St. Louis, and Milwaukee combined. Today, in the wake of economic change, not a single brewery remains in the City. New industries were born, however, and America's movie industry had its origins in New York during 1905–07. New manufacturing and shipping facilities were rising on the banks of Newtown Creek in Queens and added their taxes to the municipal treasury. Although McClellan's name is almost unknown to New Yorkers today, his administration was responsible for completing harbor improvements, beginning the municipal ferry service, and massively expanding the park and playground system. The last horsecars were removed from Fifth Avenue, in part due to pressure from the Fifth Avenue Association (1907). Eighty-four miles of subway existed by 1908 and the track to Brooklyn's Borough Hall was opened. The outer boroughs were further integrated into Manhattan when both the Queensboro and Manhattan bridges were completed in 1909. The future water supply of this thriving City was ensured when contracts expanded the Croton Reservoir system into the Catskill watershed. Not even the bank panic of October 1907 could hinder the advance for during that crisis Mayor McClellan and his Comptroller personally waited upon J. P. Morgan to arrange a $30,000,000 loan which safeguarded the City's credit and payrolls.

But the greatest human drama of McClellan's tenure was not the Mayor's conflict with Murphy; rather, it was the continuing saga of immigration to New York. Vast though the City was, its sources were strained to the utmost by the millions of immigrants arriving at Ellis Island. The cost of steerage passage from Bremen had been lowered to $33.50 (1903) and by 1907 an all-time high immigration figure of 1,300,000 was reached. The newcomers, young, ambitious, and secular minded, came primarily from Russia, central Europe, and Italy. In sheer numbers, Jews were dominant; from 1880 to 1915, fully a third of all east European Jews arrived in America. Over 1,100,000 Jews lived in New York by 1910 and the effects of that enormous transfusion of young Jewish blood into the stream of the Greater City's life has not yet run its course. Jewish businessmen ultimately rose to dominate the ready-made clothing industry even as Jewish Socialists organized unions which brought workers a greater return for their labor. Their patronage turned the Bowery into the "Jewish Rialto" and created the Yiddish theater; luminaries such as Adler, Jolson, Jessel, Cantor, Benny, Burns, Fields, Brice, and Tucker performed there. This was the training ground for impresarios such as Goldwyn, Mayer, Fox, Selznick, Cohen, and the Warner brothers who ended in California. But no matter what their status or hopes, it seemed that all Jewish newcomers read Abraham Cahan's *Forward*, a newspaper first published in 1897, and every family intended to send their children—if not themselves—to the free City College. In 1905 the elementary school population of the East Side was 95-percent Jewish and an educational revolution was being created in the crowded classrooms. Although 50,000 previous Jewish immigrants had already moved to Brownsville in Brooklyn by 1905, their removal had little discernible efect in the streets of Manhattan's tenement district. In 1906, as McClellan began his second term, 37 of the 51 New York blocks with over 3,000 people were located on the Lower East Side. The Housing Code of 1901 was meaningless when faced with the enormity of the problem—Jacob Riis estimated the population density of the area at 330,000 per square mile.

From the teeming chaos of the tenement district came countless vignettes that have been incorporated into the folklore of the metropolis. The pushcarts of Hester Street, the cry of the "seltzer man," the cross-pollination of "Abie's Irish Rose," the woes of the *Forward*'s "Bintel Brief" all convey the New York-Jewish experience. Equally impressive was the intense upward mobility of the Jewish newcomer. They fled the "eternal darkness" of tenement flats as rapidly as they could and sought the splendors of Mosholu Parkway in the Bronx, Ocean Parkway in Brooklyn, or the "Jewish City" of Harlem. It was true that many New Yorkers resented Jewish immigrants. The riot that marred Rabbi Jacob Joseph's funeral in July 1902, was tangible proof of the scorn in which they were held by other earlier arrivals. Still others believed Jews crime prone—had not famed gambler Arnold Rothstein began his career as a runner for "Big Tim" Sullivan? McClellan's own police commissioner intemperately charged that 50 percent of all New York crime was committed by newly arrived Russian Jews, only to be forced into a public retraction by the outraged Jewish community. But by whatever magic, New York successfully accommodated the flood of new immigration, and like Irish, Italians, and Germans before them, Jewish dreams became part of the Greater City.

But New York was not all Hester Street. O. Henry was in residence from 1902 to 1910 and wrote his stories of the "four million" for magazines and newspapers that no longer exist. In Greenwich Village, authors such as Frank Norris, Willa Cather, Theodore Dreiser, Sherwood Anderson, and Edna Millay were struggling toward greatness while Mark Twain, who already had achieved it, watched from his home on Fifth Avenue. Also in America's Bohemia, Eugene O'Neill was writing plays that ultimately would bring him a Nobel Prize. Popular culture reached out to the masses as movie theaters—the Fox and Loew's chains—opened across the metropolis and the Schubert brothers created similar outlets for theater. John Barrymore was the greatest actor, George M. Cohan the brightest Broadway star, and the most popular song of 1908 "Will You Love Me in December as You Do in May?" was tossed off by a young man named James J. Walker. All in all, Mayor McClellan's New York, viewed from any perspective, was the most exciting and vital City in America.

McClellan, although he chose to retire in 1909 to a life of scholarship at Princeton University, bequeathed to New York a style of integrity and accomplishment that Murphy intended to maintain. But to find such competence within Tammany Hall was not easy. Ultimately, Murphy's eye of necessity wandered across the East River and fastened on Supreme Court Judge William Gaynor. Gaynor's electability was suspect because he was a lapsed Catholic, but his conflict with Brooklyn's Democratic leadership had given him a reputation for integrity and strength. Moreover, he was an intense worker who tried more cases per month and suffered fewer reversals than any other metropolitan area justice. On balance, he seemed an ideal candidate to replace McClellan and to once again frustrate the mayoral ambitions of Hearst. After hard negotiations, Gaynor accepted the 1909 Democratic nomination and agreed to head a slate of Murphy-named officials in the race. Early in the campaign, however, the judge asserted his independence during a visit to Tammany Hall itself. Gaynor asked the assembled sachems the whereabouts of "the Tiger . . . which they say is going to swallow me up? If there is any swallowing up, it is not at all unlikely that I may be on the outside of the Tiger!" Although the race was complicated when Hearst ran an independent Fusion campaign, its result was predictable. Gaynor, with 250,678 votes easily outdistanced Republican Otto Bannard and ran about 100,000 votes better than Hearst. Tammany Hall was back in power, or at least so it seemed.

The revival of the machine never took place. Manhattan had 2,330,000 citizens in 1910 but not even that huge population sufficed to return the Tammany hacks. Gaynor won, but not the rest of Murphy's slate and the new Mayor hardly intended to trade his reputation for integrity for that of a spoilsman. He accepted Murphy's demands for patronage with a smile and a "few kind words" but he nevertheless ignored all requests. Prickly independence was the hallmark of Gaynor's administration, a trait that Murphy should have expected from a Mayor who daily walked three miles to his desk and who had unblinkingly told suffragettes that all persons aspire "to that thing which (they) are least fitted for!" Gaynor not only ignored Tammany's patronage expectations but also overhauled the City payroll; his purge of "no-shows" from the lists cost the organization over 400 positions. Gaynor worked out an accommodation with the Fusion majority of the Board of Estimate and together they reorganized the Bureau of Weights and Measures, demanded that City employees put in full eight-hour days, and launched the legislative initiatives that became the "Gaynor Charter" of 1911.

Gaynor's accomplishments were so significant that, of all New York's 4,800,000 people, only Hearst and the spoilsmen of Tammany resented his success. It seems likely that 1910 was the finest year of Gaynor's life; his prospects seemed so limitless some observers believed that his career might extend to the White House itself. Then, on August 9, as the Mayor boarded the S.S. *Kaiser Wilhelm* for a well-deserved vacation, he was shot by a disgruntled, recently discharged dockworker named James Gallagher. Instead of leaving for Europe, Gaynor spent the next three weeks in St. Mary's Hospital, Hoboken. Gaynor had always been testy and opinionated—Mayor McClellan believed he was "never normal"—but the assassination attempt changed him for the worse. The bullet could not be removed from his pharynx and the Mayor lived with pain and increasing irascibility. He feuded with John Purroy Mitchel, President of the Board of Alderman, lost his allies on the Board of Estimate, and generally lost interest in obtaining the best appointees. His intemperate behavior forced him to write three public letters of apology and the last years of his administration were constantly in turmoil.

The Mayor's instability was hardly conducive to easing the heated atmosphere of New York City in 1910. Workers, especially in those trades dominated by Jewish immigrants with militantly Socialist backgrounds, were increasing their use of the strike to obtain greater economic benefits. In 1909, the Shirtwaist girls had gone on strike led by Clara Lemlich, an epic struggle in which the "70,000 Jews became 70,000 fighters" even though they lost. In 1910, the cloakmakers and the shirtmakers struck, a battle that ended only when Louis Brandeis negotiated a "Protocol of Peace" in August. And as 1911 began, the militants of labor were again demanding changes in the intolerable conditions of the sweatshop lofts. At the Triangle Shirtwaist Company, for example, the girls were billed for their needles, taxed for their lockers, and suffered triple fines for spoilage. Nevertheless Triangle, located on the top three floors of the ten-story Asch Building at 22 Washington Place, had successfully resisted all attempts to bring unionism into its workrooms. Yet no union could have averted the Triangle disaster. Just before quitting time on March 25, a fire broke out and the elevator operator fled. Although the Fire Department was quickly on-the-scene, its ladders reached only to the sixth floor. Within minutes, the building was an inferno and 146 workers, 125 of them girls, were dead. The greatest factory disaster in New York history, the Triangle tragedy was made more terrible when a Buildings Department ruling declared the Asch Building unsafe—two days after the fire! In court, no negligence was found and Judge Thomas Crain directed an acquittal. The heritage of the Triangle was an increased labor militancy and state action. In Albany, the legislature responded to the leadership of Al Smith and Robert Wagner and produced 56 factory reform measures. And in New York in 1912, the furriers and the tailors struck their respective industries; the latter conflict was settled in part due to the mediation of a young lawyer named Fiorello La Guardia. There is no doubt that the deaths of the Triangle fire intensified unionization across New York; for example, in 1913, Jewish building workers founded their first union. And in the massive clothing industry, which produced a billion dollars worth of goods in 1914, the Amalgamated Clothing Workers Union (later the ILGWU) represented the future. New York was on its way to becoming the preeminent "union town" in the nation.

Beyond worker militancy and political strife, however, New Yorkers could ponder the awesome physical changes in their City. Buildings illustrative of the metropolis' power seemed to spring up yearly. Macy's opened on Thirty-fourth Street in 1901 while the Flatiron Building was erected in 1902. The New York Stock Exchange was occupied in 1903 while the *Times* moved into its Tower on Longacre Square. On January 1, 1908, the paper inaugurated the custom of dropping an illuminated ball to greet the New Year in what everyone now calls Times Square. Architectural *tours de force* such as Cass Gilbert's Beaux Arts Custom House (1905) the New York Hippodrome (1905), Stanford White's Colony Club (1906), and the French Renaissance Plaza Hotel (1907) were dedicated while McClellan ruled the City. In 1908, Ernest Flagg's Singer Building, at 612 feet the tallest building in the world, celebrated its opening; in 1967 it became the highest structure ever demolished. Gaynor's accession only intensified the metropolitan mania to express economic preeminence in monumental architecture. In 1909, the Metropolitan Tower surpassed the Singer Building by 45 feet. Then on September 8,

1910, the new Pennsylvania Railroad Station opened, a duplication of the Baths of the emperor Caracella which just as effectively showed the power of the railroad barons who financed its construction. It was also in 1910 that the Long Island Railroad, ultimately the line of "dashing" if sometimes immobilized commuters, first entered Manhattan on newly electrified tracks. Nor was all the construction privately sponsored. The City continued its pier modernization and in 1911 completed the Hellgate Channel to the East River to speed intracity commerce. Perhaps the most impressive statement of the City's domination of commerce and transport came with twin dedications in 1913. On February 3, the Grand Central Terminal on Forty-second Street was opened and on April 24, President Wilson turned on 80,000 bulbs which illuminated Cass Gilbert's "Cathedral of Commerce," the 792-foot Woolworth Building. For almost twenty years the Woolworth would reign as the world's tallest building; its managers carefully maintain Gilbert's Gothic ornamentation to this day. O. Henry's wry comment, "New York will be a great place if they ever finish it," seemed perfectly justified in these years.

But if buildings demonstrated New York's economic might, they also indicated its intellectual stature. Major colleges had been forced to desert the crowded streets of lower Manhattan but they had created educational enclaves of distinction elsewhere in the city. New York University moved part of its faculty to University Heights in the Bronx (1895), Columbia decamped to Morningside Heights (1897), and City College itself had moved uptown to Convent Avenue (1907). Joseph Pulitzer, perhaps partly inspired by the notoriety of Hearst and the increasing prestige of the *Times,* decided to endow a new School of Journalism which opened at Columbia's new campus in 1911. In that same year, on May 23, President Taft and Mayor Gaynor presided over the opening of the New York Public Library. Constructed at a cost of $9,000,000 on the site of the reservoir in Bryant Part, the massive Beaux Arts structure became home for the Astor, Tilden, and Lenox Foundation bequests to the city. More important to scholars was the fact that its reference resources, ably organized by John Shaw Billings, have made Forty-second Street a Mecca for generations of scholars. Only the dominant reputation of such an institution could dwarf the availability of the J. P. Morgan Library (1913) and the more modest resources of the Municipal

Reference Library. Yet another cultural landmark was also under construction in 1913. Henry Clay Frick's Renaissance Palace at Fifth Avenue and Seventieth Street would ultimately become one of New York's smallest but finest museums. Thus, New York's superiority in transportation, commerce, and intellectual life was shown in stone to all the world. It seems fitting therefore that the new Municipal Building by McKim, Mead, and White was also completed in 1913. At its apex stands Adolph Weisman's "Civic Fame"—a sculpture largely unseen by New Yorkers—symbolizing the glories of the metropolis.

Mayor Gaynor presided over the undoubted splendor of New York with ever-increasing bile and intemperance. He insisted that the police rigidly enforce peddler license laws, a measure that alienated Manhattan's smallest entrepreneurs and which proved almost impossible to accomplish. On the other hand, he prevented the force from moving without warrants to close prostitution or gambling houses; he even forbade the free use of billy clubs in crowd control. Perhaps the Mayor knew his police's capabilities, however, for when confronted with a major challenge—the July 16, 1912 murder of gambler Herman Rosenthal—the department proved singularly incompetent. Although the Rosenthal case made two careers, that of the journalist Herbert Swope and of prosecutor Charles Whitman, it did Gaynor no political good. It probably destroyed the slim chance he had to head the Democratic national ticket in 1912. Yet despite his wounds, police scandal and the enmity of Murphy's Tammany Hall, Gaynor was eager for another term in 1913; his ego led him to accept a reform coalition's nomination for the mayoralty and he sailed for Europe to recuperate for what he knew must be an arduous campaign. En route, on September 10, 1913, Gaynor died with Emerson's *Essays* on his lap. Emerson had once written that reform is dangerous, for it "runs to egotism and bloated self-conceit." There was a hint of that in Gaynor's last message to New York: "No king, no clown shall rule this town—that day is gone forever."

The "clown" Gaynor so delicately referred to was Boss Murphy's handpicked candidate, Judge Edward McCall. A loyal party man, McCall would normally have been assured of election but his candidacy was destroyed by Murphy's immoderate use of Tammany Hall's political power. In November 1912, the Democratic party had elected William Sulzer to the state house by the biggest majority in New York history, a large proportion of that majority being supplied by Tammany. When Sulzer avowed his complete independence in his Inaugural Address, Murphy responded, "like hell." And when the Governor supported a direct primary law abhorrent to the machine and refused to appoint an organization regular to the State Highway Commission, battle lines were drawn. Under Murphy's direction, the Democratic legislature led by Al Smith rejected the primary law and counterattacked by authorizing an investigation into the financing of Sulzer's campaign. On August 13, 1913, almost coincident with McCall's nomination, the Democrats in Albany impeached their own Governor on charges that he had perjured himself, submitted false financial statements, and diverted campaign funds into private stock speculations. Sulzer was tried and removed from office by October 17. Murphy had demonstrated his total control of the party but his unprecedented display of naked power provided reformers in the City with an opportunity to recover from Gaynor's death and once again elect a Fusion candidate. Murphy's eight years of patronage drought were to be extended to twelve as Fusion coalesced to win 57 percent of the vote and a stunning, unexpected victory.

John Purroy Mitchel had been identified with reform ever since he had led an investigation which resulted in the removal of several borough presidents (1907–08). Elected president of the Board of Alderman in Gaynor's 1909 victory, Mitchel cooperated closely with the Mayor on major projects and during the Mayor's hospitalization, he had been an effective acting chief executive. Since May 1913, Mitchel had served as Collector of the Port and had worked to master the patronage bureaucracy and bring efficiency into traditionally lax customs operations. When Fusion, now directed by Hearst, asked him to take Gaynor's place at the head of a reform ticket, Mitchel did not hesitate. With the support of President Wilson, Hearst, and Progressives of all types, Mitchel became the choice over McCall and led his coalition to a smashing victory. Mitchel's platform was simplicity itself. "I want to make New York the best governed City in the world."

The single greatest problem Mitchel had in governing the City was his own character; he was an elitist who constantly underestimated the important role of the machine in providing personal attention to the needs of New Yorkers. Mitchel believed that simply by naming efficient commissioners, among them several of his personal friends, he could cleanse the Augean Stable of municipal patronage. The bureaucracy was hurt but was never destroyed. Like his predecessor, Mitchel survived an assassination attempt (April 17, 1914) and then successfully led the City through a short-term currency deficiency caused by the outbreak of the first world war. That crisis was ignored by the legislature, but Mitchel successfully negotiated an $80,000,000 loan from the Morgan syndicate which put the City on a "pay as you go" footing. The Mayor's problem was that he could never convince the average citizen that his was a magnificent accomplishment; the ordinary man saw only fewer jobs and reduced public services. Mitchel won the approval of his friends who came from the upper classes but lacked empathy with the working man. He was considered a "Manhattan Mayor" unconcerned with the common folk.

Mitchel's creed was "Be right and speak out." He personally intervened to settle garment industry and transit strikes in 1916 but already he was entering political limbo. Murphy had regained the Board of Alderman, the district attorney, and the sheriff's office in the elections of 1915 and Mitchel desperately needed to show the City he was more than a passing phenonemon. In July 1916, Mitchel strongly supported a Zoning Plan which embodied the recommendations of the Conference on City Planning (1912). New York soon adopted the first Zoning Code in the nation, one which mandated "setbacks" for skyscrapers and created the ziggurat form which characterized the next four decades of New York architecture. Mitchel believed in economy and ruthlessly pruned the civil service lists while reducing taxes. The Mayor hoped to achieve major financial benefits by imposing the Gary System, an educational reform which provided vocational training and made more efficient use of school facilities. In pursuit of this goal, Mitchel dismissed the head of the Board of Education, arrogantly ignored parental objections, and vetoed most school construction projects. Although cities across the nation recognized the revolutionary nature of the Gary Plan and adopted it widely, in New York City the Mayor's political ineptness alienated many voters and ultimately destroyed the appeal of the innovations. To compound his difficulties Mitchel, although himself a Catholic, decided to

reduce public subsidies to privately administered religious charities, a battle during which he attacked religiously affiliated child-
caring institutions and actually tapped the phone of a Catholic
priest. By 1917, his Fusion coalition was shrinking and he had
lost the support of the Hearst papers. Mitchel's performance, even
as he accepted Fusion's renomination on July 30, 1917, presaged
a Democratic revival.

It had been twelve long years since Tammany Hall had enjoyed
the patronage of New York City; indeed, Murphy had been far
more effective influencing state government then in controlling
his own city. Some party lenders saw 1917 as Murphy's last
chance to prove his competence and the Boss rose to that challenge. To restore the normal Democratic majority against a weakened Fusion coalition, Murphy's eye fell upon Brooklyn County
Judge John Francis Hylan, a man who was a loyal Democrat
though many considered him rather dull-witted. Murphy arranged a scenario in which Kings County Democrats forced Hylan
"down my throat" at the party convention. In addition, Hylan won
the newspaper support of the Hearst publications. The unknown
factor in the campaign was how voters would react to the fact of
America's entry into the first world war. Mitchel campaigned
against "Hearst, Hylan, and the Hollenzollerns" while seeking to
restore his middle-class base; among the Mayor's supporters were
Presidents Taft, Roosevelt, and Wilson as well as Governor Charles
Evans Hughes. But in New York the result was inevitable. On
November 6, Hylan (and Murphy) won an overwhelming victory,
293,386 votes to the Mayor's 148,060. Not only was the "Boy
Mayor" retired, but his upper-class supporters were shocked by
138,793 votes cast for Morris Hillquit, the Socialist candidate.
Mitchel, who had ardently supported Wilson's preparedness policy, decided to enlist in the Air Force though he was 38. He died
during a training flight on July 8, 1918 and his memory was
honored when an aviation depot was given his name. Typically,
most New Yorkers believe that Long Island's Mitchel Field com-
memorates the career of bombing advocate General "Billy" Mitch-
ell, rather than giving honor to a former Mayor of New York.

"Red Mike" Hylan was elected Mayor in 1917, the year America
went to war. In 1913, the trade of New York had declined to only
58 percent of the nation's imports and 37 percent of its export
trade but the outbreak of World War I restored the losses. During

the nineteen months of American participation in the war New York and Hoboken served as major ports of embarkation for the American Expeditionary Force; over 1,500,000 "doughboys" would wave farewell to the Statue of Liberty and New York's skyscrapers. Even before April 1917, the demands placed on port facilities had been overwhelming, but as men, munitions, and supplies of every description converged on the City the situation became catastrophic. Local rail terminals could not handle the traffic and trains backed up as far as Pittsburgh. Harbor facilities, even including the 6,000,000 square feet of the new Bush Terminal in Brooklyn, were so overtaxed that some ships were forced to sail without full holds in order to make wharf space available. Only the appointment of Irving T. Bush as chairman of the War Board of the Port of New York brought order out of chaos. By mid-1918, the port was operating more smoothly than it ever had. Tonnage toward the port was increased moreover, by the widening and deepening of the Erie Canal—a long-delayed project completed in 1918. New York benefitted from the wartime trade in money as well as commerce; the City replaced London as the center of international finance and America became the world's banker. Perhaps the most impressive aspect of New York life during the war was the City's ability to avoid the animosities of the European conflict. Although Germans comprised 15 percent of the population, their lives and property were not subjected to ugly incidents which occurred elsewhere in the nation, a fact for which Mayors Mitchel and Hylan deserve much credit. The City rallied as a unit to the war effort and Hylan even dared to name Hearst, whose newspapers had been pro-German in 1914, as an official greeter for returning soldiers. Hylan called himself the People's Mayor, and he presided happily over the boom.

The New York *Times* had been appalled when Hylan, "a man of marvelous mental density," was elected and President Wilson wondered "How is it possible for the greatest City in the world to place such a man in high office?" The answer of course was the organized power of Tammany. After 1917 and for the first time since 1906, Murphy could deal with a sympathetic partisan in City Hall. This did not mean dishonest government. No fewer than three investigating panels later agreed that Hylan was honest and that the City was well administered. Not even the destructive Wall Street explosion of September 1920, an accident once attributed to terrorists, could shake the stolid progress of Hylan's administration. He pointed with pride to the opening of $30,000,000 worth of municipal piers on Staten Island (1919), the largest school construction/education budgets in City history, the elimination of police graft by Commissioner Richard Enright, and construction of the Bronx Terminal Market. Above all else, Hylan maintained, as his campaign had promised to do, the five-cent subway fare. The Mayor intended to construct a municipally owned transit system and named John Delaney to plan what became the Independent Subway System. In yet another transit innovation, the States of New York and New Jersey created a tax exempt Port Authority (April 30, 1921) "to purchase, construct, lease, and/or operate terminals and transportation facilities" and to integrate all harbor activities. Modeled after London's Author-ity and the first such agency in America, for 55 years the Author-ity has been one of the major forces in determining the future of New York. The voters obviously perceived in Hylan an honesty of purpose that compensated for his lack of humor and his unin-spired rhetoric. On November 8, 1921, once again with the support of Murphy, Hearst, and the people, Hylan was reelected by a plurality of 417,000 votes. Problems of image notwithstand-ing, he became the first modern Mayor to serve eight consecutive years and only the second since consolidation to win reelection.

Extraordinary municipal progress continued during Hylan's second term. A massive educational building program provided the City with 662 schools by 1925, an achievement duly lauded by the *Daily News* (established 1919). Pictures showed the Mayor at the Regional Plan Association; he was there when automatic telephone dialing began in October 1922; and he became the first Mayor heard over the facilities of WNYC Radio. Some of his ideas were too grandiose—the subway to Staten Island which he autho-rized is still unbuilt—but he sponsored projects such as a tri-borough bridge and a high school for the arts which would soon become reality.

Achievements notwithstanding, Hylan seemed increasingly out of place in the Jazz Age. He had the somber duty of enforcing prohibition in a City which would never surrender its God-given right to drink. In Hylan's New York, entrepreneurs such as Sher-man Billingsly, Helen Morgan, and "Texas" Guinan provided cus-tomers with all they could imbibe. Indeed in New York you could almost always find anything you wanted to drink at a relatively moderate price, a phenomenon due in no little part to the efficient distribution system created by bootlegger Francisco Costello. And if you were inventive, local supermarkets sold malt syrup while personal brewing apparatus was available at the hardware store. The worst sin a child could commit, according to Will Rogers, "was to eat the raisins Dad brought home for fermenting." The outmanned and outguessed Treasury Department had only 178 agents for the entire metropolitan region, but among them were the legendary Issy Einstein and Moe Smith. The latter two "super-cops" confiscated 5,000,000 bottles of booze and made 20 percent of all prohibition arrests in the City until they were dismissed in November 1925 "for the good of the service." Hylan doubtless agreed that Issy and Moe were too zealous. However, when his Police Department and courts absolved Miss Abby Rockefeller of blame in two speeding (and possibly drinking) infractions in 1924 the Mayor ordered official reprimands. The incident leaves little doubt that Hylan's political instincts were still highly attuned to the mind of the people.

It was in 1924 that two "nonevents" occurred which helped to determine New York City's future. The first of these incidents revolved about a "home rule" amendment that voters had adopted in November 1923. It had become obvious that the Gaynor Charter (1911), although 330,000 words in length, needed revision— the 1,700 laws specifically relating to the City enacted by the legislature between 1911 and 1921 amply proved that point. "Home rule" seemed the answer and in 1924 the Board of Estimate was combined with the aldermen to form a Municipal Assembly. Yet the "reform" accomplished nothing! The Mayor fought just as interminably with the new body; fifteen additional years would pass before a new City charter could be approved. The second happening that might have changed City history, yet did not, was the convocation of the Democratic National Convention in Madison Square Garden. America's preeminent Democrat was New York Governor Al Smith, a politician groomed for national office by Charles Murphy. Many assumed that Smith would inevitably lead the ticket and focus his party's program on the needs of urban America. However, on April 30, 1924, death removed Murphy's sure hand from the political scene. Senator James Walker lamented, "The brains of Tammany lie in Calvary

Cemetery," and when the Democrats met on June 24, their convention lacked a directing authority. It proved to be the greatest debacle in America's party history. A record 103 ballots were taken before the delegates, hopelessly divided between urban and rural constituencies, chose John W. Davis as their compromise nominee. Smith, Catholics, and urban America had been rebuffed and not for another 52 years would a Democratic Convention dare meet in New York City.

Others did come and marveled. When the great French architect Le Corbusier visited the metropolis in 1920 he called the City "a catastrophe, but it is a beautiful catastrophe." Manhattan, which Le Corbusier referred to, had reached its greatest population figures in 1910 and had already begun a slow decline. Yet to visitors and to the New Yorkers of the outer boroughs it remained "the City." But even Manhattan was an amalgam of neighborhoods, a varied patchwork which encompassed the Bohemian life-style of Greenwich Village, the staid residential enclaves of Murray Hill, and the wildly exciting, exploitive yet depressing, enclave of Harlem. Good housing was everywhere at a premium and in Manhattan that fact was indicated by housing cooperatives such as Tudor City, Hudson View Gardens, and London Terrace. In 1922, when revision of the state housing code permitted insurance companies to participate in housing projects, Metropolitan Life began a development in Queens. In Woodside, also in Queens, the garden apartments of the Steinway Company took rapid shape. Moreover, architects such as Otto Eidletz, August Heckscher, Adolph Zukor, and Louis Horowitz added their visions of beauty to the urban skyline. Completion of the Equitable and Straus buildings, the Paramount Theater, Gimbel's Department Store, and the McAlpin, Ambassador, and Waldorf-Astoria hotels punctuated the twenties. In November 1925, a third Madison Square Garden replaced the structure in which the Democrats met disaster. In sum, the vitality of New York during the Jazz Age was overwhelming—a vast contrast to its plodding, if efficient, Mayor.

Within the sacred precincts of Tammany changes became apparent after the death of Mr. Murphy. The leadership had fallen to George W. Olvany, a lawyer who had previously directed only the Polar Bear Club at Coney Island. The state's leading Democrat remained Al Smith, who made no secret of his disdain for Hylan, an "imperfect demagogue" and his prime supporter, Hearst. When the *Times* documented the fact that the Mayor had taken four vacations in the last six months of 1924 Smith decided to act. He joined with Olvany and the new leader of Bronx County, Ed Flynn, in opposition to Hylan. The stage was set for the bitter primary battle of 1925 when the three agreed to support popular State Senator James Walker, an effective legislator who had provided the public with Sunday baseball, boxing, and movies. Robert Moses later wrote that Walker "had genuine charm, not charisma" and events would prove this true. However, the issue in 1925 was raw political power and the primary was a war with the Manhattan and Bronx machines arrayed against the outer boroughs. Walker won the September primary by 100,000 votes and relegated Hylan to the sidelines. The November 3 victory over Republican Frank Waterman was almost anticlimatic. Walker, a loyal party man, took over as Mayor and his accession seemed to promise the continuation of good times for Tammany and the entire metropolis. If New York ever really was "Fun City," it was during the "Night Mayor's" first administration.

Walker possessed a glittering personality, lots of show business pals, and an intuitive sense of public relations. But he had an abysmal lack of knowledge of City government. He was a dilettante with style, and it seems somehow fitting that he was the first Mayor whose inauguration was live on the radio. Voters greeted major appointees as police and health commissioners with universal approval; few carped that Tammany men retained 20 of the 25 Commissionerships. Moreover, Walker's excellent relations with the Municipal Assembly were a welcome respite from the acrimony of Hylan's last years. Walker believed he had a responsibility to enjoy both his office and his City. At the Inner Circle Dinner in March 1926, he sang "By every test, I'm at my best, Under electric lights!" No civilized man, said Walker, would go to bed the same day he woke up and so he established himself as New York's "Night Mayor." Walker came to symbolize the Jazz Age in New York, a time of heavy drinking and rather loose private and public morals. Yet despite his perennial lateness, Walker presided with flair over the ceremonial aspects of his office. He helped bury Rudolph Valentino, greeted channel swimmer Gertrude Ederle with a tickertape parade and starred at the Tercentary Celebration of the City. The Mayor frequented the theater, an all-time high of 268 attractions appeared on Broadway in 1927, and he rooted shamelessly as Babe Ruth hit 60 home runs for the "Murderer's Row" Yankees of 1927. City business was not entirely neglected—the Mayor settled a subway strike, improved the Sanitation Department, and encouraged the Police Department to continue gambling raids—but Walker was always happier when in the public eye. No Mayor could have equaled the greeting he arranged for Charles Lindbergh as millions cheered the "Lone Eagle."

But official business intruded little on Walker's life. He took 149 days of vacations in his first 30 months in office, and often men who hoped to do business with the City paid his bills. Although New York had 7,000,000 residents and a budget of half a billion dollars the Mayor simply ignored his day-to-day responsibilities; his commissioners administered the City and Tammany Hall took care of patronage. In 1928 Walker named Grover Whalen New York's official greeter, to handle the ceremonial aspects of his office. The onerous weight of the mayoralty was lifted from his shoulders so that "our Jimmy" could fully devote himself to other pursuits—largely that of a dancer named Betty Compton, who was literally half his age.

In the vernacular of show business, 1928 was a year of mixed reviews for the "Night Mayor." He decided to leave his wife and took up residence with Betty Compton at the Ritz Carlton. Reporters tolerantly ignored the scandal but Governor Smith, a staunch Catholic, was appalled. Potentially as disruptive was a court decision on May 2 which granted the IRT an increased transit fare of seven cents. Walker, whose political sense of survival was always alert, ordered an immediate appeal and later, when an IRT accident killed sixteen people in the Times Square Station, he used the tragedy and the fare hike to flay the transit operators. But Walker's attention always returned to Miss Compton, and he ignored rumors of corruption everywhere. Even after the borough president of Queens was convicted of rigging sewer contracts, the Mayor did nothing. Despite all evil portents, Walker persisted in taking more vacations and having yet another drink.

The Great Depression began in 1929, but the year turned out a triumphant one for New York's Beau James. In March, John F. Curry, a fine organizer, replaced George Olvany as Grand Sachem of Tammany Hall. On April 8, the Supreme Court denied the IRT its fare increase—and even ordered it to pay the City an additional $6,300,000 in overdue revenues. The electorate cheered the decision as a Walker coup and was also impressed when the Mayor created the metropolis' first Department of Hospitals. His reelection chances suddenly seemed more secure and, as if to highlight his good fortune, a new Central Park Casino opened in May. Inside its gilded rooms, Walker was never presented with a bill. Both the Mayor and the City were thoroughly enjoying the Jazz Age—a jury even decided that "Texas" Guinan was innocent of running a speakeasy. Walker's only complaint was; "I have not had as much [fun] as I get the credit or the blame for." On July 18, August Heckscher led a group of public-spirited citizens who demanded that Walker accept renomination. The Mayor honored that petition and, despite his loss of support from Smith and in the face of Republican charges of citywide corruption, Walker won easily; his plurality was 865,000 votes. The only shadow on his victory was the collapse of the Stock Market on October 29, a Crash that signaled the onset of the Depression. Blithly ignoring that catastrophe, Walker accepted a $15,000 raise in December. "Our Jimmy" was made to govern New York in the Jazz Age and he was one of the few of New York's 6,930,000 people who would receive a raise in the thirties.

Aside from his increased salary, the decade did not begin well for Walker. In January 1930, he was warned to alter his life-style by no less a personage than Patrick Cardinal Hayes. In March, more than 100 were injured when Communists clashed with police in Union Square; a new police commissioner hastily had to be found. By year's end Judge Crater had vanished and the Bank of the United States had failed. Moreover, U.S. Attorney Charles Tuttle discerned that there was massive incompetence or corruption in New York's magistrate's court system. As a result of Tuttle's charges an investigation was launched in September by Judge Samuel Seabury. From Tammany's point of view, the Seabury probe meant danger. Corruption was discovered not only among the magistrates but also in the Women's Court and the police vice squad. The scandal grew even more ominous when eight Democratic district leaders refused to waive immunity and give testimony. The great Democratic machine was suddenly threatened with disaster.

Tammany fought back with an attempt at intimidation. Early

in 1931, the City's Corporation Counsel refused to honor salary vouchers for Seabury's staff of investigators—and only a court order forced release of the money. It was becoming clear that corruption in the magistrate's courts was so transparently present that an additional question had to be answered—Why had the district attorney's office failed to exercise its oversight function? When in March 1931 a prospective witness was murdered, Governor Franklin Roosevelt authorized an expanded investigation into the DA's office. By April 8, a general investigation of all City government was underway. A picture of municipal incompetence on a gargantuan scale soon emerged as the "tin box" brigade, led by Sheriff Thomas Farley of Manhattan, was summoned to give testimony before Seabury. It was soon discovered, among other revelations, that the Board of Standards and Appeals had no standards; that City condemnation procedures cost the municipality millions; that the new Department of Hospitals was a bureaucratic nightmare; that the clerk of Queens Surrogates Court did not know his duties; that 90 percent of welfare went to Democrats; that George Olvany's law firm could "expedite" City contracts; that one witness could not remember where he borrowed $500,000. The list of maladministration and theft seemed endless.

Despite all revelations, however, it became apparent that while Tammany leaders had often waved the flag they now had no intention of waiving immunity. Why should they have to when, despite all disclosures, their machine swept the City elections of November 1931. After all, wasn't Jimmy still Mayor? But embarrassing questions now were being raised about the Mayor's actions. Who had paid for his many vacations and why? Why did Walker's personal financial agent refuse Seabury's invitation to return from Mexico? What, if anything, had the Mayor contributed when he participated in certain stock speculations? The long-anticipated confrontation between Beau James and Judge Seabury took place on May 25–26, 1932, only days after the Mayor had triumphantly led a quarter-million New Yorkers in a Beer Parade down Fifth Avenue. Walker once said that every man must be "born, die, and testify" alone and in sparring with Seabury the Mayor was brilliantly evasive. Women threw roses at Walker after his testimony but newspapers threw brickbats! On June 22, the Governor ordered Walker to formally reply to

Seabury's allegations. Walker did so only after his return from the Chicago Democratic Convention that nominated Franklin Roosevelt for the presidency. There the unrepentant Mayor had voted for Smith and joined in Tammany's refusal to make Roosevelt's nomination unanimous. Inevitably, the Governor in turn was less than pleased with Walker's response to Seabury. Therefore, as mandated by Section 122 of the City Charter, Roosevelt decided to hold public hearings on the Walker case. Once again Walker confronted Seabury and this time the investigators questions were so cunningly prepared that a denial of one charge implied guilt in another area. After that session, Roosevelt probably had no option but to remove Walker. The Mayor, however, resigned his office on September 1, 1932. Walker bravely claimed he would go to the voters in November for vindication but he never did; he embarked shortly thereafter for European exile. His departure signaled the end of the carefree Jazz Age in New York.

* * * * *

After suffering through the tenure of reform mayors, the Hylan-Walker years provided Tammany with an opportunity to prove it could effectively administer New York. By 1932 the organization was thoroughly discredited and the prosperity of the "roaring twenties" was replaced by welfare rolls approaching 900,000. Nevertheless, reform remained in eclipse and the organization remained the single most potent force in New York politics. In the special election of November 1932 the machine swamped the hopes of interim Mayor Joseph McKee, whose independent character made him anathema to professionals, and easily elected John J. O'Brien to complete the final year of Walker's term. O'Brien's talents were perhaps best summarized by his oft-quoted response when asked the identity of his new police commissioner. "I don't know," said the Mayor of New York; "they haven't told me yet."

But if Tammany had experienced political disaster, the fundamental vitality of the world's metropolis could not be doubted. Depression had reduced the port's percentage of imports, but only to 50 percent of America's total. Despite the crash, membership on the Stock Exchange had expanded and assessed valuation of City real estate reached an all-time high in 1931. Manhattan remained the most valuable land on earth but even in an outer borough like Queens values had risen 1,000 percent from 1905 to 1929. While the construction industry was temporarily depressed, previously begun projects surged toward completion. In 1928 the Port Authority completed the Outerbridge Crossings to New Jersey and in 1931 the Holland Tunnel and the George Washington Bridge opened. Old institutions such as Pulitzer's *World* might die (1931) but they were soon replaced. New landmark buildings soared upward. In 1930, Art Deco received its grandest monument when William Van Alen's 77-story Chrysler Building was occupied and for a brief moment reigned as the world's tallest building. With strengths such as these, it seemed that all New York needed despite the Depression was enlightened leadership to match its economic powers. But where was that political strength? Reform had frittered away several opportunities. Low, McClellan, Gaynor, and Mitchel had all proven less than inspiring. Tammany had brought prosperity, but its regime had culminated in scandal and cynicism. When if ever would the "world City" receive the leadership its eminence demanded?

BRIEF BIBLIOGRAPHY

Gurock, Jeffrey. *When Harlem was Jewish, 1870–1930.* New York, 1979.

Howe, Irving. *World of Our Fathers.* New York, 1976.*

Johnson, James Weldon. *Black Manhattan.* New York, 1968.*

Kessner, Thomas. *The Golden Door: The Jews and Italians of New York City.* New York, 1976.*

Kurland, Gerald. *Seth Low: The Reformer in an Urban and Industrial Age.* New York, 1971.

Laidlaw, Walter, ed. *Population of the City of New York, 1890–1930.* New York, 1932.

Lately, Thomas. *The Mayor Who Mastered New York: The Life and Opinions of William J. Gaynor.* New York, 1969.

Lewinson, Edwin R. *John Purroy Mitchel: The Boy Mayor of New York.* New York, 1965.

Lowi, Theodore. *At the Pleasure of the Mayor: Patronage and Power in New York City, 1898–1958.* New York, 1962.*

Riordan, William L. *Plunkett of Tammany Hall.* New York, 1963.*

Smith, Mortimer. *William J. Gaynor: Mayor of New York.* Chicago, 1951.

Syrett, Harold, ed. *The Gentleman and the Tiger.* Philadelphia, 1956.*

*Paperback

VIII

The La Guardia Era

THE HEDONISM AND exuberance of Jimmy Walker perfectly suited the roaring spirit characteristic of the 1920s. In New York City that glorious decade saw the traditional dominance of Tammany Hall reestablished after a long hiatus. Equally dominant across the nation was a deep respect for business enterprise and corporate leadership. But the great Market Crash of 1929 put an end to the dreams of the decade and in a sense foreshadowed the demise of both the Tiger and the Mogul; these two fabled forces could never be the same in a depression-plagued America. Although Walker's personal mystique and fabled luck was sufficiently strong to enable him to win reelection, the scandals of the "tin box brigade" were already closing in on his administration. Though he was to linger as Mayor until forced to abdicate, the slow decline of Tammany was apparent during his second term. Walker's was a failure of character which Tammany might hope to overcome through better candidates, but there could be no such quick fix for the reputation of the American business community. For half a century the economy of both the nation and its greatest City had proceeded in a never-ending upward spiral, a wondrous joyride for which the American businessman took full credit. Americans had come to believe in the expertise, the acumen, and the style of business leadership just as much as Democrats had come to expect huge vote majorities from New York City. By 1930 both capitalism and Tammany Hall seemed to be tottering. As the impact of scandal and economic catastrophe worked their way into the consciousness of Americans, it became suddenly apparent that events and not the old verities were now in control. Tammany Hall would be unable to save Jimmy Walker and the formerly all-wise business leadership simply did not know what to do in the face of market collapse. As the 1930s began, a palpable sense of failure had begun to envelop both the nation and its largest City. The Great Depression had truly arrived.

* * * * *

The U.S. census reported that the population of New York in 1930 was 6,930,416 and the assessed valuation of City properties in 1931 reached an all-time high of $19 billion. It seemed almost ludicrous to imagine that so vast a conglomerate of people and power could be threatened by financial collapse, especially since the metropolis was well within its legal debt and taxation limits. Nevertheless, a sense of disaster pervaded Tammany and their chants of praise for the Walker administration seemed as hollow as were President Herbert Hoover's platitudes about prosperity returning to America. As the deflation which characterized the early years of the depression deepened, the ability of the City to meet its obligations to its people became suspect. In 1930–31 the harassed Walker administration had been forced to fire 11,000 schoolteachers in a desperate attempt to balance its budget but the savings were temporary at best. All municipal welfare moneys that existed were spent and private charity agencies, many of whose services had been funded by quiet handouts from the City Treasury, proved incapable of providing much relief to the growing legions of unemployed New Yorkers. Horror stories about people routing amid the garbage for scraps of food began to appear and Governor Franklin D. Roosevelt convened a special legislative session to consider the twin issues of local relief costs and emergency food supplies. By 1932, a third of the City's manufacturing plants had closed and up to 1,600,000 New Yorkers were receiving some sort of relief; fully a quarter of the population was out of work and many would never again hold a job. In such a situation what did it really matter if Jimmy Walker would or would not be forced to resign? Never had the City of New

York been faced by such an overwhelming economic crisis. Never had there been a better opportunity to effect profound, even revolutionary, changes in American life.

If New Yorkers had anything to cheer about in these bleak years of the decade, it was the continued development of the cityscape. We have noted how the Chrysler Building was completed in April 1930 and its stainless steel spire, taller by far than the Eiffel Tower, seemed to say that the metropolis could still reach for the skies. Even more impressive was the construction of the Empire State Building, begun on October 1, 1929, which proceeded upward despite all financial and union difficulties. New Yorkers watched enthralled as the marvel grew, often at the rate of four stories in a single week. On May 1, 1931 the doors opened—but there were too few renters and the Empire State Corporation would teeter on the brink of bankruptcy for years. Shreve, Lamb, and Harmon's massive structure had displaced New York's finest hotel for its construction, but in October, less than a mile up-town, a new Waldorf-Astoria Hotel opened for business. And also in 1931, another gigantic project was emerging from the rubble of construction. Otto Kahn had secured a midtown site for develop-ment of an Opera House but the crash had made that dream impossible. The land was obtained by the Rockefellers and, in late 1929, John D. Rockefeller, Jr. announced his selection of an architectural consortium whose task was to design a grand busi-ness and entertainment center which ultimately encompassed 14.5 acres. The project was Rockefeller Center, the "Acropolis of America," and to construct its 14 massive buildings would be the work of a decade. In 1931 workmen on the girders decided that they deserved a little Yuletide celebration. They decorated a small Christmas tree and so began a tradition which has flourished in New York for over half a century. By Christmas, 1932 there was not only a tree but also an $8,000,000 theater offering 16 acts and featuring Ray Bolger, Martha Graham, and the Flying Wallendas. This first offering at the Radio City Music Hall failed, of course, because there simply were too few people with money to spend on frivolities. For despite the completion of such gargantuan pro-jects, the structures most typical of New York's agony were not skyscrapers but rather the "Hoovervilles" located in Central Park.

It seems clear that 1932 was the nadir of the Depression in New York; the metropolis lurched ever closer to bankruptcy even as

Walker's political troubles came to a conclusion. On July 22, the Mayor told his 148,557 municipal employees that they must accept a wage cut if the City was to survive. Already the City debt of $1.9 billion was equal to that of all 48 states combined and a full third of the City's budget was being used to service its obligations. Yet even as Walker spoke he was negotiating further loans with a banking coalition which demanded $40,000,000 in budget reductions before further loans were made. As events turned out, it was not Walker who implemented the agreement, however, but his successor "Holy Joe" McKee. In the two months he governed following Walker's abdication, Joseph McKee carried out the painful job of slashing jobs and reducing salaries. His ruthlessness was one factor that allowed Tammany Hall to elect John O'Brien to finish the last year of Walker's term. O'Brien was a hack given to malapropisms and he attempted to approach the continuing crisis on a "business as usual" basis. The hardheaded bankers were not convinced by rhetoric, however, and in 1933 they forced the City to accept another "Bankers Agreement." In return for high interest cash over a three-year period, the City granted limitations on real estate taxes, created a budget reserve, and made a serious effort to penalize those in tax arrears. New York also agreed to drop proposed new taxes on stocks, savings banks, and insurance companies. The agreement saved the City and protected Tammany's padded payrolls, but it only provided further evidence that the business/clubhouse alliance which had operated during the twenties still functioned. Was O'Brien and constantly rising debt service all New Yorkers could hope for? Was it impossible for the nation's greatest City to receive leadership comparable to that of Franklin Roosevelt's, with his "hundred-day" domination of Congress? Responding to such demands, the old coalition of reformers and Republicans stirred once again. They made plans to wrest control from the hated machine in the election of 1933.

The disgrace of Tammany and Walker rather than the Depression provided the backdrop for the reform campaign. The ideal reform candidate for Mayor would have been the incorruptible Judge Seabury himself, but his eye was on the governorship and he adamantly refused to run. His prestige gave him veto power over the reformers' selection, however, and he disdainfully rejected such proposed candidates as Robert Moses and General

John F. O'Ryan. Ultimately, and perhaps inevitably, reform turned to the independent-minded candidate the Republicans had sacrificed to the Walker landslide of 1929. In that race, Fiorello La Guardia had not carried a single assembly district despite his incessant charges of Walker administration larceny. By 1933, corruption had been proven and the wild ravings of 1929 now became the words of a prophet before his time. La Guardia demanded an opportunity to run as a Fusion nominee; he was available to run because he had been ousted from Congress during the 1932 Democratic landslide. Yet even that defeat had been put to good use as the "Little Flower" cooperated with Roosevelt's incoming New Deal during the transition months. From Vice-President John Garner he had received the ultimate accolade—"He's a good little wop."

Perhaps most importantly, a La Guardia candidacy would assure Fusion of Roosevelt's neutrality in its campaign against Tammany. Adlof Berle arranged a meeting between Seabury and La Guardia which resulted in a "meeting of minds" and the judge's approval. On August 3, 1933 La Guardia received the Fusion nomination and launched his campaign in a typically frenetic style. The Seabury revelations had so thoroughly discredited Tammany that the real contest was between Fusion and a Recovery Party led by Joseph McKee. La Guardia secured the increasingly influential Jewish bloc by accusing McKee of youthful anti-Semitism, a potent charge in the year Hitler came to power. Naturally reformers backed him rather than "Holy Joe." In November, to strains of "Who's Afraid of the Big Bad Wolf," the Four-Leaf Clover ticket of Fusion was victorious although it received only forty percent of the total vote. On January 1, 1934 La Guardia took his oath as Mayor in Seabury's office and reform had the leader it deserved. A new era in City history was about to begin.

Fiorello H. La Guardia, ninety-ninth Mayor of New York, was born in Greenwich Village on December 11, 1882. Historians have called him an ethnic ticket all by himself since he was the child of a Jewish mother and an Italian father, was raised in Arizona and Italy, and followed the Episcopal faith. Moreover, as an employee of the Consular Service (1900–1906) and the Immigration Station at Ellis Island (1907–10) he had learned to speak half a dozen languages. As a young lawyer La Guardia nurtured a hatred of Tammany and its corporate allies; it became the hall-mark of his style. He joined the Republican party and in 1916 became the first Italo-American ever elected to Congress. After a brief military career, he won the Presidency of the Board of Aldermen in 1919. There his independence alienated his own party, although he effectively cooperated with Mayor Hylan. When the Republicans ignored him as a mayoral candidate in 1921, he again won a congressional seat and served brilliantly in Washington for the decade 1922–32. He learned where the levers of power were located and how they operated. No man had ever been more suited to the task of governing New York.

La Guardia took over a City in crisis and promised it only difficult times; there would be "no more free lunch" for New York, its employees, and its people. His aim was simply to prove that "nonpartisan, nonpolitical local government" was possible and that principles of good government could overcome a heritage of corruption and the reality of depression. The Mayor's immediate concerns were a budget $30,000,000 in deficit, the 142,000 families on relief, and the fact that the City was mortgaged to the terms of the Bankers Agreement; only $39,000,000 remained of the $70,000,000 relief loan and the rest would be gone by August. La Guardia dedicated his own "hundred days" to "clearing away the debris and repairing the ruins" left by Tammany misrule, but it was evident that his only possible action had to be a tax increase which could keep the relief program operative. Therefore, his Economy Bill, proposed on January 2 contained as its centerpiece a major La Guardia concession. He dropped his life-long opposition to a sales tax and proposed a 2-percent levy which would finance the City's share of relief costs. When combined with a 3-percent utility tax, a one tenths of 1-percent gross profits tax, and modifications of the Bankers Agreement, the "temporary" sales tax would keep the City solvent. Since the City was the creature of the state, such a major tax program had to receive legislative approval, and it had a stormy career in Albany. Democratic Governor Herbert Lehman criticized its provisions as leading to a mayoral "dictatorship." The measure came close to defeat many times before it was reluctantly signed in April. After his "hundred days" La Guardia had a tax program but, as he wrote to Senator Wagner, "I am so tired . . . at times I can hardly stand it." Nevertheless, the program was in place by the fall. La Guardia then proceeded to balance his budget by breaking his campaign pledge of no reduction in civil service salaries. Economy measures included payless furloughs, but the cruel job was accomplished. Hundreds of municipal workers were abruptly terminated, not all of them Tammany drones. But the result of La Guardia's harsh measures produced 20 years of financial stability for the City.

Although the economic recovery of New York took years, the Mayor only days after taking office had dramatically shown his feelings about corruption and crime. His symbolic first act was to order the arrest of mobster "Lucky" Luciano; the Mayor's physical attack on slot machines came later after the City won legal injunctions against federal acceptance of the gambling equipment. These were public relations spectacles and more lasting was La Guardia's conviction that "to the victor belongs the responsibility of good government." He intended to purge the City government of patronage hacks and named to his Fusion cabinet men free of political strings; their prime concern would be the proper management of their departments. The roster of his commissioners read like an honor roll of the most expert and capable New York public servants: Adolf Berle, Paul Blanchard, Edward Corsi, Sigismund S. Goldwater, Austin MacCormick, Robert Moses, John Rice, Louis Valentine, and Paul Windels. Not only were these men whose dedication to the public weal could not be doubted but also their nonpolitical character was not the least factor easing the Democratic legislatures acceptance of La Guardia's financial program. In all, the City's "hundred days" saved its credit, laid the foundation for a balanced budget, and began a massive program of governmental reorganization. Moreover, Democratic fears that "the Hat" would build a Fusion machine from his commissioners' expertise were soon dispelled. La Guardia's intention was far more noble; he intended to create an electoral force based on the trust and empathy the people felt for their eccentric Mayor. La Guardia was at times a tyrant, an autocrat, a showman, and a clown but he was always wooing his electorate. Their strange love affair was to last 12 years and revolutionize both the forms of City government and the physical structure of New York.

La Guardia's administration had tremendous problems in its first winter. It was so cold that armories had to be opened to the homeless lest they freeze to death. So much snow fell that the City was able to pay for its removal only by selling short-term city notes to the Teacher's Retirement Fund. Strikes by taxi drivers, waiters, and laundrymen bedeviled the Mayor, while 164 bread lines were hardly sufficient to deal with an army of reliefers equal to the population of Detroit. The WPA administrator for New York even accused La Guardia of not trying to move people from welfare to work relief, and a special Committee on Welfare—the first of many such investigations—had to be appointed. The police commissioner decided he could not work with La Guardia and so the harassed Mayor named Chief Inspector Louis Valentine as commissioner. With full mayoral backing Valentine "got tough" with criminals and approved a "third degree" form of questioning. Above all else, he tolerated no trace of police corruption. Valentine ousted 244 cops during his tenure and some said he had caused another 83 suicides. He provided one of the NYPD's periodic cleanings and actually reduced the upward surge of crime statistics.

Of all La Guardia's commissioners none figured more prominently in the news of 1934 than did new Parks Commissioner Robert Moses. Moses, who had built the state's park system, began his tenure by dismissing the five borough Park Boards, and firing hundreds of CWA workers. He thus began with a controversy his 34 year career as the remodeler of New York City. Beyond his talent, vigor, and administrative expertise, Moses had one additional virtue. Only he, of all La Guardia's men, dared yell back at the "testy tyrant" of City Hall. La Guardia kept his parks commissioner despite the antipathy in which Moses was held by Franklin Roosevelt. By the end of 1934, 60 new parks had already been constructed and the City was feverishly providing plans to justify the allocation of PWA project funds to the metropolitan area; $68,000,000 became available in the spring of 1934 alone. No single factor weighed as importantly in the federal-funding process as did La Guardia's budget achievements of that fall. When he balanced the City budget, the federal government approved funds for a series of major construction projects which provided the foundation for New York's economic recovery. In welfare aid alone, New York received over a billion dollars from 1933 to 1939. La Guardia also received invaluable assistance from Al Smith who convinced Washington to take leases on the vacant floor space of the Empire State Building. Within a year the heartbeat of New York had perceptibly quickened, and the Mayor's new crew, with some difficulties, had taken firm hold of the governmental oars.

The people of New York, over 7,000,000 citizens representing every religion, race, and nationality, watched in amazement as a revolution sparked by a "24-hour" Mayor swept across their jaded town. They saw the Little Flower wear out relays of secretaries, they were amazed when he showed up at fires, they chuckled as he awarded oxbones after mistakes by commissioners, and they howled with laughter when he attacked confiscated slot machines. Tammany Hall gnashed its teeth as patronage jobs were ruthlessly eliminated. The prime sufferers of the purge were Irish Democrats, and one historian estimates that only 5 percent of government jobs under La Guardia went to that ethnic group. Far more favored, with 15 percent of the jobs, were the Italians who had given Fiorello over 60 percent of their votes and the WASP reformers who had provided the crucial victory margin for Fusion. Most fortunate of all were the second- or third-generation descendants of the great Jewish migration. By the thirties, more than half the doctors, lawyers, dentists, and teachers of the City were Jewish, and for them La Guardia represented the finest opportunity for good government in their lifetime. They rallied to La Guardia en masse and ignored whispers that the Mayor made both anti-Semitic and anti-black comments in private. Jews received even more jobs than Italians did from La Guardia, and they were to remain his most electorally loyal supporters.

One further factor enormously complicated the ethnic politics of the La Guardia years. The arrival of immigrant groups and their acculturation had long been a feature of New York life but suddenly the administration discovered that the City's newest immigrants had arrived almost unnoticed. They were there, however, and they were black. Passage of restrictive quota laws in 1924 had briefly removed the question of immigration from the consciousness of New York's politicians. Yet even then the movement known as the Great Migration—which was to quietly transfer the black farm population of America into its urban centers—had been underway for a decade. This immigration was internal and, since it was black, it had not impressed itself upon the minds of any politician of note. Indeed in 1933 only Mayor O'Brien had wooed the black voters of Harlem, a neighborhood he called the "garden spot of the world." In his usual bumbling fashion O'Brien told unreceptive audiences, "My heart is as black as yours." Yet suddenly and unexpectedly La Guardia's New York was 5 percent black. Almost all these people were poor, and their future welfare became an important political consideration for the dynamic Mayor. This latent concern was intensified after March 1935 when a sudden riot exploded in the streets of O'Brien's "garden." White shopkeepers had been threatened and the black presence in the world's greatest metropolis had to be discussed as profoundly, or as cursorily, as former questions of Irish, Italian, or Jewish immigration. A Mayor's Task Force discovered enormous black resentment "against racial discrimination and poverty in the midst of plenty." So was initiated, in words that bring progress into question, a debate which has lasted to this day.

Although the La Guardia Administration seemed surprised to discover that it had a racial issue on its hands, it should have not been surprised. There had always been blacks in New York and their relationship to the City stretches across the entire span of its history. There had been black farmers tending crops in the boweries of New Amsterdam and the arrival of the first slaves here was recorded in 1626. In the seventeenth-century City both the Dutch and English had enacted slave codes to regulate the blacks who lived in Manhattan. Economic competition between races and the abuse of blacks led to violent conspiracies in 1712 and 1741 which solved nothing. Yet the City also fostered a countervailing tendency to prejudice. As early as 1750 blacks who met property requirements were entitled to vote, and additional blacks won their freedom during the Revolutionary era by serving in the Continental Army. By the time the Constitution was adopted in 1787, fully 10 percent of the City population was black though only a third was free. Slavery as a legal institution did not end in New York until 1827, but in Manhattan before that year blacks had their own Free Schools and comprised a voting bloc important in municipal elections. Until the 1820s Tammany Hall identified itself with abolitionist thought and it was only as Irish and German immigrants began to outnumber blacks that the anti-slavery commitment waned. The European newcomers usurped black jobs as well. In 1830 50 percent of Manhattan's servants were black but by 1850 that number was reduced to 10 percent; the Irish serving maid had become the new symbol of gentility. And as the Irish came to dominate the docks and cartage trades, the only accepted jobs for black men was as strike breakers or scabs. In the face of enduring prejudice, fewer jobs, and political impotence, blacks began to drift away from New York and by the time of the Civil War only 12,472 remained in the City.

Proportionally the ratio of blacks in the City declined all during the nineteenth century even as their numbers grew slowly in real terms. The black community was slowly forced to migrate from the Five Points (1830s) toward "Little Africa" in the Village (1860s) to the west midtown areas of the Tenderloin and San Juan Hill by 1900. Everywhere, prejudice followed them and often they were the victims of police brutality. On August 15–16, 1900 a knifing incident led to confrontations between blacks and white mobs, sometimes abetted by policemen, that continued sporadically for a month. The first census of the new century showed that New York had 60,666 blacks, a mere 2 percent of the consolidated City's total population. But the internal Great Migration away from the rural South and toward the Northern cities was beginning and by 1910 New York's black population had risen to 91,709. The outbreak of the first world war made the metropolis even more attractive for jobs once again were available and because for the first time in American history, a place for black hopes was being created. It was called Harlem.

Harlem, founded in 1657, is probably the oldest true suburb of New York City. Only eight miles from City Hall, it first held the country homes of the gentry and been the scene of horse races along Harlem Lane, later St. Nicholas Avenue. When elevated tracks reached the area in 1878–81 it became accessible to downtowners fleeing Italian and Jewish immigration. As a result a building boom soon changed the bucolic face of Harlem into posh elegance: the new character of the area was symbolized by the magnificent rows of townhouses commissioned by David King in 1891 and designed by architects like James Lord, Price and Luce, and McKim, Mead and White. It was true that Irishmen dominated the streets west of Eighth Avenue, that a "little Italy" was growing east of Third Avenue, and that a "little Russia" could be found below 125th Street between Fifth and Seventh avenues, but Harlem proper remained the home of the elite. Then in 1904–05 the inevitable bust after a speculative boom occurred and

Harlem suddenly had a glut of housing that had to be let. Until this time black presence in Harlem had been restricted to the role of menials. However, the riot of 1900, the massive dislocations caused by the construction of Pennsylvania Station and the completion of the Lenox Avenue subway line suddenly coincided with uptown housing availabilty. The Afro-American Realty Company was organized to place blacks into the vacant apartments—and it mattered little how many tenants combined to pay a single rent. Within a decade, 50,000 blacks came to Harlem and their downtown churches soon followed the northward exodus. Harlem, a black community with good housing, community churches, and a turbulent sense of growth became the natural goal of migrating blacks.

By 1920, when over 109,000 blacks lived in Manhattan, it was clear that the continuing influx of newcomers was overwhelming the resources of Harlem. Real estate ownership remained in white hands but repairs were inadequate and the area was already becoming a slum. High rents remained the rule but the low income jobs available to blacks made it impossible for all but a favored few to avoid overcrowding. With increasing density of population the pathology of ghetto life took stronger hold. Vice and policy gambling, narcotics addiction, and juvenile delinquency were in the 1920s recognized as community issues along with the most shocking infant mortality and tuberculosis statistics in New York. Yet Harlem had no effective political voice to plead its cause; its nominal representatives were white and uncaring. Flamboyant leaders such as Father Divine, Marcus Garvey, and Sufi Abdul Hamid offered charisma rather than cogent reform proposals and still had to compete with more traditional political types such as Charles Anderson and F. Q. Morton for the allegiance of a community in chaos. Ultimately no one spoke effectively for the Nigger Heaven that was Harlem. By 1930 over 200,000 of the 327,706 blacks in New York City were packed into the two square miles of Harlem, but their potential power was dissipated by ignorance, lack of leadership, and poverty; half of Harlem's population was on relief as the Depression began.

Yet amazingly, out of the decay of the 1920s came the discovery of hope and pride through knowledge of the black past. The Harlem Renaissance set a literary standard of excellence though a "new Negro" failed to emerge from its exhortations. The white theater at least recognized blacks in plays such as *Green Pastures, The Emperor Jones,* and *Porgy and Bess,* while the undoubted glories of jazz and the blues were centered in Harlem. White visitors from downtown, led by Jimmy Walker himself, made certain cabarets nationally prominent. In 1934, two white businessmen purchased a failed burlesque house, refurbished it, booked Bessie Smith, and opened the Apollo Theater on 125th Street. Painful and brutal though Harlem might be, it was undoubtedly as alive as Queen Bess's music. Though other black ghettos were emerging in New York in the 1930s—South Jamaica, and the tenements of Bedford-Stuyvesant offered equally miserable conditions—but the eyes of observers focused on Harlem. Could La Guardia, who had emerged from Italian East Harlem, act to help a community without leaders? He at least knew better than to call it a garden spot and perhaps he would be able to integrate blacks into the life of the metropolis.

La Guardia had almost immediately made a symbolic administrative gesture of great importance to blacks; he created the New York Housing Authority in 1934. Black areas had the fewest social services, a paucity of park land, and the greatest concentration of crime and illiteracy in the City. Beyond this, a majority of New York's working blacks in the 1930s earned less than $1,000 yearly. If the City made it a policy to provide the most deprived with better housing it would show a concern that not even the black elite of 139th Street's "Striver's Row" felt for the residents of Harlem. La Guardia tried, but he failed! When La Guardia took office, there had not been a school constructed in Harlem for 25 years despite all its population gains. It would take another four years before a new school was built. Even more sadly, despite the vast park construction undertaken by Robert Moses, only a single playground was opened in Central Harlem during this bleak decade. Harlem River Houses, a PWA project of 574 apartments at 151st Street opened in 1937, but again it did not help the heart of the distressed black community. La Guardia attempted to placate black feelings with several high-level appointments; he named Hubert Delaney tax commissioner, Myles Paige a magistrate, and Jane Bolin a judge. In addition, Gertrude Ayer became the first black woman principal in the school system. However, these were "tokens" before the word came into use. Harlem believed itself ignored and a deep sense of alienation and frustration was born which persists to this day.

But ethnic dreams beyond those of blacks also rode on La Guardia's broad shoulders. Italians, on their way to becoming the City's single largest ethnic group, saw in the Mayor the culmination of fifty years of progress. The "Little Flower" had won power by using the system, and no one could doubt his total Americanism. Their pride in La Guardia was intensified because of the terrible publicity Italian-Americans endured due to the illegal activities of men such as "Lucky" Luciano, Thomas Luchese, Joseph Adonis, and Frank Costello. Their path to prominence was also a typical one for immigrants, but the control they held over vice, gambling, and liquor was already fostering the legend of an Italian crime syndicate. La Guardia abhorred these "thugs" and racketeers and, in combination with Commissioner Valentine and State Attorney Thomas Dewey he forced many of them to flee—to cheers from law-abiding Italians. The schizophrenic nature of immigrant ambition was also evident in the Jewish community. There were Jewish gangsters—Arthur "Dutch Schultz" Flegenheimer and Meyer Lansky are leading examples—but the Jewish community saw such men as pariahs and aberrations. Their pride was the phalanx of CCNY graduates, and the prominent role that Jewish commissioners and magistrates played in the La Guardia administration. That tradition of intellectual excellence was augmented during the thirties as émigrés from Nazi Germany flocked to New York; the "University in Exile" was grafted onto the existing New School in 1934.

A third major ethnic group became increasingly prominent during the La Guardia years. Archer Huntington had founded the Hispanic Society in 1904, but by La Guardia's administration that group was dominated by Puerto Ricans. In 1930, the number of Puerto Ricans in the East Harlem "Barrio" above 125th Street had passed 45,000 and their neighborhood was, if anything, even more miserable than that of Harlem. Battles between teenagers from "Little Italy" and the "El Barrio" punctuated the thirties—the arena often being the turf of Benjamin Franklin High School. Clearly one of La Guardia's greatest challenges was to foster ethnic cooperation by establishing a sense of common purpose for the heterogeneous elements of New York's population. That he failed to do so is hardly surprising, because overcoming prejudice and anger has been a task that no Mayor has yet been able to accomplish.

La Guardia could not afford to focus his attention on any single group, however powerful; his concern was the salvation and rehabilitation of the suffering whole of New York. To that end, he made countless trips to Washington to argue for extension of New Deal programs to the City. Although he was assured of a sympathetic hearing from FDR, Harry Hopkins, Harold Ickes, and Louis Johnson—none of whom wished the metropolis to fail—he constantly had to overcome their skepticism. The Mayor's ability to do so is perhaps his single greatest achievement for when he pledged to turn money into construction projects and jobs La Guardia delivered. The great metropolitan construction boom of the twenties ended with builders either bankrupt or unwilling to start new projects in a depression-ridden City. Yet no single industry was as crucial to the economic recovery of New York as was construction. La Guardia, who had a love for buildings, engineers, and architects, understood that new construction depended on the availability of federal funding. The great community projects of previous years, New York Medical Center (1928), Riverside Church (1929), The Museum of Modern Art (1929), The Daily News Building (1930), Brooklyn College (1930), The Whitney Museum (1931), and The Museum of the City of New York (1932) could no longer be financed by individuals or by the City. The Independent Subway system (1932) was already in federal receivership and the magnificent Knickerbocker Village housing development (1934) had been forced by the depression to alter its financing and become a limited dividend project. In 1934, the only building money available was that provided through the National Industrial Recovery Act and the only labor that could be paid was that of the CWA. La Guardia's task was to obtain as much labor and cash as possible and use it to stimulate New York's recovery.

Henry Miller, in *Tropic of Cancer* (1934) wrote that only New York "makes a rich man feel his unimportance . . . The buildings dominate"; but individual structures such as the Chrysler or Empire State buildings were unimportant. What New York needed were public works projects on an unprecedented scale and their construction depended on federal largess. The Mayor fortu-

238 · A BRIEF HISTORY OF NEW YORK CITY

nately had available—in the ten volume *Regional Survey* (1929) as brilliantly adapted by Robert Moses—a rough outline of needed community projects. This vision he preached on his begging expeditions to Washington. La Guardia knew little of the genesis of these blueprints, but he was the necessary catalytic agent to their implementation. Moreover, the Mayor trusted Moses, kept him on despite FDR's antipathy and Moses's disastrous defeat in the Governor's race of 1934, and used his commissioner's extraordinary record to convince Washington. Only La Guardia could have so successfully played the bureaucratic and personal game of obtaining those moneys. La Guardia obtained for his City fully one seventh of all WPA funds by 1936 and they became the leaven to lift New York out of the Depression.

None of La Guardia's achievements was more significant than his legacy in concrete. During his regime the City built a comprehensive highway and mass transportation system as well as developing the most extensive public-housing program in the United States. Merely to list the most prominent projects staggers the mind and indicates the awesome scope of the construction. In 1933 New York's harbor and waterfront had been disaster areas, subway construction had halted, and the anchorages of the Triborough Bridge stood like tombstones in the East River. Yet in the next seven years, three major bridges (the Triborough, the Whitestone, and the Henry Hudson) and at least 100 smaller ones were completed as were 50 miles of intracity expressway. By 1940, there were more miles of nonintersecting highway in New York than in the next five largest American cities combined. In addition, a traffic tunnel under the East River had tied Queens to the Midtown area. Twelve miles of track were added to the Independent Eighth-Avenue Subway while the Sixth-Avenue line was completed by 1941; plans were already afoot for the merger of all subways into a unified City rapid transit system. By 1939, La Guardia Airport was opened before a cheering throng of 325,000 people and plans were well advanced for another field, Idlewild, which was constructed during the second world war. The Docks Department constructed 14 new piers and put superstructures on four others; the City suddenly could easily accommodate mammoth ocean liners such as the *Rex*, the *Normandia*, and the *Queen Mary* that were the height of luxurious travel in that era. Parks Commissioner Moses built 255 playgrounds, 5,000 acres of new parks, and a dozen swimming pools. Using varied financing schemes, La Guardia saw 13 housing projects for 17,000 families open by 1941. Construction ended by 1940 due to several factors; the end of the New Deal, the start of the European war, and the fact that New York had reached its capital-spending limit. Indeed, La Guardia's 1940 budget contained only a symbolic one dollar for capital construction. But the physical revolution remained and the achievement of these years is still evident in New York. As with Christopher Wren's London, if you seek La Guardia's greatness you need only to contemplate the City he loved and rebuilt.

"The Hat" also provided New York with a governmental reconstruction as profound as its physical revival. The existent City charter of 1911 had limited the authority of the executive while increasing the powers of the Board of Estimate and the borough presidents. Amendments approved in 1924, although limiting state control over the "property, affairs, or government" of New York, had not altered that situation. La Guardia believed that only a strong Mayor could master the metropolis, but his first attempt to revise the charter through a commission headed by Al Smith collapsed in August 1934. La Guardia was undaunted, however, and after obtaining the necessary legislative approval, appointed a nonpartisan commission which studied the issue for 19 months. La Guardia himself testified with characteristic vigor— and ultimately was given a charter which centralized more power in the hands of the Mayor, created a City Council, authorized creation of the office of Deputy Mayor and the City Planning Commission, and clearly established the responsibilities of the comptroller. "Home rule" for New York was strengthened and in addition a proportional representation system was established for election to the City Council. The gains of this "reform" proved questionable, since it did not guarantee the selection of at least some representatives of the electoral minority. On November 3, 1936 the City electorate, while contributing to Roosevelt's landslide national victory, also gave its approval to a 40,000-word document opposed by all borough presidents and Tammany Hall. Effective January 1, 1938, the new charter strengthened the Mayor while preserving the autonomy of the Board of Estimate. In November 1937 the voters would decide whether they would entrust La Guardia with the opportunity to lead under the charter he had sponsored.

Never in New York history had Fusion been able to win reelection for its candidates against the entrenched power of Tammany and the ennui of the voters. But never had Fusion been represented by a dynamic figure whose preferred habitat seemed to be the front page. Never had an administration been able to "point with pride" to so many enormous alterations in the physical face of the City. What other reformer had ever been able to rely on the vote of Italians, Jews, most blacks, and also organized labor; could anyone but La Guardia have held the allegiance of the anti-Fascist Jews and the rather pro-Fascist Italians? And Fiorello shamelessly emphasized his political independence. In twelve years as Mayor he was never to endorse a Republican for any state or federal office. The GOP bitterly resented his lack of partisan spirit and his meritocratic view of patronage, but they had little choice but to renominate him in 1937. So too did the Fusion organization. The Mayor's reelection was also endorsed by the American Labor party, an organization created in 1936 so that liberal Democrats might support Roosevelt without voting for the Tammany ticket; that line was to give the Mayor an astounding 482,000 votes in the election. Progressives, Socialists, and even Communists supported La Guardia in 1937, and an effective Democratic charge attempted to identify La Guardia with the Communist support he found it expedient to repudiate.

To run against this phenomenon of American politics, the Democrats chose Jeremiah Mahoney, a man who probably deserved a better fate. Mahoney charged that the Mayor had broken his word on sales taxes and that he was maneuvering to obtain a Cabinet position. However, when La Guardia presided over the opening of the West Side Highway on October 12, 1937, less than a month before the election, the canvas was effectively over. Fusion won over 60 percent of the vote. La Guardia amassed 1,344,336 votes and held a plurality of 450,000 while his candidates controlled 15 of the 16 Board of Estimate votes as well. Tammany in fact barely held control of the incoming City Council. The election of 1937 was a triumph of ability and personality unprecedented in the history of New York.

La Guardia was now a national figure. His administration continued to build with federal money and slow economic recovery made possible other projects financed by the City. In 1938 alone, the Bronx High School of Science was opened, Jacob Riis

Park was made available to millions of bathers, and a Master Plan for future construction was published. Expansion of the subway system continued, port trade was definitely on the upswing, and the Civil Service continued to be reformed. So evident was the progress that newly elected Comptroller Joseph McGoldrick was able to issue $375,000,000 in revenue notes at interest rates as low as 1.35 percent. An ebullient Mayor not only declared the Bankers Agreement at an end but also approved pay raises for City workers; that action effectively underminded five years of economizing. Yet after years of depression wages, the political reality of worker pressures could not be denied. Besides, argued La Guardia, the 1939–40 property tax rate was only $2.82 per $100, hardly excessive when compared to the tremendous physical improvement of the City. One vignette is most revealing. A Latin American diplomat toured the metropolis and was awed by the construction underway. At each stop he asked who let the contracts and the proud Mayor answered "I did." By the end of the day candor overcame tact and the diplomat remarked: "Ah, La Guardia, you must be a very rich man." But the fact was that La Guardia still resided in his East Harlem neighborhood, still cooked Italian meals for his friends, and lived on the Mayor's salary. Not even his opponents accused him of personal dishonesty, although many believed he was anxious to serve a national constituency.

La Guardia's second term initiated an administrative revolution within City government. Under the new charter, the first Deputy Mayor was appointed although, as Henry Curren remembered it, La Guardia proved constitutionally incapable of delegating authority; the "job came swiftly down to handling some of the mail and sitting for the Mayor in the Board of Estimate." Not for another three decades would the office reach its potential. More immediately profound in its impact on City government was reform of the Civil Service structure. By 1939, 74.3 percent of all employees had to take competitive examinations to obtain City jobs, a gain of 20 percent in five years. The merit system imposed by La Guardia guaranteed better qualified workers and made a career in municipal service extremely attractive. From 1933 to 1939, the number of applications for Civil Service jobs rose 3,884 percent and an improved level of performance by the government toward its citizens resulted. Better economic conditions also became apparent as the City slowly recovered from the depression. Despite a downturn in 1938, economic statistics advanced steadily during the La Guardia regime. By 1939 for example, the City carried on 23.4 percent of United States wholesale trade as compared to its 7.6 percent of retail trade. New York exported 40 percent of all America's goods in 1940, a percentage that was to increase as the global war intensified.

The international eminence of New York was enhanced when it welcomed the World's Fair of 1939–40. Completion of the Trilborough Bridge, the Midtown Tunnel, and their connecting highway systems made central Queens accessible to millions of travelers. When the City obtained the right to honor the one hundred fiftieth anniversary of George Washington's inauguration with a World's Fair, Parks Commissioner Moses insisted that Flushing Meadow in Queens be the site. The alternative was that the "Master Builder" would have nothing to do with the project. Naturally he had his way. Two years and $591,000,000 later he had transformed the Corona dumping grounds, which "boasted" a 90-foot ash mountain and river rats the size of dogs, into an elegant Fair site extending over 1,216 acres. The result was perhaps the finest of all World's Fairs. Over a two-year period, some 5,000,000 visitors toured the seven fair areas centered around the 700-foot Trylon and its 18-story futuristic companion, the Perisphere. They saw the Metropolitan Museum's "Life in America," a replica of the Crystal Palace that dominated New York's first fair in 1853 and gaped at Ripley's "Believe it or Not" or Hex's "Strange as it Seems." Millions reverently looked at the Magna Carta and visited the League of Nations Pavilion while other tourists simply enjoyed the Parachute Ride or Billy Roses's Aquacade Revue. The child in La Guardia thoroughly enjoyed the fair but was quick to remind visitors that the greatest display of all was the City of New York and its 7,454,995 citizens.

The last of La Guardia's great services to New York also took place in 1940; he achieved the century old reformers dream and consolidated the subways and elevated lines into a unified, municipally owned transit system. Experience had proven that the Independant Subway constructed by La Guardia could never be self-supporting at the five-cents fare level. Moreover, the private companies which operated the once profitable BMT and IRT systems were bankrupt, and subsidy payments to them by the

City had become a sad fact of budgeting. In 1938, New York asked the state to approve an exemption from debt limitations so that it might purchase the bankrupt companies, combine service with the Independent line, and create a self-supporting system. Authorization was granted and in June of 1940 the three systems were unified at a cost of $326,000,000. The City suddenly was running a 1,300-mile system valued at $1.5 billion, and doing it profitably; merger produced an operating profit of $28,000,000 in its first year. Soon, however, union cooperation waned and as costs rose praise for La Guardia's foresight turned bilious. The unified systems became a deficit operation, an albatross to burden all future City budgets. One planning benefit did accrue to the City. The removal of surface elevated lines which duplicated subterranean routes eased traffic flow, increased property values, and vastly improved the aesthetics of many New York vistas. The Civic Center-Cadman Plaza redevelopment near Brooklyn's Borough Hall is perhaps the best example of this welcome offshoot of subway unification.

La Guardia's reelection in 1941 should have been far easier than it actually proved, for in eight years of Fusion rule the City had been fundamentally altered due to his vision and talents. Yet the office itself, often described as the second most difficult job in America, had somewhat soured the Mayor. Always an imperious boss, La Guardia now seemed increasingly intolerant of failure, delay, and opposition; bitter personal conflicts often erupted between "the Hat" and his staff. He seemed to recognize he would never hold national office, but willingly accepted service on the Canadian-American Defense Board and as Roosevelt's coordinator of Civilian Defense. As America moved ever closer to war against the Axis powers he despised, La Guardia seemed almost to have lost desire to govern his city.

Nevertheless, serve he must and as he stood for reelection in 1941, Fiorello proudly flaunted an explicit endorsement from FDR. A June Gallup Poll gave him 59 percent of the voters before his intemperate personal attack on popular Democratic Governor Herbert Lehman alienated a great many of La Guardia's natural liberal constituency. La Guardia berated Lehman for always endorsing Democrats and used some hard language to describe such thinking. Moreover, he refused to apologize and only said that his choicest epithets had been intended to describe political bosses, not Lehman. The Mayor's gaffe gave Democrat William O'Dwyer of Brooklyn, an adept campaigner with great personal charisma, an issue which allowed him to cut deeply into La Guardia's lead. In November, the Mayor trailed his Fusion ticket and won reelection by only 132,000 votes. Although the victory made the Little Flower the first 12-year mayor since Richard Varick (1789–1801) it also indicated that the rigors of mastering the metropolis might ultimately be too great for even this Mayor. Democrats argued that he was only a part-time Mayor and, since New Deal construction had halted and rancorous animosity was in the air, the question of what La Guardia could achieve in his third term was much debated. That issue became moot, however, only a month after his reelection. Pearl Harbor made it certain that the Mayor and his City must become a vital part of the national effort to win the war. The great era of achievement was over.

Governing the City of New York during wartime was neither glamorous nor easy. The lights of Broadway were dimmed and La Guardia's star seemed to set with them. In February 1942, La Guardia resigned his position as head of the Civil Defense Agency, a job in which he had not been able to obtain many results. Yet the "Little Flower" made no discernible attempt to refocus his attention on the City. After Pearl Harbor, the Mayor placed security guards on all bridges and tunnels as well as in many factories. He had interned some 200 Japanese on Ellis Island and did his best to cope with a loss of City labor to private industry and to the U.S. Army. La Guardia in reality ached to serve America in another war and believed it was his destiny to lead men against fascism. One of the greatest disappointments of his life was that the call to the colors never came. La Guardia was restricted to a civilian's role, he was only allowed to make propaganda broadcasts. Indeed he knew little of New York's great wartime achievements—the Columbia experiments that split the uranium atom, the creation of the M–3 submachine gun in Brooklyn, and the breaking of the Japanese master code at the Public Library. La Guardia simply presided as 891,923 of New York's men and women left to serve the nation; he grieved with his City when 16,106 of them never returned. His role was not battle but to appear at Harvest shows where thousands of New Yorkers displayed the produce of their "victory gardens" and to uphold morale via Sunday "Talks to the

People" over WNYC radio. In fact, so often did the Mayor recommend fish that punsters proclaimed him the "Little Flounder."

Two further developments of wartime New York should be mentioned, one cosmetic and the other pregnant with meaning. In May 1942 La Guardia and his family moved into an Executive Mansion refurbished for them by Robert Moses. Gracie Mansion had once been home to a Scottish merchant and later housed the Museum of the City of New York; it now became the symbolic power center for the metropolis even though La Guardia had to order an iron fence to keep the staring public at a distance. The second happening was far more sobering. On the night of August 3, 1943 Harlem once more exploded in a spasm of looting. Sparked by high rents, wartime discrimination, and economic deprivation, the riot resulted in five deaths and hundreds of arrests. Once again reforms were promised and a rent control law was adopted but nothing fundamental was changed. The Mayor and his family happily lived out the rest of his term less than two miles from Harlem, a cesspool of misery, whose continued decay would represent a fundamental challenge to the very survival of the City he governed.

Neither war nor riots, however, could totally darken the Broadway stage; the early forties became a boon time for the theater, cabaret, and entertainment industries. La Guardia recognized both their economic and morale value, and won praise for his refusal to enforce a midnight bar curfew. He argued, most reasonably, that servicemen were entitled to a full share of fun. Moreover, the war years produced an unexpected theatrical revival. *Tobacco Road* had closed in 1942 after seven years of performances but its place was quickly filled by such hits as *Pàl Joey, Lady in the Dark*, and, of course, the revolutionary musical comedy *Oklahoma* (1943). Frank Sinatra first played the Paramount in 1942 and many other careers were launched on the fabled "Sidewalks of New York." Indeed, in a foretaste of the future, the first TV station in America (WNBT-NYC) was founded in 1941. But when all is said and done, perhaps the single most famous event of the entire La Guardia regime took place on Sunday, July 1, 1945. Faced with a newspaper strike, La Guardia read the "funnies" to the children of the City. It was "show biz" at its best and demonstrated once again that he had not lost the common touch. In all, his City maintained its position as the artistic, communications, and economic center of the nation all during the war. When the news of the Japanese surrender came after Nagasaki on August 14, the City's celebration lasted an entire day and served as a fitting climax to the La Guardia Era.

* * * * *

Fiorello always understood that New York set the tone for urban life in the United States; if he seemed always in the forefront of events, it was because the City itself was the focus of national and even international attention. When in May, 1945 he announced that he would retire after 12 years of the harshest kind of testing, he knew enormous achievements had been made. New York had been placed on a firm financial basis by Fusion. Despite the enormous additions to the physical reality of the metropolis, its bonded debt in June 1946 amounted only to $2.194 billion, and that total represented a half billion dollar reduction since 1941. Construction had halted during the war but blueprints existed to complete the massive plan of the 1930s, and Commissioner Moses would remain ubiquitously present to see that the projects were built. Wartime employment gains had ended the relief problem—but the Welfare Department stood ready to assist indigent New Yorkers; it would soon again be dispensing millions in aid. A hundred thousand City workers were content under the generous pension plans La Guardia had approved and his initiatives had led to the creation of a Health Insurance Plan which had nationwide impact (1947). In the vexing area of race relations La Guardia's Administration enacted housing and fair employment laws which outlawed discriminatory practices well in advance of any national initiatives. Moreover, his reelections proved that Fusion need not be temporary. Havemeyer, Low, and Mitchel had all failed to be reelected but in La Guardia's three terms New York became more governable than it had been in decades. His legacy was a happier, more livable, more prosperous City.

One final note is mandatory; on October 21, 1945 a ceremony officially changed Sixth Avenue into the Avenue of the Americas. Although City natives refused then and now to utilize the new name, it was inescapably true that New York's true constituency had become the world community. Probably the change in name was also part of a grand strategy that New York adopted to win a great prize—this World City wished to become home to the newly created United Nations. And although the initial meeting of the world body had been held in London, by the end of 1945 the Bronx campus of Hunter College was designated the organization's temporary headquarters. Internationally famous planners opposed putting the United Nations in an existing City, but the lures of New York were undeniable. If the City could provide a permanent home there was little doubt the U.N. would choose to remain here. In 1946, while formal sessions were held at Lake Success (Nassau County) and in Flushing Meadow Park, a Mayor's Committee ultimately arrived at a consensus; a permanent home would be offered to the United Nations in eastern Manhattan on Turtle Bay. A seventeen-acre development site organized by William Zeckendorf was purchased by the Rockefeller interests and donated to New York. The U.N. accepted the proposed site on December 11, 1946. Plans were drawn, in part by Wallace Harrison who had helped create Rockefeller Center, and by the end of 1947 the glass-curtained, forty-five story Secretariat began its climb toward the sky. La Guardia, who had headed the Relief and Recovery Agency of the U.N. during 1946 certainly was thrilled. He had always believed the metropolis a symbol of hope for the millions who came here; now it could play a similar role for all mankind. The Mayor was never to see the structure completed, however, for he died of cancer of the pancreas on September 29, 1947. Nevertheless, he must have known that he and the United Nations had together helped make of New York the "world's capital City."

BRIEF BIBLIOGRAPHY

Bayor, Ronald. *Neighbors in Conflict: The Irish, Germans, Jews and Italians of New York City, 1929–1941.* Baltimore, 1978.

Caro, Robert A. *The Power Broker: Robert Moses and the Fall of New York.* New York, 1974.*

Carter, John Franklin. *La Guardia.* New York, 1937.

Cuneo, Ernest. *Life with Fiorello.* New York, 1955.

Fowler, Gene. *Beau James.* New York, 1949.

Garrett, Charles. *The La Guardia Years: Machine and Reform Politics in New York City.* New Brunswick, New Jersey, 1961.

La Guardia, Fiorello H. *The Making of an Insurgent: An Autobiography,* Philadelphia, 1948.

Mann, Arthur. *La Guardia Comes to Power, 1933.* Philadelphia, 1965.*

Mitgang, Herbert. *The Man Who Rode the Tiger: The Life and Times of Samuel Seabury.* New York, 1963.*

Nevins, Allan, and Krout, John A., eds. *The Greater City: New York, 1898–1948.* New York, 1948.

Osofsky, Gilbert. *Harlem: The Making of a Ghetto.* New York, 1966.*

Ware, Carolyn F. *Greenwich Village: 1920–1930.* Boston, 1935.*

*Paperback

IX

The Long Slide

WITH THE END of the global conflict in 1945, the City of New York seemingly had every reason to be confident of its future prosperity. Since consolidation, its population had virtually doubled from O. Henry's "Four Million." The census of 1950 counted a City of 7,891,957 people, larger in population than 45 of the 48 United States and far surpassing in size many of the original members of the United Nations. The manufacturing vitality of New York, honed to a fine edge by the trauma of war, was unsurpassed anywhere in the country. A magnificent harbor made it America's commercial capital and 40 percent of national freight traffic passed through the City each year. Each year its transit system carried the equivalent of the world's population, and its streets bustled with newcomers from both the Old and New World. The metropolis was truly a world City, yet the newest statistics showed that it was rapidly becoming ever more American; in 1948 only 30 percent of its population were accounted as foreign born. Nevertheless, whether perceived from a national or international perspective, the wealth and power of the giant on the Hudson was envied, respected, and conceded.

The immediate task faced by the metropolis as it welcomed back America's armies and accepted thousands of the world's refugees, was a severe housing shortage. The resultant construction boom of the late 1940s proved to be extraordinary. In the decade from 1946 to 1956, public housing constructed unprecedented numbers of rental apartment units. The first such accommodations were temporary wartime-style Quonset-hut apartments in sites such as the East Bronx and Queens. The City Housing Authority rapidly evolved as high-rise apartment buildings that have come to characterize modern urban scenery were built. Even more significant for America's future, was the desire of young married couples to purchase their own home and thus tangibly participate in the American dream. In the counties surrounding New York, tract housing—the model for which was Levittown in Nassau County—rapidly proliferated. Of necessity, the Long Island Railroad adopted as its symbol a harried commuter called Dashing Dan and a symbiotic relationship between these burgeoning suburbs and the central core City was soon established. Nassau County alone received more home mortgage loans from the Federal Veterans Administration than all of New York City. Within only a few years, 400,000 commuters entered the City daily to take advantage of its seemingly inexhaustible supply of job opportunities. In 1947, for example, New York City held 37,870 of the 240,881 manufacturing establishments in the nation. Among these were a clear majority of all apparel factories. Clothing had been New York's greatest industry since before the Civil War and provided jobs to more workers than did the autos of Detroit or the steel of Pittsburgh. With a manufacturing base this powerful, the stability of City finances was secure even though much of its working population now resided outside its geographical boundaries.

The postwar era was thus a time of population flux and physical alteration in New York City. Perhaps no single phenomenon illustrated the change so graphically as did the onset of the City's battle with the automobile. As Detroit began once again to manufacture cars for consumers, the metropolis discovered to its chagrin that it had lost control of its own streets. A surge of postwar buying and the increasing numbers of commuters made traffic control a nightmare that even today is unsolved. It was estimated that if the autos entering New York each day were put end to end they would span the nation. Bowing to the new auto god, in 1946 the famous double-decked buses of Fifth Avenue were phased out and in November the Forty-second Street crosstown trolley made its last trip. All trolley service, even in the outer boroughs, had terminated by April 7, 1957.

But not only automobiles congregated in the crowded streets of Manhattan. As always, New York remained a City of hope for the "storm-tossed" refugees of the world and nation. Displaced persons, veterans anxious to try their luck in the "Big Town," blacks fleeing Southern racism, and economic refugees from depressed Puerto Rico all seemed drawn to New York as if by magnetism. Somehow no one doubted that the metropolis would accept and assimilate all their dreams and skills but that goal was not so easily accomplished.

One fact was undeniable; in May 1945 Fiorello La Guardia announced his intention to leave the office he had revolutionized. Thus the first item on the political agenda was the selection of the man who would serve as New York's hundredth Mayor, a leader whose task it would be to cope with the myriad of new realities and marshal and direct the energies of the world's greatest city.

* * * * *

After twelve years in the political wilderness of opposition, Tammany Hall desperately needed to field a winning ticket. The candidate they selected to make the mayoral race was almost a prototype New Yorker. William O'Dwyer had immigrated to New York from Ireland in 1910, arriving here with only twenty-five dollars in his pocket and a driving ambition to succeed. He worked at a variety of menial jobs until he obtained his citizenship in 1916 and immediately thereafter became a policeman, the almost traditional road for Irish advancement. His aspirations were higher than those of the patrolman and he soon entered Fordham Law School; he also participated in Democratic politics at the precinct level. A law degree and political advancement both came easily to Bill O'Dwyer. By 1939, as the crusading district attorney for Brooklyn, he was given the lion's share of credit for the effective prosecution of gangland's infamous Murder Incorporated. In 1941, he ran and was defeated in the mayoral race, but he gave La Guardia a far closer race than expected. O'Dwyer then served his country well in the war; he was chief of the Allied Control Commission in Italy and left the army with the rank of brigadier general. While in Italy, he had been almost unanimously reelected as district attorney. In 1945 he was clearly Tammany Hall's best hope of returning to power.

Against this paragon, the Republicans offered Jonah Goldstein, a former Democrat and once himself a member of Tammany. In a weird reversal of history, the Democrats accused Goldstein of being "boss nominated." Moreover, they mocked La Guardia's chosen successor, Newbold Morris, the third candidate in the race, as an unwanted legacy of the past. Both his opponents claimed that O'Dwyer's official record was really less than met the eye—Morris, in fact, claimed O'Dwyer left Brooklyn a "rotten mess"—but there was never any doubt about the outcome. On November 4, Bill O'Dwyer became New York's one hundredth Mayor and the darling of Tammany Hall.

O'Dwyer's career had always been based on loyalty to the Tiger, but the new Mayor was hardly a typical Tammany hack. Often described as a leader who knew the City more intimately than any elected Mayor, O'Dwyer astutely recognized that his major task would be to oversee and control New York's transition to a peacetime economy. Accordingly, he decreed that the housing needs of returning servicemen and women should take immediate priority and decided that the wartime rent controls drawn up in 1943 should be expanded. Although often controversial and amended incessantly over the decades, these regulations still remain in force today. The unrelenting crusades of the real estate industry to dismantle the system provided renting New Yorkers with a convenient caste to despise, the landlords. It should be remembered that the metropolis has always been largely a rental market; in 1948, for example, 76 percent of its residents lived in apartments. Thus it is hardly surprising that the rent control system institutionalized by the Mayor became the most sacred of sacred cows.

Bill O'Dwyer proved to be remarkably in tune with, and adaptable to, the changing human face of the City he governed. As with all modern incumbents of the Mayor's office, the perennial problem of finance dogged his administration and in order to bring the power of expertise to bear in that area, O'Dwyer created the Analysis Section within the Bureau of the Budget. Among his many administrative initiatives were Traffic and Smoke Control Bureaus created to deal with environmental problems; equally important was the reorganization and purported improvement of the Welfare Department. Reconstructing City government was facilitated when the voters, in November 1947, approved the abolition of proportional representation on the City Council. This vote fundamentally was due to the onset of the Cold War, because the American Labor party's vote, if combined with that of other leftists, might have given legitimate representation to a Communist. The voters decided that councilmen henceforth would have to command majorities, a mandate which enhanced not only the dominant position of the Democrats but also the power of the Mayor. Another of O'Dwyer's early successes was a vigorous campaign against a smallpox scare; in 1947 almost 6,350,000 persons were efficiently vaccinated by a reconstructed Health Department. Although administrative reform is exceedingly dull, O'Dwyer's endeavors contributed in many long-range ways to the welfare of his City.

Perhaps no single administrative action had more import for the future than the creation of a Division of Labor Relations. It was inevitable that the City's labor force should demand catch-up pay increases once the necessity for patriotic sacrifice was ended. By May 1946, a strike by tugboat workers severely curtailed the commerce of the port and also caused fuel shortages. O'Dwyer first issued a mayoral Declaration of Emergency and then helped mediate the dispute. His intervention established a precedent of executive participation in labor disputes with City employees which subsequent Mayors have ever since attempted to repudiate. In the growing metropolis, all of New York's Mayors simply would have to deal with the growing militancy of labor, even if it was represented by leaders such as "Red" Mike Quill of the Transport Workers Union (TWU). Since the City did not wish to deal with so-called Communist unions, the Condon-Wadlin Act was passed by the legislature in 1947 with the intent of outlawing strikes by government employees. The provisions of the statute—including loss of jobs—were so severe, however, that no politician was ever able to invoke the full force of the law. Nevertheless, whether the City recognized the TWU or not, it was unthinkable that any Mayor could allow a transit strike. The subways and buses of New York carried 8,000,000 riders daily and so a 1948 wage settlement with the unhappy transit workers was ultimately negotiated. Its cost was the nickel fare which had lasted since

1904. On July 1, 1948, the cost of a subway ride rose to a dime, the first of eight such increases in the next 33 years. Moreover the City in 1949 accepted the principle of collective bargaining with its employees; a new era of power for the army of 180,000 City employees was thereby inaugurated.

Daily life in O'Dwyer's New York was exciting in many ways; the atmosphere was not dominated by the grim business of commuting, earning a living, reorganizing the administration, or living with strikes. In 1947, over 5,500,000 patrons attended baseball games at the three New York major league ball parks. That fall, the metropolis thrilled to a "subway" World Series as the New York Yankees, led by Joe DiMaggio, defeated the Brooklyn Dodgers, who boasted the first black ball player in the majors, Jackie Robinson. The next decade was to be a golden era of sports for New York with the invincible Yankees constantly winning over the Brooklyn "Boys of Summer" and the Giants. The sports mania spread to professional football, boxing, and college basketball as well; in 1950 the City College of New York won both the National Collegiate Athletic Association and the National Invitational tournaments.

High on the municipal agenda was the celebration of the Golden Anniversary of Greater New York in 1948. At the age of 50 the City encompassed 320.26 square miles with 5,719 miles of street and 578 miles of waterfront. Its 80 high schools and 569 grammar schools served a million pupils. In density of population New York was 500 times the national average, but no one seemed aware of it as they went about their teeming City. People preferred to talk of the power of New York's economy; its retailing of cloth led the nation and fully 20 percent of all American wholesale transactions took place within its boundaries. As part of the Golden Anniversary festivities Idlewild International Airport was dedicated on July 1, 1948; by 1960 activity on its new runways allowed it to surpass La Guardia as the major entry point to the City. In 1949 the long awaited Brooklyn Battery Tunnel opened to relieve the auto congestion and the President of the United States arrived to dedicate the cornerstone of United Nations Plaza. Across the metropolis signs of growth abounded. Even the housing crush seemed to be alleviated in 1949 when Manhattan's vast Stuyvesant Town housing project, funded by Metropolitan Life Insurance, began renting. Urban planners took additional heart after federal Urban Renewal funds for slum clearance won congressional approval. In all, O'Dwyer and his administration were nicely positioned for the reelection campaign. All the voters recognized that the difficult transition years had not been passed without problems, but most agreed that O'Dwyer had done a creditable job.

Despite all celebrations, openings, and expectations, the Mayor constantly delayed the announcement that he was again a candidate. Whispers began to be heard that he had allowed his town to become too "wide open" and that scandals were imminent. There were claims that fewer than 1,000 policemen were on patrol some days and that the "Mob" had too much political influence. There was little doubt that among the most influential men in Tammany Hall was Frank Costello, the "Prime Minister" of American organized crime. The leader of Tammany was to be quoted as saying, "If Frank Costello wanted me, he would send for me" and the Mayor himself supposedly visited with Costello. On January 24, 1949, when Costello hosted a $100 a plate dinner to benefit the Salvation Army, the dais and tables were crowded with Democratic leaders. Tammany apologists argued that the Mayor was equally on good terms with the new archbishop of New York, Francis Cardinal Spellman, and that neither mobster nor churchman had any political control over the City's decision-making process. Nevertheless rumors charged that O'Dwyer had secret ties to organized crime which could be proven by an inmate in Sing Sing Prison. As if in confirmation of the charge, it was not until after that prisoner had died in the electric chair that the Mayor finally decided to again offer himself to the public as a candidate. Despite all the innuendos and rumors, once O'Dwyer made the decision to run he became the instant favorite. The campaign was easily won by the Democrats as the City basked in the afterglow of another "subway series" won by Casey Stengel's Yankees.

The scope of the Democratic victory in 1949 was overwhelming. Not only did O'Dwyer win 59 percent of the vote, but also the Democrats won all borough presidencies (Robert F. Wagner, Jr. was elected in Manhattan) and 24 of the 25 council seats. Once again O'Dwyer's major victim was Newbold Morris who ran as the Republican-Liberal-Fusion nominee and denounced an administration of "plunder and corruption." A fascinating aspect of the race was the relatively strong showing of Socialist Victor Marcantonio who demanded a return to the five-cent fare, mandated rent rollbacks, lower utility rates and an end to police brutality against black and Hispanic New Yorkers. He also claimed that "you could fill Central Park with the . . . labor unions Bill O'Dwyer has tried to smash." Nobody seemed to listen to either Morris or Marcantonio.

Yet hardly had the election dust settled when their charges suddenly took on substance. A series of well-documented exposé articles in the Brooklyn *Eagle* charged that an alliance of policemen and judges illicitly protected 4,000 bookies in return for payoffs of over $1,000,000 annually. Although the evidence was overwhelming, O'Dwyer refused to accept it. He insisted that the charges were a press vendetta and defended the NYPD even after an accused policeman committed suicide. Yet the evidence of corruption was clear and so overwhelmingly hostile was the public's reaction that in January 1950, the Mayor fled to Florida because of "nervous prostration." Despite his oath, "as God is my judge," to serve his term, O'Dwyer began to cast about for release from the griddle that New York suddenly had become. The flame became even hotter when better than 110 police resigned in the face of an investigation that the Mayor had termed a "witchhunt." Corruption was hardly new to the New York police but never since Tweed days had a Mayor seemed so obtuse. Finally, Bronx boss Ed Flynn arranged a deal whereby O'Dwyer resigned (August 31, 1950) to accept appointment as Harry Truman's ambassador to Mexico. "There he would be safe from the petty annoyance of transportation problems, dirty sidewalks, snowstorms, a recalcitrant district attorney digging up scandals about corruption in the Police Department, and racketeers always showing up to be photographed at important functions of Tammany Hall." But O'Dwyer's sudden flight did not remove his name from newspaper headlines. After bookmaker Harry Gross told of contributing $20,000 to the former Mayor's reelection fund O'Dwyer was subpoenaed to testify before the Kefauver committee investigating organized crime. This famous committee successfully questioned Frank Costello who admitted he knew ten of the sixteen Tammany leaders "well," and "maybe they got a little confidence in me." The famous film of Costello's nervous hands clenching under Rudolph Halley's inquisition preceded the mobster's abrupt walkout. Then on March 19–20, 1951 O'Dwyer testified. He ultimately admitted his awareness of Police Department corruption and aquaintance-ship with various mobsters; he had also once visited Costello's apartment. He denied receiving any illegal contributions and ever afterward was able to assert, "I have never been charged with a crime, let alone convicted." But the final report of the Kefauver committee was damning. O'Dwyer's actions, the committee asserted, "often seemed to result favorably for men suspected of being high up in rackets." Moreover," his failure to follow up evidence of organized crime . . . contributed to the growth of . . . gangsterism in New York City." No hard evidence of malfeasance was provided, however, and Bill O'Dwyer remained American Ambassador until he resigned in 1952 and established a law practice in Mexico City.

Long before O'Dwyer's personal ordeal, New York had met its one hundred first Mayor. Automatically on O'Dwyer's resignation, president of the City Council Vincent Impellitteri took office under the charter until a special election could be held in November 1950. Impellitteri was a Sicilian-born New Yorker who had an excellent reputation as a successful racket's prosecutor and an "unbossable" lawyer. Although nominally a Democrat he was determined to win election as an Independent candidate in the Fusion tradition. Proclaiming his freedom from Tammany influences, Impellitteri entered the mayoral race as the nominee of the Experience party. Pehaps the most interesting feature of the brief campaign was that it marked the debut in municipal politics of the new boss of Tammany Hall. Carmine DeSapio had actually been Manhattan's Democratic leader since 1949 but O'Dwyer's easy reelection had not brought him to prominence. Now he selected Ferdinand Pecora to make the race against "Impy" and Republican Edward Corsi. As might be inferred, the campaign often resembled a balance sheet accounting which of the three candidates was the best Italian. Appeals to that voting bloc was important for by 1950 it had become the single greatest element of New York's electorate. No candidate could claim all Italian voters, however, and the real key to Impellitteri's 225,000 vote plurality was the precious word *independent*. The voters seemed alienated by the continuation of corruption and the seamy politics of the Tammany clubhouse. It was impossible to argue, even though it was true, that DeSapio as leader was systematically purging his party of its ties to Costello; he was making the democracy "saintly." Few, even among Democrats, believed that in November 1951 and it was not surprising that New Yorkers once again enlisted behind the standards of independence and reform as waved by Impellitteri.

Vincent Impellitteri was the "best-dressed, best-rested" Mayor New York had since Jimmy Walker, but his two years in office proved insufficient time for him to make a substantial record. In fact, his tenure severely disappointed reformers because the Mayor failed to reach out for the reins of power. It was true that as an Independent he lacked a firm party base and was thus at a disadvantage when dealing with a Board of Estimate and City Council more mindful of DeSapio than the Mayor. In those arenas, Impellitteri's few initiatives were ignored. But the Mayor had often made political blunders as well. For example, in 1952 he presented New York's fourth consecutive billion-dollar budget, its largest yet at $1.336 billion. In order to finance the spending, the sales tax was increased to 3 percent and a long-range financial plan to prevent deficits was presented to Albany. The proper legislative spadework had not been done, however, and in February 1953 state officials rejected the proposal because the City was taxing itself into "economic paralysis." Like O'Dwyer before him, Impellitteri tried to convience Albany that New York City received far less a proportion of local aid than it contributed in taxes but his analysis was ignored by the legislature. "Impy" did make good appointments however, and, like all mayors since La Guardia, one of his best was Robert Moses. Moses was selected to head the Slum Clearance Committee which would use federal urban-renewal appropriations to build largely middle-class housing. Under this program, Moses pushed through the construction of cooperatively owned developments at Morningside Gardens and Corlears Hook. Since the projects resulted in removal of site residents who could not afford the new housing—the Mayor took that heat—the political gains were few. And credit for the housing increases went to "Master Builder" Moses—his public relations men saw to that! The Mayor's reputation was also slightly tarnished when an investigation of waterfront corruption focused attention on one of his oldest friends. And finally, to complete "Impy's" discomfiture transit fares had to be increased to fifteen cents in July 1953. The Mayor's critics said he was indifferent to the increase since he spent most of his time on vacation. In all, the Impellitteri performance proved less than his promise and his mayoralty was to be only an interlude in Tammany's reign.

Regardless of who was Mayor, the glamor and allure of New York City continued to attract new immigrants. The census reported the City's 1950 population as 7,891,957 with Italians compromising the single greatest ethnic component. Yet the Immigration Act of 1952 provided the lowest quota ever for Italians, less than 6,000 annually, and their continued influence in the metropolis was thus to depend in the future on natural increase. New York still remained a cauldron of social mobility; an amazing 56 percent of all its citizens were still either foreign born or first-generation Americans. Economic mobility, however, was less apparent among the 10 percent of the population that was black. That segment of the City remained segregated in ghettos and suffered under the slogan of Last hired, first fired. Even middle-class blacks were stigmatized by color. For example, they were tacitly excluded from renting apartments in projects such as Stuyvesant Town.

The single most rapidly increasing ethnic group in New York, however, was the Puerto Rican community which in the early 1950s numbered 325,000. There had been sizable numbers of Puertoriqueños in Manhattan since the time of the Spanish American War and "barrios" had been established adjacent to the Brooklyn Navy Yard and in parts of East Harlem by the 1920s. In the 1930s Puerto Ricans had settled in Washington Heights, while the South Bronx assimilated the influx of the war years. But few New Yorkers were ready for the vast migration that began at the end of the World War; over a million immigrants fled the collapsed agricultural economy of Puerto Rico from 1945 to 1960. As the island government launched Operation Bootstrap for its economic revitalization, thousands of unemployed or underemployed Americans left Puerto Rico for the mainland and America's traditional City of opportunity. Not only were these newcomers citizens of the United States, but also they were the first immigrants to arrive in New York by plane—their flight took up nine hours yet cost $50 or less! Mayor O'Dwyer had recognized their growing numbers and had ordered his Welfare Commission to examine the problems Puerto Ricans would face in adapting to an urban environment. A 1949 report discovered that fully 98 percent of Puerto Ricans came to New York to better themselves economically but due to a lack of education, a language barrier, or simply due to discrimination, most failed to achieve the success they sought. By 1952, as an estimated 1,135 Islanders arrived each week in New York, Puerto Ricans already constituted the most rapidly increasing segment of the welfare rolls. By 1953 Puerto Rican New Yorkers comprised fully 5 percent of the City and increasingly they sought a sense of community; in 1959, for example, the first Puerto Rican Day parade was held. The vitality and ambition of these newcomers was as important to New York as were the problems they faced in becoming part of the metropolis.

But Puerto Ricans were not the only Caribbean migrants of the 1950s. Refugees from dictatorships or from revolutions arrived constantly in New York and Haitian and Cuban elements in the population grew rapidly. Moreover, thousands of Hungarians were admitted to the United States as displaced persons after the abortive revolution late in 1956. By some estimates a total of 2,000,000 persons arrived in New York during this decade, and many stayed to make new lives for themselves. The City made strenuous efforts to house and care for these new arrivals, but fell ever further behind. It is interesting to note, however, that the enormous influx of the 1950s did not substantially alter the total central City population because the continuing middle-class move toward suburbia drained residents from the metropolis at an almost equal rate. In time the increasing percentage of minority residents in New York that resulted from these dual migrations would become the most explosive issue facing the City's political leadership.

But that future crisis was inconceivable in 1953. The immediate concern then was the mayoral race in which Tammany once again hoped to return to power. Democrats recognized that simply to assert that they had purged themselves of mobster influence and corruption was not enough; they needed a "superclean" candidate in order to defeat Impellitteri. The long-time chief of Bronx politics was Ed Flynn, a realist who recognized DeSapio's internal party achievements. Moreover, DeSapio was "the first Tammany man since Murphy I can sit with and not have to talk out of the side of my mouth." Accordingly in early 1953, the two reigning bosses selected as their candidate the young borough president of Manhattan, the Honorable Robert F. Wagner, Jr. Wagner boasted one of the most revered names in New York politics, and had proven himself an effective administrator. Perhaps more importantly, he believed in party regularity. Although Ed Flynn died in August 1953—this made DeSapio supreme within Tammany—the joint effort of the Manhattan and Bronx machines routed Impellitteri in the Democratic primary race and secured for Wagner the nomination. When "Impy's" forces failed to collect enough Independent signatures to qualify the Experience party for a November ballot line, the race effectively ended. There remained for the Democrats only the formalities of dispatching Republican and Liberal candidates, and of bringing to heel the remaining outer borough dissenters to DeSapio's rule. On November 3 Wagner was elected Mayor, a position he held with some distinction for the next twelve years. A triumphant DeSapio proved magnanimous even to Impellitteri, who had regularly refused patronage to Tammany. He allowed Wagner to appoint "Impy" a judge of Special Sessions.

The incoming Wagner slate had been elected on the slogan, "Promise means performance"; no one could doubt they certainly had promised. The administration was committed to providing more policemen, improving civil service performance, protecting and expanding civil rights, constructing more and better public housing for every class of citizen, cleaning up the dilapidated waterfront, eliminating and replacing 170 "firetrap" schools, and embarking on "a genuine pattern of collective bargaining" with its municipal unions. The magic touchstone by which all this might be accomplished was a City economy which remained the greatest single marketplace of the nation. In 1954 New York still had 40,000 manufacturing firms while its 104,000 retail outlets sold $10 billion worth of goods annually. Its great port handled 40 percent of the total value of America's water trade; 12 railroads and 750 trucking firms served its needs. More impressive still was the fact that its airports serviced 37 percent of all domestic fares. Almost half a million commuters entered Manhattan daily to ply their various trades and business was getting even better now that the war in Korea had finally been settled.

Wagner capitalized on the glowing optimism of these prosperous years. He proved politically adroit in making above average appointments while remaining on excellent terms with the DeSapio machine. Not only was there continued labor peace but also the City managed to provide substantial new services for its residents; for example, the first of the City's current eight community colleges was created in 1955. The ubiquitous Robert Moses was kept on to push through the redevelopment of the Columbus Circle area and renovation of Manhattan's brownstone housing slowly marched up the West Side of Manhattan. Committed to provide additional housing, the Mayor lent his full political weight to support the passage of the state's Mitchell-Lama legislation which would provide moderate rent apartments for middle-income families. Today over 100,000 New Yorkers live in those units although the rents are no longer very low.

Wagner's first administration was also a time of optimistic expectations in race relations. Everyone was proud that a black man, Hulan Jack, had replaced the Mayor as Manhattan's borough president and most New Yorkers were confident that this presaged the incorporation of blacks into the political system. So many ethnic groups had previously been successfully assimilated that there seemed no reason to expect that full societal acceptance of blacks would be more difficult. Indeed there was more concern about "gangs" of youths and their battles than fear about the larger issue of successful integration. On the national scene, the Supreme Court's decision in *Brown* v. *Topeka Board of Education* (1954) declaring "separate but equal" schooling unconstitutional was hailed by liberal New York, while locally Wagner's appointment of a Commission on Intergroup Relations won universal plaudits.

In all, the mid-1950s appear as a time of lost innocence. The political system seemingly embraced all groups while the economy was universally praised as impervious to ordinary forces of decay. The tremendous reality of the metropolis was the subject of E. B. White's famous essay, "Here Is New York" which first appeared in 1955. Beyond its political and economic importance, White chose to focus on the implausible nature of the "miracle" that was New York. "The subterranean system of telephone cables, power lines, steam pipes, gas mains, and sewer pipes is reason enough to abandon the island . . . By rights New York should have destroyed itself long ago, from panic or fire or rioting or failure of some vital supply line . . ." No catastrophe occurred, and the constant renewal of the City continued as the Third Avenue Elevated Line, the oldest in Manhattan, was demolished and daylight as well as new construction took its place. New York's greatest problem seemed its inability to pick up trash, and Wagner launched an "anti-Litter Bug" campaign to meet that crisis. It came as no surprise that he was renominated and in 1957 won an overwhelming million vote victory over weak Republican opposition.

Although the 1950s are often derided as a dull and uninteresting decade, in New York they were highlighted by a construction boom which once again transformed the cityscape. Not only were high-rise apartments and slum clearance projects going up virtually overnight but also major architectural projects long under development were now rapidly brought to completion. Architectural historians may decide that the new corporate style had its origins in the glass curtained walls of the U.N. Secretariat but suddenly the format was being adapted for office buildings such as Lever House (1952) constructed by Skidmore, Owings, and Merrill. The stone and brick of an earlier age was now superseded by metal and glass constructs which dramatically altered and often enhanced the streets of New York. Glass walls and open ground spaces added a quality of airiness to the traditionally constricted spaces of Manhattan. Many skyscrapers, it must be admitted, had been ugly monoliths destructive of light and air but this new form of building seemed totally different. Perhaps the greatest single achievement of the decade was the 38-floor Seagrams Building designed by Miles van der Rohe with interiors by Philip Johnson. Dramatically set back from the whiteness that predominated along Park Avenue, this bronze and glass tower lured pedestrians into its "piazza." It set such a high standard that major zoning changes were enacted by 1961 in an effort to duplicate its enhancing effect on urban space. Unfortunately, the quality of the Seagram Tower was never matched in the decade that followed.

The massive nature of the construction boom in New York is indeed difficult to contemplate. From 1947 to 1963 over 58,000,000 square feet of office space was added to the City stock, a total greater than that built in the next 22 cities combined. Among the most prominent additions to the skyline were the Chase Manhattan, Time-Life, and Equitable buildings—each of which was constructed with pedestrian plazas. By 1959, the assessed valuation of the City soared past $32 billion, $22.5

billion of it fully taxable. In 1956, moreover, the $35,000,000 nine-acre Coliseum was opened to the public, a structure intended to solidify Manhattan's claim to be the "world's exposition capital." Among the public facilities added to New York's infrastructure were a third tube on the interstate Lincoln Tunnel, and the Verrazano Bridge across the Narrows at the entrance to the harbor. Ground was also broken to construct a major arts complex at Lincoln Center. It was not surprising that President Eisenhower in 1960 designated New York to host another World's Fair in serene expectation that the City could repeat its triumph of 1939–1940. The exposition was even to have the same *maître d'* because Robert Moses ultimately resigned several of his posts to oversee fair arrangements. The fifties were a decade in which physical change seemed the greatest reality of the giant metropolis at the mouth of the Hudson.

Yet, as so often is the case in a seemingly healthy organism, a cancer was slowly growing within the vital framework. The disease grew slowly even as the population of the City crept up to 7,781,984 persons in 1960. The underlying reality of the 1950s was that the economic fabric of the metropolis was altering itself in such a fashion that it would no longer be able to support the weight of all the dreams of its residents. For almost a century, the basic strength of the metropolitan economy had been its manufacturing sector, and despite the size of New York the small factory had been its most typical business establishment. Amid the myriad of smaller enterprises the unending immigrant waves of the past had traditionally found employment. The wages they earned, though often meager, provided millions with the means for their first steps toward dignity and independence and inspired them to higher goals—if not for themselves then for their children. Similarly, the immigrants of the 1950s were expected to conquer not only their poverty but also the unique burdens of racial and linguistic discrimination. Perhaps this might have been possible had not the lowest rung of the job ladder been suddenly narrowed. During Eisenhower's presidency, from 1953 to 1960, the national economy experienced three recessionary interludes and their cumulative effect on New York's manufacturing employment was substantial. And even within surviving factories, an accelerating trend toward automated methods demanded more educated and skillful workers even as it reduced the absolute number of men needed to maintain production. Finally, as evidenced by the enormous surge of office space construction, New York's white collar needs were increasing as the urban economy became more service oriented at the expense of manu-facturing.

Economists and social science researchers were quick to dis-cover these trends and to speculate on their import for the prospects of New York. In 1959, a massive report on the future of the three-state metropolitan region was issued by a team led by Raymond Vernon; the results of this three-year study made som-ber reading. While forecasting general growth for the entire re-gion, nine separate volumes uniformly predicted a troubled fu-ture for urban communities, and especially for New York City, within the tristate area. Studies indicated that both public facili-ties and private enterprise were suffering from obsolescence; factory techniques, housing, transit systems, streets, and schools had simply not been able to keep pace with changing needs. Vernon was certain that New York City's "position as the nation's business and financial capital seems virtually unassaila-ble for the next few decades," but predicted that future growth in jobs and commerce would be largely outside its boundaries. As if to punctuate this conclusion, from 1958 to 1964 metropolitan factory employment reportedly fell by 87,000 jobs. Although it was widely criticized for undue pessimism, the Vernon study holds up remarkably well after 20 years. It is also interesting to note that one volume of the study, Oscar Handlin's *The New-comers*, has become a minor classic for accurately defining the difficulties that blacks and Puerto Ricans were to face in the changing metropolis.

Just as economists analyzed the urban situation, so too were political scientists active. At least three major studies of New York's government had been undertaken and completed by the start of Wagner's second term; the Committee on Management (1950–53); a Temporary State Commission (1953–56); and the Joint City-State Fiscal Committee (1955–56). Though of varied quality each of the studies found serious inadequacies in the political-fiscal stance of the City. Their suggestions for reforms were largely ignored by Mayor Wagner who believed he had mas-tered the techniques of City government. An administrative structure which tolerated many layers of overlapping authority was allowed to perpetuate itself without interference and inevitably corruption appeared. In 1959 alone there were scandals in the Market Department, in city fuel oil purchases, and within the office of the Manhattan Borough president. Only a month after the latter affair led to the indictment of Hulan Jack, a fourth study of the City was issued (February 1960). The New York State "Little Hoover" Commission, led by Otto Nelson, charged that the government of New York City was inherently ineffective due to one party predominance, a weak Mayor's Office, a hack-ridden Board of Education, and a rubber stamp City Council, the "weakest but highest paid" in America. The Nelson committee scathingly attacked Wagner personally for compounding governmental inadequacies by inaction; the Mayor apparently has "no appetite, willingness, or capacity to initiate or carry out . . . substantial changes" as suggested by previous studies. Nevertheless, the Nelson panel did propose a series of specific reform programs dealing with increased cash flow, staggered real estate tax collections, and particularly debt service adjustments which, had they been implemented, would have served the City well. Indeed, they might have spared New York the national humiliation it experienced in the 1970s. However, the too general nature of the Nelson Commission's mismanagement and corruption allegations enabled Democrats to excoriate the entire report as a "partisan political document" funded by the Republican legislature. Wagner, Comptroller Lawrence Gerosa, and Council President Abe Stark united to reject Nelson's conclusions and, as was the case with the Vernon Commission, nothing of substance was changed.

Yet despite all intimations of economic decline and governmental disorder, the Wagner years represented the last really good times for New York. They also became the last hurrah for Tammany Hall. Although the immensely popular Eisenhower twice carried New York State in presidential years, DeSapio was successful in nominating and electing Averell Harriman as Governor in 1954. The "Boss" served as New York secretary of state and had as much patronage to distribute on the state level as he enjoyed in the City. Although DeSapio's appointments were given to capable but loyal party men, his reputation as a manipulator remained strong. His very successes as party manager made DeSapio increasingly prominent and, whether due to vanity or to his desire to overcome the "Boss" label, he began to himself seek the political spotlight. In 1958 he crushed an attempt to win the senatorial nomination for a liberal and imposed his own candidate, District Attorney Frank Hogan, upon the Democratic State Convention. The losers inevitably raised the old cry of "bossism" and DeSapio's dark-glassed image—he had an eye disorder—seemed to give substance to the cry. When both Hogan and Harriman were defeated, his regime was suddenly shaken. Not only had DeSapio become so visible as to become himself an issue, but also he had committed the unpardonable sin of backing losers!

DeSapio's once sure touch also deserted him during the presidential campaign of 1960 when he only belatedly joined the John F. Kennedy bandwagon. When Kennedy won, he decided to chastize DeSapio by awarding patronage not through Tammany but rather through Mayor Wagner. Thus was the stage prepared for perhaps the most outrageous of all the amazing mayoral campaigns in New York's history. The Republicans, anxious to run against a Mayor widely perceived as weak, vacillating, and machine dominated, would not be allowed to do so. Instead, Wagner openly broke with his mentor, announced his support for a different borough president in Manhattan, and denounced as "bossism" the political record he himself had constructed over eight years. It was 1961—a year for miracles—and just as a New York Yankee was shattering the "unbeatable" home run record of Babe Ruth, so Robert F. Wagner set out to destroy the myth of the invincible Tammany machine. In September, as Roger Maris hit his sixty-first home run, the Mayor crushed DeSapio's candidate and won the Democratic primary; he immediately therefore became the odds-on favorite for reelection. A despondent DeSapio was forced to back an independent candidacy by Comptroller Gerosa in November. Almost no one paid any attention to Gerosa's claim that the "real issue is whether the City is to become solvent or go bankrupt"; everyone knew that the only issue was DeSapio. On November 7, Wagner won 1,237,421 votes to soundly trounce Republican Louis Lefkowitz; Gerosa amassed only thirteen percent of the total vote.

And DeSapio's humiliation was not yet ended. He had concentrated so completely on the citywide campaign that he had neglected his own position in Greenwich Village where a group of liberal insurgents led by James Lannigan and Edward Koch successfully ousted him as district leader. Not only had "bossism" been routed by Wagner, but the Boss himself had fallen. Never again was a Tammany chief to dominate New York. In retrospect the election of 1961 signaled the demise of the great machine first built by Aaron Burr; an era had come to a sudden, unexpected end.

The demise of Tammany was not immediately apparent, of course, for a new leader replaced DeSapio. Edward Costikyan represented the Liberal coalition which had ousted the boss and was the first Protestant leader of the Hall since Boss Tweed. His prickly independence made it difficult for him to work with Wagner, however, and critics of the Mayor—who were legion— soon were asserting that bossism had only relocated into City Hall. After his reelection, Wagner demanded resignations from 400 City workers identified with DeSapio and he let be known his intention to lead both City and party; he cited charter revisions approved by the voters in 1961 to prove that the people wanted strong leadership. In September 1962, a select panel was appointed to review all judicial nominees and to remove courts from politics. Yet despite the rhetoric, nothing really changed. It was a bitter Costikyan who summed up Wagner's style as Mayor: "Create no potential opponents, eliminate those who appear, take care of yourself, and never make a decision until it can't be avoided."

Nevertheless, the third Wagner administration began in the glow of political independence and good economic times, even if both were in part illusory. The City had never been more populous and internal improvements such as the Throgs Neck Bridge (1961) and second deck for the George Washington Bridge (1962) tied it even closer to its hinterland. Yet under the surface titanic forces were growing which gradually undermined the City's self-sufficiency. The key element was financial. From the early 1960s to the present day New York has lived with a sense of budget crises. In 1960, the City received over $150 million in federal grants yet even that enormous sum was inadequate to provide all the services New Yorkers needed. Wagner had to negotiate a special infusion of state aid from Governor Nelson Rockefeller before he could achieve budgetary balance. As the Mayor began his third term, a quarter of his money came from state and federal sources. In the next two decades, the proportion of City expenses provided by subsidies was continually to grow. But all transfusions provided only temporary help. By May 1963 the City Council, as part of a general revenue raising package, gave its reluctant approval to a sales tax increase. The outcry was naturally clamorous yet temporary. Even though the City has never used all its potential taxing authority, the beleaguered New Yorker was already the most heavily taxed type of *homo Americanus*, a title that residents have learned to almost flaunt. More seriously, by the time Wagner left office the expense budget had reached $3.4 billion and was still rapidly rising.

As the economic base of New York eroded, the question of race relations within the metropolis assumed even greater importance. Inevitably reductions of City services would have greatest impact upon already struggling minority populations. It was Mayor Wagner who was forced to confront the racial revolution that stemmed from the 1954 Supreme Court decision against segregated schools. But how was this to be implemented in New York where the minority population was clustered into ghettos? Wagner's administration had made housing discrimination illegal, in theory if not in practice, and thousands of units of urban renewal apartments available to all New Yorkers were constructed. The Mitchell-Lama housing program offered middle-class housing to thousands and in the decade of the 1950s, New York City constructed more housing project units than the rest of the nation. Still the demand grew. In 1960, a Housing and Redevelopment Board was established in order to coordinate the multiplicity of City efforts. In the West Side Renewal Area, the Mayor argued that any minority residents displaced by construction would have the "right of return" to one of the projected 2,500 units. The harsh reality of high rent levels however, made it difficult for many displaced minority families to do so. Despite good intentions, much of New York's educational system and housing remained *de facto* segregated.

As part of the City's efforts to deal with the depressed economic status of most of its minority groups, a major educational innovation was announced in 1961. The City University of New York was created in order to provide a free college education to any qualified New Yorker. The consolidated institution would guarantee to anyone the opportunity to advance as far as their talents allowed. The leavening effect of education, it was argued, would ultimately raise both the income levels and status of the City's minorities. In

1962, Wagner increased the antidiscrimatory powers of his commission on Human Relations and created a Rent and Rehabilitation Administration to deal with specific complaints by the poor. The optimism that these efforts would be successful seems almost utopian today, but was looked upon as realistic in the benign era of John Kennedy's national "Camelot."

Despite all efforts and expectations the situation of most minority individuals remained dismal. In 1960, for example, blacks comprised 13 percent of the City population but received 45 percent of welfare payments. Even more depressing was the discovery that Puerto Ricans, who had arrived with such high hopes and who then constituted 8 percent of the City, received 30 percent of public assistance. Tragically, there seemed few rungs on the upward ladder for minorities. Equally troubling was the increase in animosity evident when middle-class white residents spoke scornfully of a "welfare class." Slum conditions spread when public housing was neglected, crime statistics soared as joblessness grew among the unskilled, and neighborhood communities in New York moved further apart. In April 1964, as the long-awaited World's Fair opened in Flushing Meadows, disgruntled black leaders threatened to bring their cause to national prominence with a "stall-in" on the roads leading to the fair. It did not happen but clearly only a single misstep could have precipitated violent confrontation. Later that year, during a July heat wave, a policeman shot and killed a black boy and four days of sporadic violence erupted in Harlem; before it ended there were fires, 140 injuries, and one death. Harlem provided the first harbinger of the "long, hot summers" to come but its import was ignored. A troubled racial future was also indicated in the striking but unpublicized fact that during the Wagner era 800,000 white residents left New York for the suburbs. They were replaced within the City by various minorities with lesser skills who could not be provided with jobs. Yet they required at least an equal amount of public service as did the exiting whites.

In order to deal with the myriad of urban crises confronting the City and the nation, an accepted cliché of the 1960s argued that stronger executive leadership was imperative. On the national scene President Kennedy labored to invigorate a reluctant Congress and on the local level mayors like Bob Wagner tried their best to imitiate his example. A major revision of the City Charter had been approved by the voters in 1961 and when it took effect on January 1, 1963 the Mayor suddenly was given unprecedented budgetary authority. He alone was given the right to estimate revenues as well as to determine the level of debt that the City could afford for its capital construction program. Subsequently the Mayor was to overestimate general fund revenues by $68,400,000. Of equal importance for the City's fiscal future, Governor Nelson Rockefeller on April 3, 1964 approved an amendment to the Local Finance Law which permitted mayors to include current expense items in their capital construction budgets. Thus were put into place two of the techniques which were to result in the fiscal disaster of the 1970s.

Toward the end of Wagner's third term, it was obvious to everyone that race and finance were the most important long-term issues facing New York City. Beyond cosmetic announcements and short-term improvision, little effective action in these areas was undertaken by a Mayor both famed and blamed for his "dedicated inactivity." Wagner found it far more politic to emphasize the continuing strengths of the metropolitan economy than to respond to the discovery of slow hemorrhage. In 1963 the City still was home to 33,000 manufacturing establishments employing 927,000 workers, a total surpassed by only five of the fifty states. Its clothing factories created 28 percent of the total apparel value for the nation while its myriad of small print shops and publishing houses handled a full 19 percent of America's printing business. Retail trade surpassed that of 43 of the 50 states while the City maintained its traditional position as the leading wholesale market in the nation. With statistics such as these, it proved easy to ignore statistics which showed that the port's total share of national cargo handling had dropped by 10 percent in the previous decade, that the local job market grew only 1.6 percent from 1958 to 1963 against a national average of 11 percent, and that 227 manufacturing firms left the City during Wagner's third term. Nor was it incumbent on the administration to explain why with more teachers instructing fewer pupils and with more police on the streets, the City was plagued by ill-educated, truant children, and ever-increasing crime statistics. If the public perceived any threat, it probably was in the area of racial tension, a reality most apparent in a series of battles to achieve more integrated schools that were waged in 1964–65. Since these disturbed public serenity Wagner professed great concern, but his answers proved to be soothing words and a new superintendent of schools who promised increased institutional sensitivity to minority concerns.

Few noticed that the greatest casualty of the Wagner years was the Democratic machine. After the Mayor's rout of DeSapio in 1961, that last Boss's return to power was frustrated first by Greenwich Village reform groups and later by legal battles. No universally accepted leader succeeded DeSapio in ruling Manhattan. The Mayor selected officials on a merit basis and each long-term appointment further cut into the sinews of the machine. In 1964 Charles Buckley, Boss of the Bronx since the death of Ed Flynn, was also defeated by a reform Democrat; his death three years later removed another tie to the past. Although perceived as an ineffectual, vacillating Mayor, Wagner proved a veritable tiger when it came to dispatching his foes. During his third term he purged the Democratic party of its machine-oriented politicians, organization men capable of delivering the vote. They were easy prey now, for the ethnic groups they represented were exactly those who were relocating themselves to the suburbs. Like a row of dominoes, their dominions collapsed before Wagner's onslaught. It is one of the great ironies of City history that even as the Mayor destroyed the remnants of the Tammany machine, the legislative apportionment law which had for 50 years underrepresented the City in Albany was being declared unconstitutional. The gains that a unified City delegation elected by machine vote might have won for the financially troubled City would not be forthcoming. The areas of New York that most benefited from reapportionment were the suburbs. Thus the end result of Wagner's twelve years in office was a Democratic party sadly lacking in organizational leadership when the Mayor announced he would not stand for a fourth term in 1965.

Wagner's timing was as usual correct. His personality hardly was compatible with the temper of a year when diverse protest movements seemed high on the public agenda. Causes as disparate as womens' rights, consumerism, student activism, black power and anti-Vietnam protests all would have to be confronted by a strong Mayor. Across the nation new young leaders were attempting to don the mantle of an assassinated JFK. It was a time when a rather shell-shocked public hoped and perhaps even believed that one man might still make a difference. Manhattan Republicans believed they could exploit Democratic disarray and the public's psychological malaise and return to power. The young leader who was to accomplish this was John Vliet Lindsay, a 44-year-old graduate of Yale Law School, who since 1958 had represented the "Silk Stocking" District of East Side Manhattan in the Congress. Lindsay's appeal was summed up in his campaign advertising: "He is fresh and everyone else is tired." He seemed anxious and able to master the City's problems; not only did he win both the Republican and Liberal nominations but also he enjoyed the unanimous backing of the press. The *Times* looked forward to "renewal" for the City while the *Herald Tribune* found in Lindsay a "capacity to inspire"; he offered the vision of a City physically and spiritually transformed. The press warned that if the electorate rejected Lindsay it meant a return to "backroom government," a signal that the City was a "haven for mediocrity" which they equated with the sedate Democratic nominee, Comptroller Abraham Beame. Yet all of these advantages might have meant nothing had not Lindsay also benefited from the third-party candidacy of conservative columnist William F. Buckley. In November 1965 the 339,127 votes that Buckley won from potential Beame voters provided the Liberal Republican Lindsay with a narrow margin of victory. It now remained to be seen if the man and the times had met.

Immediately after Lindsay's election, on November 9, the infamous "blackout" of the Northeast power grid took place. In the City, there were areas which lacked electricity for up to fifteen hours; not unexpectedly, nine months later there was a minor "baby boom." Although the power outage was inconvenient, it was temporary, yet perhaps it symbolized the plight of New York. The metropolis was increasingly the victim of outside forces it could not control. Even more figuratively, it might by asserted that there was a blackout of effective thinking about the nature of the City in the 1960s, a failure of political will which led to its humiliation in the 1970s. Simply to read the newspapers and magazines of these years is a sobering experience; author after author accurately identified the nature and the causes of the looming urban crisis. In *Commentary* Nathan Glazer asked "Is New York City Ungovernable?" and wondered if the vice of the City might not be bigness itself. The *Herald Tribune* in 1965 ran an extended analysis of the awesome problems and concluded that "New York is the greatest City in the world, and everything is wrong with it." Almost all writers agreed that the City was living beyond its means and that financial reforms were necessary. During the Wagner-Lindsay interregnum, yet another Temporary Commission on City Finances concluded that "sooner rather than later (New York) will find itself unable to meet current charges" due to its widening budgetary gaps.

Closely tied to the financial conundrum was the dawning recognition that a permanent welfare class of minorities was coming into existence in New York. Many welfare recipients were unemployables who lacked the technical skills to serve modern business and whose raw muscle power was not useful in the shifting economy. Most of the welfare class, however, consisted of women and young children. Politicians seemed to ignore or to offer platitudes about this issue rather than to face up to its serious implications. Indeed, when Buckley's eccentric campaign had proposed alternatives to constantly rising welfare rolls, opposing politicians and the press had united to label him a crypto-racist. It was far easier to cite the victory of Puerto Rican migrant Herman Badillo as borough president of the Bronx to prove that New York's minority population would be successfully integrated. Any alternative was not worth thinking about! In any case, the future of New York was now Lindsay's problem. In a Christmas Day editorial, *Business Week* suggested that "the worries are catching up" with America's greatest City, but there was still the expectation that vibrant leadership could overcome the rising tide. Undeniably, when Lindsay took office New Yorkers shared a feeling of expectant hope. Maybe he was another La Guardia who would be able to master the crisis and build the "Fun City" he promised.

On January 1, 1966, a beautiful 61-degree day in early winter, that hope died. At 5:00 A.M. that morning 33,000 public transport workers led by Mike Quill—whose union that had always talked tough but which had never struck the City—shut down the greatest transit system in the world. The resultant 12-day strike has been described as the "greatest catastrophe since the Great Depression," a disaster in both economic and psychological terms. The economic effects of the walkout were devastating of course, with business losses totaling $800,000,000, lost wages reaching $25,000,000 daily, and ripple effects spreading across the nation. Even more destructive, however, was the damage done to Lindsay's "can-do" image as he ineffectively attempted to cope with the calamity. He did the expected things—walking to work and issuing clarion calls of solidarity with the walking masses—but he flailed about wildly searching for solutions. He denounced the "power brokers" of New York, coyly adding that "they know who they are," as the real culprits behind the strike. Yet on January 4 he allowed Quill to be jailed for leading the walkout. "Red Mike" loved it and called on the judge to "drop dead in his black robes"; he even scornfully refused to correctly pronounce the Mayor's name. Harried and desperate, Lindsay ultimately approved a settlement twice as large as the TWU had originally asked. Not only did he accept a contract the City could ill afford but he also obtained no labor support for doing so. The other municipal unions perceived his political tentativeness and subsequently whipsawed the reform Mayor into granting each of them settlements larger by far than they had obtained from easygoing Bob Wagner. It seemed after all that New York's glamorous new Mayor was a politician just like all the others, though perhaps less gifted with tact and strength. As a reformer, Lindsay attempted to recoup administratively. In January 1966 he created by Executive Order a massive Transportation Administration to rebuild the defective system. He also attempted to replace the extraordinary Robert Moses as head of the Triborough Bridge Authority. The superagency came into existence but was never effective and the powerful Moses shrugged aside Lindsay's challenge as efficiently as he had warded off all such attacks in the past.

But Lindsay's "on-the-job training" did not end with his inept performance in transit affairs. His early denunciation of "power brokers" had not been forgotten by the New York establishment which had supported his election. When the Mayor chided businessmen for not contributing enough time or money to help the City it was interpreted as another gratuitous slap at his natural friends, and as an indication of political paranoia. By March, Lindsay had alienated major elements of the coalition which had elected him (bankers, businessmen, and nabobs of the Bar Association and Century Club) and it would be many months before they forgave him. If this was not enough, he then decided to challenge the single most visible bureaucracy in his City, the New York Police Department. In a move to appease both liberal and ghetto critics of the department, the Mayor suggested that a Civilian Review Board be established to assess and control police performance. In a City where 150,000 felonies were committed each year, the public at large perceived this suggestion as a mechanism to tie the hands of the police and to coddle criminals, especially those from minority groups. When Lindsay appointed a new police commissioner whose task was to implement the proposal and "reform" the department, that poor man was virtually destroyed by the entrenched police establishment and driven from the City.

To cap a generally dismal initiation period, Lindsay also isolated himself from political support by feuding with Republican Governor Nelson Rockefeller. Both men were liberal politicians with presidential aspirations and their one-upmanship battles continued over a period of years. On the local front, moreover, Lindsay treated Democratic City Council President Frank O'Connor with studied contempt, even though O'Connor at least understood how the City operated. It played as magnificent theater, the Lone Ranger in a white hat surround by enemies, but it resulted in terrible government. Wagner, whose maligned performance in office suddenly seemed admirable, was quick to indicate the gaps between Lindsay's rhetoric and his accomplishments; he predicted a fiasco. As early as June 1966, *Fortune Magazine* echoed that judgment in an article entitled "This Lindsay Takes on that City" which lamented the confrontational attitude of New York's new leader. At a time when the metropolis was running out of time, the Mayor was mired in a series of battles which changed little and ignored the slow deterioration of the City.

In July 1966 yet another commission—this one led by Earl Schwulst—reported to no one's surprise that the basic New York problem was a lack of money. "The City at present borrows for everything it possibly can, including some truly current expenses which the state permits it to fund." The result was enormous debt service charges and too high taxes. The report did acknowledge that the City provided "unusual and costly" services such as the municipal hospital system, high employee pensions, and CUNY, but it insisted that additional revenues were needed in order to support them. Lindsay naturally was aware of the conclusions long before they were published and he blithely responded that "the situation in New York is always desperate." In a fireside chat to his City, he conceded that taxes would have to rise but he never moved to alter the systematic use of the bogus deficit financing techniques he had inherited. Indeed, other methods of "creative bookkeeping" were pioneered! The immediate budgetary issue was solved on July 1, 1966 when after a protracted struggle with the legislature, an income tax for City residents and a commuter tax were established. Great as the new revenues were, however, they still did not bring the books into balance. In order to run the subways another transit fare increase to 20 cents was enacted and additional bond issues had to be floated that fall to fund a budget suddenly in excess of $4.5 billion. The budget had doubled in ten years and projections said it would double again by 1974; in reality, it would be far greater. John Lindsay presided over the City in those eight years and he never gained control of his budgets. He accepted the ramshackle system, the poor managers, and the questionable financial practices that had begun under Wagner and by ignoring the fundamental problems compounded them. It was not all his fault, of course, for banks, the legislature, the Governor, and the people must bear their share of the blame. But the task and the promise of leadership were his responsibility and in that regard, he failed.

The inability of Lindsay to come to grips with the financial question represents a fundamental failure, yet its effects were long-term. In the short run, the Mayor achieved the dream of every politician—he dominated the headlines. Sometimes the stories were disastrous, as when the voters in November 1966 defeated his Police Review Board by almost two to one, and sometimes they were triumphant, when the Mayor negotiated $30,000,000 in Model City aid from the federal government in 1967, but always it was Lindsay who "got the ink." He created a Public Development Corporation to relocate firms to New York and to halt the slow ooze of jobs toward the suburbs. By 1968 three of ten planned superagencies to restructure City administration were in operation. Others were stillborn or, like Transportation, defeated. One clear problem was the Mayor's inability to retain able commissioners; fourteen quit during the first two years of his administration. One effective bureaucrat was Thomas Hoving in the Parks Department who shared the same flair for headline grabbing as did the boss. In sum, after its rocky start, the Lindsay administration settled down to maintaining the system rather than mastering it.

Lindsay's greatest success clearly lay in the race relations sphere where he managed to keep New York's streets "cool" during the many discontents of the late 1960s. It had been shocking to discover, in 1966, that in the schools of New York whites were now the minority and that the system was virtually segregated. The fears and traumas thus released led to the "Great School War" of late 1968 as blacks contended with Jewish-dominated teacher organizations for control of the educational process. Lindsay ultimately moved the City into a decentralized educational system which lasted into the 1980s. In the greater arena of violent protest, Lindsay was also successful. Violent protests led by the Students for a Democratic Society wracked Columbia University and anti-Vietnam demonstrators often filled the streets, but the race issue was muted. Probably only Lindsay's leadership spared New York the trauma of riot that devastated cities such as Detroit, Newark, and Washington. Although welfare rolls soared beyond 800,000, the attendant costs were minor compared to the Armageddon of race war which some commentators had expected. It was not a payoff that prevented this in New York; it was the almost heroic figure of a shirt-sleeve Mayor walking ghetto streets and really caring. It bids fair to remain Lindsay's finest hour.

* * * * *

As New York reached the end of the troubled 1960s, there was little public recognition that the metropolis was undergoing fundamental economic and social changes. Probably on a subconscious level everyone recognized the danger, but minds tended to focus on headline happenings rather than underlying realities. It was the age of TV war in Vietnam, a nightmare of political assassinations, an era of "long hot summers" of racial confrontation, and of a race for the moon. To expect budgetary trivia or sociological jargon to compete with all this for the attention of the public was foolish. Besides, how could New York City be in trouble? It still was larger than 67 of the 122 members of the United Nations and its Mayor supervised the second largest budget in the nation. Lindsay often spoke of having the "second toughest job" in America and many suspected he longed to try the first on for size, especially when he used his membership on the Kerner Commission (1968) to become the spokesman for urban America! There was no doubt that New York City in 1968 was still strong, but each day its finances worsened, its restive minorities grew more sullen, its institutional fabric weakened, and its resilient spirit eroded just a bit more. A time of testing was approaching when both New York and America would have to face up to the sobering realities of our contemporary world. The City would have to face the most basic question of all; could it survive the 1970s?

BRIEF BIBLIOGRAPHY

Carey, George W. *New York, New Jersey: A Vignette of the Metropolitan Region.* Cambridge, Mass., 1976.*

Connable, Alfred, and Silverfarb, Edward. *Tigers of Tammany.* New York, 1967.

Costikyan, Edward N. *Behind Closed Doors: Politics in the Public Interest.* New York, 1966.*

Glazer, Nathan, and Moynihan, Daniel P. *Beyond the Melting Pot.* Cambridge, Mass., 1963.*

Hacker, Andrew. *The New Yorkers: A Profile of an American Metropolis.* New York, 1975.

Hamburger Philip. *Mayor Watching and Other Pleasures.* New York, 1958.

Moscow, Warren. *What Have You Done for Me Lately?* New York, 1967.

Pinchot, Ann. *52 West.* New York, 1962.

Robbins, Sidney M., and Terleckyj, Nestor E. *Money Metropolis.* Cambridge, Mass., 1960.

Sternlieb, George. *The Tenement Landlord.* New Brunswick, New Jersey, 1969.

———, and Hughes, James W. *Housing a People in New York City.* New York, 1973.

Wakefield, Dan. *Island in the City: Puerto Ricans in New York.* New York, 1960.

*Paperback

X

Disaster and Rebirth

DURING THE TURBULENT 1960s the grim face of the urban crisis took a tangible form in the mind of the American nation. Violence in great cities such as Detroit, Newark, and Washington resulted in scores of deaths; ethnic immigration to urban centers continued to exacerbate racial tensions; an increasing gap between city revenues and the services they were expected to perform haunted the thoughts of the nation's mayors; and thousands of jobs were lost from the urbanized East to the balmier climes of the Sunbelt. Taken together all these phenomena brought the reality of urban transformation to the center of the national stage. Learned panels were convened to discuss if the present city form was viable or if it could be salvaged only by imposing "metropolitan solutions." Cassandras of many persuasions despaired that problems of ethnic diversity, poverty, mass transit, and manufacturing dislocation could ever be successfully met by the existent system. Since the entire discussion took place in the shadow of a foreign war increasingly detested by most Americans the atmosphere at the end of the 1960s was gloomy indeed.

* * * * *

In no American City were the contradictions between the boundless dreams of urban residents and their troubled present

281

so apparent as they became in New York. Mayor John Lindsay had won election by a narrow plurality not because he was a Republican but rather because he offered the promise that somehow he could confront and conquer the myriad of imposing urban problems. Typical of the situation he faced was an article which appeared in *Fortune* magazine shortly before his election; it was called "A City Destroying Itself." Early in his first month of office, as New York clawed its way out of the debris of the transit catastrophe, *U.S. News and World Report* asked "Does New York City Have a future?" (January 24, 1966) Besides the 12 days of the transit strike, Lindsay's first-year experiences were to include a 25-day newspaper blackout, a 33-day dock strike, and a 75-day hiatus of shipping deliveries. It was a year of unending racial conflict typified by battles over educational priorities, police-minority relations, and a welfare system whose expenditures had doubled in five years. As if these afflictions were not enough, the metropolis was in the throes of a five-year drought which forced restaurants to halt serving water with dinner. Finally, the major felony rate was to triple in the course of the decade and "crime in the streets" would become a preoccupation of city residents. Many New Yorkers by 1968 were prepared to concede the validity of a Lindsay's commissioner's despairing comment; "The City has begun to die."

Yet despite all difficulties, the social fabric of the national metropolis held firm. While urban centers across America were convulsed by racial conflict New York remained relatively unscarred and for this Lindsay deserves much of the credit. The Mayor served with distinction on Lyndon Johnson's National Advisory Commission on Civil Disorders. In March 1968 he was instrumental in proposing to the nation an Urban Bill of Rights suggesting "a cooperative attack on the problems that beset the under-privileged"; the project was ignored. Lindsay's New York benefited from a still powerful economy which provided many jobs for its residents. In fact in 1969 the City's unemployment figures were lower than any major American City except Dallas. When in the spring of 1969 the Mayor proposed an operating expense budget of $6.1 billion, a figure which had tripled in only a decade, no one was shocked. The *Times*, a staunch Lindsay supporter, commented that it was a budget of "wisdom and equity" and informed its readers that the administration had consistently "applied the City's resources with skill and sound discretion." The role of the metropolis as the urban flagship of the nation remained unchallengable.

Yet to Lindsay's critics, and they were legion, the praise of the *Times* rang hollow. Some charged that he had purchased racial calm by offering to New York's minorities the most generous welfare benefits available anywhere in the nation. Others held that he was mindlessly expanding the public payroll to offset the decline in private job creation. Almost all his detractors agreed that the Mayor had cravenly agreed to extortionate labor settlements with militant City workers so as to avoid a repetition of the calamity of January 1966. The costs were not merely in salary gains but in pension obligations as well. In 1966 policemen were granted full pay pensions after 35 years of service and firemen received equal treatment the next year. Sanitation workers won 20-year half pay pensions in 1967, as did transit workers in 1968. Board of Education, City University, and other employee unions were quick to follow, and New York even agreed to "sweeten" some contracts by paying a larger percentage of pension costs. How, asked Lindsay's opponents, could New York hope to pay its bills in the future when its high taxes quickened business and white flight? There was little doubt that such an exodus was underway as New York became the "Land of Taxes." "Money providers" were leaving while service demands on City resources were constantly increasing, especially from a welfare population about to reach 1,000,000 persons. Rationality counseled caution! Yet despite all warnings, the City persevered in its policies and its Mayor walked tall.

In retrospect, the election year of 1969 represents a watershed in New York history; it was the last good economic year the City was to enjoy for a decade. Employment reached the astronomic figure of 3,884,000 citizens, establishing a municipal record which may never be broken. The census of 1970 showed that New York grew only 1.5 percent in a decade to its peak population level of 7,895,563; a precipitous fall was to be the demographic reality of the 1970s. But beyond mere statistics of jobs and people, the metropolis experienced a series of emotional highs and lows which marked the year as memorable indeed.

Certainly the year began with a definite ego trip for a City buffeted by winter winds. On January 12, an underrated but confident New York Jets football team led by brash Joe Namath ambushed the mighty Baltimore Colts and gave the City its first and only Super Bowl victory. The celebrations were hardly concluded, however, when in February a sudden snowstorm turned the economic hub of the nation into a wasteland. Manhattan was rapidly excavated but the outer boroughs were ignored for up to a week. City Hall's seeming indifference to their plight left a residue of anger at Lindsay among many citizens which he never was able to thaw. The Mayor, who was about to publish a book extolling his achievements and arguing that New York City must lead the nation to an urban renaissance, suddenly became "only a politician" who could not even keep the streets clear. Beyond this dissatisfaction, however, the Mayor was in deep political trouble within the Republican party. He was perceived as being interested only in minority voters and the "beautiful people" of the East Side of Manhattan, not in traditional Republican principles. Many believed he had "given away" the City. Moreover, the seemingly endless series of strikes and confrontations which had marked his first term had raised up a bevy of Democrats anxious to oppose him. Antipathy toward all officialdom was in the air as the nation entered its fifth year of heavy fighting in Vietnam. Though Lindsay opposed that war, he became suspect simply because he represented authority. Under his aegis welfare costs had risen beyond $1.7 billion and were being dispensed to a clientele as large as the population of Baltimore. In the spring of that discontented year, "Lindsay Must Go" signs proliferated like rabbits across a City which seemed to have lost faith in his style and perhaps also in its own future.

It came as no surprise to knowledgeable New Yorkers that Lindsay was routed in July's Republican Primary by a respected conservative state senator named John Marchi. Less predictable but still not unexpected was the fierce, five-way Democratic dogfight which resulted in victory for Mario Procaccino, an almost unknown and somewhat inept clubhouse politician. What was shocking was that Lindsay displayed no intention of quitting the race and had arranged surprises of his own. The Mayor not only obtained the nomination of the Liberal party but also managed to have his name appear on the ballot as an Independent. Both Marchi (Republican-Conservative) and Procaccino (Democratic-Nonpartisan) obtained two ballot lines, but in the campaign they competed viciously for essentially the same groups of conservative and ethnic voters. Neither appealed greatly for the support of the minority-poor and Manhattan-based liberal blocs which were the staples of Lindsay's power. Moreover, it was a tested truism that no one could ever win in New York City by calling for vigorous economy, and certainly Lindsay promised to maintain his activism on behalf of the least successful residents of the metropolis. In the end, the Fusion-Liberal coalition of 1965 had just enough power to successfully coalesce one last time; John Vliet Lindsay was returned to office with only 42 percent of the vote.

Many pundits asserted that Lindsay's triumph was a political wonder but the average New Yorker understood that a far more profound miracle had occurred a month earlier. In October 1969 the formerly hapless New York Mets had won the World's Championship of baseball. Many believed that the euphoria of seeing a perennial last-place team transform itself into champions had been Lindsay's greatest asset in the last days of the campaign. That argument was unquantifiable of course, but there was little doubt that Lindsay's triumph continued the process of declining party influence. Democrats, with 70 percent of the registration, had proven incapable of uniting behind their candidate and the remnants of their once-vaunted organization could not deliver the vote for the slate. Despite all the campaign hoopla, voters displayed a fine apathy toward all candidates; the Democratic vote was the lowest since the O'Brien disaster of 1933 while the Republican total hit a 40-year low. Despite all the fire and brimstone, it seemed that citizen indifference was as responsible for Lindsay's second term as were his real accomplishments and the New York Mets. The continued decline of party loyalty was again proven on August 10, 1971 when the Mayor announced that he was leaving the Republican party and becoming a Democrat.

During his second term, Lindsay worked hard to obtain administrative control of the monstrous corporation called New York City. There had always been two aspects to his mayoralty, one being the job itself and the other the far more glamorous role of spokesman for urban America. During his second term, the Mayor was to prove himself a more capable administrator than previously. He continued with his grand scheme of consolidating the myriad of City managerial agencies into ten superunits as well as voicing with ever greater urgency his conviction that the upper levels of the federal structure must do more for America's urban centers. A major package was lifted from his burden when Albany created a Metropolitan Transit Association (1969) to deal with subway and commuter problems. Nevertheless, Lindsay was able to build only a mixed record as an administrator; his jumble of City agencies never effectively spent even the moneys they received. For example, it took 10 City agencies up to 71 steps in order to purchase a single sanitation truck. The bureacracy moved so slowly that in 1969 the City failed to spend $65,000,000 received from the federal Model Cities program, while in fiscal 1970 the City was to lose $16,000,000 in state education aid because of its failure to disperse previous funds. Such administrative failures became rarer in the course of Lindsay's second term but they were never completely eliminated.

Perhaps the greatest shortfall of Lindsay's term was an inability to cope with the City's perennial housing crisis. In 1965 the Mayor had promised to build 160,000 low-and moderate-income housing units by 1970 to meet the growing demand. Private builders had simply opted out of constructing any housing except for the well-to-do and thus it fell to the City, with state and federal support, to fill the residential gap. It failed miserably to do so. Only 34,167 units were initiated over a five-year-period, 8,920 of which were low income apartments. In the same period of time, some 200,000 existent units in sound buildings, were either abandoned by their owners or fell prey to fire or vandalism. Arson for insurance profit suddenly became one of the most prevalent crimes in the City and in the early 1970s it would transform the South Bronx, already depressed and decrepit, into a national symbol of urban decay. Although the metropolis already owned 189 housing projects and although its Housing Commission argued vehemently that they were generally well run and less crime ridden than other areas of the City, not even their presence could compensate for the continued attrition of precious residential stock. Zoning changes, the introduction of "scatter site" projects, and the integration of retail and recreational facilities into new construction were all tried but nothing seemed to arrest the juggernaut of decay. Betweeen 1970 and 1975 the South Bronx alone lost 16 percent of all its housing (43,000 apartments) as an estimated four square blocks were lost each week to physical decay and to fires. Faced with such a future, the white middle class—already leaving in great numbers—began an accelerated exodus from the City. White Bronxites fled northward in droves though many others ended in the massive development of the East Bronx's Co-op City which began to fill its 35 apartment towers in December 1969. Other segments of the white middle class simply decided to leave New York completely.

It was not only in New York that the movement toward suburbia was apparent, although it was there that its effects became most apparent. Statistics proved that practically all the growth in urban America during the 1960s took place not in center cities but in suburban enclaves. The commuter's life-style was pioneered by New York and its bedroom communities, but in the early 1970s a new and potentially disastrous trend became apparent. Not only were City residents fleeing but they now appeared to be carrying their jobs with them as they traveled. Figures indicated that the number of commuters from Westchester to Manhattan had risen 50 percent since 1950, but the percentage of New Yorkers traveling northward to jobs had risen an amazing 500 percent in the same 20 years. By 1971, 115,000 Westchester residents were coming south each day but an almost identical number of City residents went north. The metropolis in 1970 still held 125 headquarter operations among the nations Fortune 500 companies, but in that year six others decided to leave the City. Discontent with the atmosphere of New York—its crime, its dirt, its taxes—seemed common in executive suites and resulted in a corporate exodus which was to reduce headquarter operations to only 94 by 1975. Most important for the City economy was the fact that after a corporate relocation, often to Connecticut, Westchester, or New Jersey, 80–100 percent of all executives retained their positions as opposed to only 10–25 percent of all lower level workers. Perhaps the unkindest cut of all was the loss of an institution identified with the City; in 1972 the New York Football Giants decided they preferred Hackensack, New Jersey, as a home rather than remaining in their Bronx stadium. The Brooklyn Dodgers and the New York Giants baseball teams had gone to California in 1958, and now the beloved Giants ran to a swamp in Jersey. Perhaps corporate America knew something?

Undoubtedly, a major reason for the hemorrhage of corporate executives was the soothing attractiveness of suburban living as opposed to the unceasing hustle, excitement, and danger of the

City. But the flow had objective causes as well. Costs of doing business in Manhattan constantly increased. In 1970 transit fares rose again while the sales tax increased to 7 percent of all purchases. Although City employment was at an all-time high, the quality of the work force was perceived to have deteriorated and the unending burden of supporting over one million welfare clients lay heavy on the back of all City taxpayers. Despite an operating budget beyond $6.6 billion, the delivery of City services seemed increasingly irregular and the creation of superagencies such as the Hospitals Corporation did not improve the situation. Moreover, crimes and fear of violence had become a pervasive reality of City life. Major racial violence had so far been averted in New York, but a riot at the Tombs prison in October 1970 indicated that it was never very far from the surface. Lindsay himself termed the Tombs hostage situation his most difficult moment. In all, the upper or middle-class white leaving the City had many arguments to justify his flight.

Essentially Lindsay's second term represented a constant struggle to provide his City with the services it demanded and required if it was to maintain itself. Yet the Mayor was forced to wage his battle with ever-decreasing resources. Revenues would continue to increase slowly and new expedients such as Off-Track Betting added millions to the City's coffers, but the accelerating costs rapidly outstripped such marginal increases. Between 1961 and 1975 the City debt was to almost triple while the costs of debt service rose beyond 500 percent. To a substantial degree the City suffered because of national forces beyond its control. The exchange of 1,600,000 whites for a similar number of minority residents from 1950 to 1970 was due to the mechanization of the farms, the availability of airline immigration, and the undoubted appeals of suburbia. Nevertheless migration altered the character of the City and led it to spend far more on welfare and health programs than it expected. Whether Lindsay compounded the difficulties he inherited with a Manhattan-centered tunnel vision as his critics charged will long be debated. But he presided as the effects of the transformation became ever more apparent. Certainly he was the center of the City's life and a stream of press releases, averaging almost two a day for eight years, told everyone of his efforts to cope with the developing crisis. But the obvious enthusiasm with which he approached his task proved inadequate to deal with welfare rolls of 1,100,000 clients, an accelerating decline of jobs, and the inexorably growing cost of funding New York's short-term debt.

Although assessments of Lindsay's two terms differ widely dependent upon partisanship, he certainly must be ranked as one of the master builders of modern New York. His accomplishments in that field rankled Robert Moses who became one of Lindsay's harshest critics and was quoted as saying, "If you elect a matinee idol as Mayor, you get a musical comedy administration." Lindsay was deeply interested in City planning and had the courage to insist that the special needs and desires of local groups be considered when building City-sponsored projects. An Urban Design Group was created within the City Planning Commission and consulted with 62 Community boards while bringing to completion scores of police and fire stations, playgrounds, pools, and libraries. Under Lindsay, the metropolis was deeply involved in Lyndon Johnson's Model Cities and would construct the first residential units to emerge from that program. Special offices to plan and develop Midtown and Lower Manhattan, Jamaica, Downtown Brooklyn, Staten Island, and Fordham Road in the Bronx were organized to develop projects within the spirit of a new Master Plan (1969). As a result of the "incentive zoning" initiated under Lindsay, 17 skyscrapers were added to the skyline of New York during 1970 alone.

The climax of this extraordinary construction boom occurred in 1972 when the 110-story "Twin Towers" of the World Trade Center (WTC), a project launched in 1966 by the Port Authority, were finally opened. Designed by Minoru Yamasaki and Emery Roth Associates, these 209-foot squares contained over 9,000,000 square feet of office space and were expected to spur a major revitalization of Lower Manhattan. They would serve as a center for the port's international trading community and their sponsors dismissed charges that the complex displaced too many small businesses and would be unrentable. Advocates of the WTC megastructure emphasized its sheer size and magnificent engineering; the buildings had their own zip code, consumed daily the electricity of Schenectady, and hosted 50,000 workers and 80,000 visitors each day. Although condemned by some critics as "General Motors Gothic" with high lobbies of "pure schmaltz," the public readily accepted the structures. They rapidly became a fixture of downtown activity and an integral part of the world's most famous skyline. A decade later the trade complex included 6 buildings while the excavated earth from the project had been used to create 23.5 acres of new landfill on which the long-planned Battery Park City was being constructed.

Yet critics of the WTC were proven correct in a fundamental sense; the trade center turned out to be a financial white elephant which never became attractive to private renters. Perhaps it was the fact that the surge of new City construction completed in the Lindsay years came on line just as the mammoth complex opened, or perhaps it was only a matter of location. In any event, the only long-term occupants of the buildings turned out to be the Port Authority itself and the State of New York. As early as 1978 Governor Hugh Carey of the Empire State began to suggest that the complex be sold into private hands, a sale that would require the approval of New Jersey and perhaps even Port Authority bondholders. If such a sale could be negotiated, and it seemed a growing possibility by 1983, the new ownership would contribute many more millions in taxes to New York City than does the Port Authority. In such a case, the WTC might become finally more than a valued part of the skyline. It could be a vital component in keeping the metropolis of the 1980s economically viable.

As the Lindsay years drew to a close, there was little public or private recognition that New York was about to be traumatized by a fiscal nightmare. New York had been providing the widest possible spectrum of services to its citizenry for almost twenty years and the bills were about to come due. Lindsay left office in 1973 before the bankruptcy storm broke, but as he concluded eight years in the mayoralty his remarks contained not a hint that he saw crisis ahead. An accounting of his stewardship was issued listing vast gains in seventeen separate areas. The Mayor claimed that he was "turning over the government . . . in the best shape it has ever been." In an interview with editors of the New York *Times*, Lindsay proudly cited substantial gains in worker productivity, City accountability, and improved management techniques. He professed himself glad to have exchanged his seat in the House of Representatives for the mayoralty; the experience had afforded him the "best eight years of my life." That he himself believed the litany of accomplishment seems certain. Yet that so gifted a leader could be so blind to the long-range results of his fiscal profligacy stands as a remarkable testimony to the lack of technical skill possessed by many modern politicians.

A more realistic accounting would have begun with the fact that New York City had never recovered from the recession of 1969. Job erosion had continued as had white flight, and in Lindsay's second term a staggering quarter million jobs had vanished. Many of these lost positions were due in large part to the construction boom of which the metropolis was so proud; the World Trade Center alone was responsible for the virtual decimation of thriving small print shops. Because of inflation revenues for City use had continued to rise under Lindsay, but the cost of providing and upgrading social services to an ever more demanding population was outstripping revenue by at least nine percent each year. Despite this gap new commitments were constantly added to the budget; in 1970 for example a policy of Open Admission to the City University for all high school graduates was initiated a full five years before originally planned. Lindsay worked closely with his comptroller, Abraham Beame, and together they would announce each year that the City had somehow managed once again to achieve budgetary balance. It would be fruitless to rehearse even one of these yearly sagas for they all blended into a farce. "Inventive accounting" was the order of the day and precarious stability was achieved only by issuing ever greater amounts of short term debt. During the 1965–73 period the size of the metropolitan operating budget quadrupled; pay increases for a City labor force of 300,000 surpassed the cost of living while pension benefits trebled in size though they remained largely unfunded. In all, the outstanding debt of the City was over $8 billion. Facts such as these were ignored by Lindsay and indeed by most New Yorkers. Despite a changed population, capital flight, and an ever-increasing agenda of services, it was somehow assumed that the good times would last forever.

What is perhaps most striking was that the dismal fiscal facts were equally ignored by the man who was soon to be Lindsay's successor, Comptroller Abraham Beame. During June of 1973, when it was obvious that Lindsay would not seek reelection and when Beame's path to Gracie Mansion seemed assured, the two leaders had worked together to create an Expense Budget for 1973–74. The document that emerged from those deliberations was jointly fashioned and it was to elect Beame. Unfortunately, it was also filled with budgetary "gimmicks" fashioned specifically to obscure the City's fiscal plight. Among its innovations were placement of $564,000,000 of operating expenses in the capital budget; a rollover of $308,000,000 in 1971 notes; the virtual draining of the "rainy day" fund; and simply inventing $100,000,000 in "special" revenues to be uncovered by the comptroller. Yet despite all such expedients, the budget still contained an official deficit of $211,000,000 which the two smiling leaders called upon the state legislature to close. Two years later, as the City struggled to survive insolvency, Beame would claim that Lindsay left him with a $1.5 billion budget gap but there was little hint of such a chasm in 1973, the last summer of fiscal "business as usual." As comptroller, Beame surely understood the dangers of excessive short-term borrowing but he nevertheless certified that City revenues met expenditures for each of the last four Lindsay budgets. In fact, he accepted the Democratic nomination and ran as the man who "knows the buck!"

To many observers Abraham Beame is a tragic figure who played a pathetic role in the great New York fiscal crisis. Yet from another perspective he represented the marvelous opportunities for growth and advancement which New York traditionally had offered to the "storm tossed" of the world. Beame's family were immigrants from Poland. His father found employment as a paper cutter and matured in the socialistic tumult of the Lower East Side. As a child young Abe had been taken to many rousing meetings of the faithful but he himself decided that education and politics provided a more promising road to success. The young man graduated from City College and worked faithfully within Brooklyn's Democratic machine for decades. In the 1960s he served as comptroller only to be defeated by Lindsay for the mayoralty. Yet in 1973 persistence had been rewarded and Beame was positioned to win the Democratic nomination. Given his service, his loyalty, and his competence as well as the fact that he would be the first Jewish Mayor of the City of New York, the Democrats willingly turned to him. Beame's critics believed he was and always would be a hack without abilities or ideas but perhaps the voters believed in miraculous transformations. Had not the amazing Mets won another National League pennant that fall? Might not Beame be capable of giving the metropolis constructive leadership? In any case, the Democratic tide once again drowned Republican candidate John Marchi and on November 6, 1973 Abe Beame was elected New York's one hundred fourth Mayor. It had to be the crowning achievement of his life. Then in December 1973, even as Beame prepared to take his oath, a section of the West Side Highway collapsed under the weight of a repair truck loaded with asphalt; the entire length of roadway between the Battery and Forty-Sixth Street had to be closed. Whether the accident was due to age or improper maintenance is irrelevant. The rain of concrete which closed a major City artery was only the first harbinger of the disasters which were about to fall on the City of New York.

Beame took office in January 1974, a year featuring economic stagflation and the resignation of a President. With American society in the throes of a crisis, it was inevitable that New York would be affected greatly particularly since it had not yet recovered from the previous Nixon recession during 1969–70. Yet it seemed inconceivable that the economic sands of time were running out for a City which earned 10 percent of all the money made in America and which still was headquarters to 96 of the Fortune 500 corporations. New York after all had 6 of the 10 largest American banks, 4 of our biggest 6 insurance corporations, 9 of the 10 most prosperous advertising agencies, and a full third of the nation's most prestigious law firms. The latest tally reported that the City had 28,000 restaurants, 1,000 foreign corporations, about 500 galleries, a similar number of Off and Off-Off Broadway theaters, 61 museums, and 30 major department stores. It was totally beyond the power of reason to expect such a amalgamation of power and talent to collapse.

These institutions and businesses did not collapse of course but their host City did. The real disease after all was not in its supporting mechanisms but rather in the urban heartbeat as it was heard by accountants. With a population greater than that of Sweden and a budget virtually equal to that of India, the metropolis had provided more for its citizens in education, medical care, and social services than did any American city or most nations. New York spent more than twice as much per capita on its people than did any other city. The operating expenses of programs were far too often simply shifted into capital bugetary accounts; by 1975 about half that budget was being used to finance current expenditures. What could not be hidden, was financed by short-term revenue anticipation notes. By the early 1970s the City was regularly unable to repay all such outstanding notes at the end of its fiscal year in June. For about a decade it had simply rolled over its debt and borrowed more to pay current expenses as well as the accumulating interest on its previous notes. The practice was inherently destructive, but as long as no one complained and as long as the banks were willing to accept the City's IOU's, the system worked magnificently. After all, the more debt the City contracted the more business it represented for the banks themselves. Even when New York was marketing 30 percent of all the short-term paper being sold in the nation apparently no one was unduly concerned. A short-term City debt of $4.5 billion clearly did not seem to bother Abe Beame as he settled in for what he confidently believed would be the greatest four years of his life.

By May of 1974, however, the wages of fiscal sin began to appear. New York State declared that the City was in an "unprecedented fiscal crisis" and Governor Malcolm Wilson, who was running hard for reelection, responded by approving a special bill which gave the metropolis the right to borrow even further. In July, City Comptroller Harrison Goldin was forced to pay interest charges of 8.586 percent in order to market one-year City notes, and the City's long-term bonds yielded to investors an unprecedented 7.9 percent. When Goldin issued his Annual Report in November, it contained the dire warning that unless the City lessened its borrowing the comptroller's office might not be able to market future bonds. On November 8, the Mayor joined the dismal chorus by conceding that his budget for fiscal 1975, which had gone into effect only months earlier, was already $430,000,000 in the red. To rectify this Beame disclosed that several thousand City employees would have to be fired in phased stages. By December, the beleaguered City had to pay an "outrageous" interest rate of 9.479 percent in order to market a $500,000,000 short-term loan; it had not had a single taker for a smaller issue in October. Finally, the state-funded Urban Development Corporation (UDC) collapsed that winter and brought the credit rating of the state into question as well.

If there was any redeeming quality found in the events of 1974 it was the key role that Beame played in the party maneuvering which allowed Hugh Carey to become the Democratic nominee for Governor of the Empire State. A former member of the House of

Representatives from Brooklyn, Carey was elected in November 1974, in large part by an outpouring of New York City votes. In retrospect the survival of New York, if it can be attributed to any individual, certainly can be claimed by Carey. His judicious and compassionate concern for the metropolis was to prove its surest bulwark for the next several years. Even as he assumed office, the new Governor was forced to deal with the threat to state credit which the default of the UDC posed. He did so quickly and effectively. However, the drama at Albany also had the disquieting effect of focusing the minds and thence the wallets of investors southward where an infinitely worse fiscal disaster appeared to be imminent.

In a decade the expense budget of New York had tripled; the total debt exceeded $13 billion, and the 1975–76 estimate for debt service alone was beyond $2.3 billion. A horrified investment community began to withdraw its support, and an abandoned City was to need all the guidance and leadership it could find. When Beame defaulted in this regard, Hugh Carey would almost by default take the point position.

On February 27, 1975 lawyers for a banking syndicate considering upcoming City bond issues asked to examine the municipal books in light of the recent UDC default (February 25). They professed themselves shocked at what was discovered, even though it could hardly have been a surprise to the banks they represented. As word of irregularities and shortfalls swept the investment world, the City failed to obtain any purchasers for its pending note issues; moreover, the value of its outstanding bonds plummetted to two thirds of face value. Standard and Poor's proved indecently quick to suspend the *A* credit rating of the metropolis in April and during that month only a state-supplied emergency loan of $400,000,000 kept the City solvent. Beame's contribution to this first salvage operation was to constantly reiterate his faith in New York and to cancel the phased layoffs he had ordered in 1974. He seemed to wander in uncertainty while searching desperately for someone to blame. He did not seem to know or care if his afflictor was Washington, Albany, the banks, the unions, Lindsay, or God; as long as the culprit was not Abe Beame! On May 29 he even decided the newspapers were to blame for creating an "atmosphere of doubt and uncertainty" by reporting the fiscal news. Still, with the touching faith of a child, Beame would assert on July 7 that "the crisis is behind us!" Rarely had a political man been so out of touch with reality. In truth the affairs of New York City were in the process of being taken away from Beame and for the rest of his term he would be only a figurehead.

The key institutions which shepherded New York through its extended crisis were created by Governor Carey and the state legislature; they were the Municipal Assistance Corporation (MAC), irreverently known as Big Mac, and the Emergency Financial Control Board. In May, President Gerald Ford had made it clear that the nation's greatest urban center could expect no special aid from Washington. Once again that month, an advance of revenue sharing funds from Albany, this time a transfusion of $200,000,000, allowed the City to pay its current expenses. Nevertheless, the City University had to be closed temporarily and its faculty went briefly unpaid along with other workers as New York tottered on the edge of formal bankruptcy. In Albany, late night negotiations and frantic maneuvering took place because the public bond market had completely spurned all New York City offerings just as millions of dollars worth of municipal obligations were coming due. Finally, early in the morning of June 10, the legislature agreed on the creation of the Municipal Assistance Corporation, an agency expressly designed to alleviate the immediate cash flow crisis by refinancing New York's short-term debt. Big Mac would also oversee the long-range borrowing policies of the City. Revenues raised by City sales and stock transfer taxes were specifically earmarked to provide Big Mac with an initial billion dollars. The state asserted its "moral obligation" to protect any investors who purchased MAC bonds against their default, and a billion-dollar reserve fund in Albany backed this promise. Despite unrelenting protests from Beame, the control of both current City revenues and its fiscal future had been given to a state-created body. "Home rule" temporarily ceased as state, City, bank, and union officials worked desperately to save New York.

The Mayor was not only not in charge but also he was ignored. In the terrible weeks that followed he would defiantly assert that never would he impose a wage freeze on municipal workers yet he would do so. After claiming that a budget ceiling was impossible, he would agree to one. He would be forced to sacrifice his friend, the First Deputy Mayor, to the fiscal watchdogs. Transit fares increased to half a dollar, CUNY was informed of harsh cuts, and services were reduced everywhere. The City was told it would have to adopt new accounting procedures and to gradually excise operating funds from its capital budget. Many workers suddenly realized they were about to lose their jobs and policemen responded viciously by distributing pamphlets urging tourists not to come to "Fear City" or to walk the streets after 6:00 p.m. Not to be outdone, sanitation workers staged a wildcat strike which allowed 58,000 tons of garbage to accumulate on the streets and even firemen protested with a "sick-in." By July 25 even the City Council, a kind of long-running joke, was roused from its lethargy to recognize that the situation was indeed serious; it responded mightily by raising the round-trip fare on the Staten Island Ferry from ten cents to a quarter. At such times it seemed as if the City was only one step from anarchy or madness.

Big Mac sold a billion dollars worth of new bonds in June and prevented default but the constant tensions between itself and the Beame administration made a second sale unlikely. Only on August 6, after the Mayor agreed to a three-year budgetary plan including absolute spending ceilings, was Big Mac able to market another $960,000,000 which maintained solvency. The August package was made possible only because of another advance from Governor Carey, and the timely participation of several City employee pension funds. It was the "monthly miracle," said MAC's chief financial negotiator Felix Rohatyn, but it was undermined almost immediately. Accountants studying the City ledgers discovered that the looming budget deficit for 1975–76 was $2.8 to $3.3 billion rather than Beame's stated figure of $641,000,000. As it became increasingly obvious that the Mayor lacked the political will to make harsh political decisions, investors shunned further MAC bonds. It appeared certain that the City must soon default.

Governor Carey now openly intervened and convinced the legislature to take a last "gamble," one ultimate "major effort to save a City and secure a state." On the evening of September 9 a $2.3 billion aid bill was passed in Albany which not only set harsh financial curbs on the City but also gave control of all monetary decisions to a state-appointed Emergency Financial Control Board (EFCB) whose chairman was to be the Governor himself. As of November 1, all City revenues would go to the board which would disperse them for three years in accordance with an overall financial plan. A special state deputy controller for New York City would be named to monitor the City's compliance with this Draconian regime. The existing municipal wage freeze was incorporated into state law and any further employee contracts could take effect only after approval by the EFCB. Only the harshest measures, affirmed Carey, would save the City, the state, and the nation itself from "inestimable harm for an indefinite time." The control board included Mayor Beame as one of its members but the Governor dominated its proceedings; the EFCB legislation completed the process which turned New York's Mayor into a figurehead.

Despite the chaos in New York and the inevitable effect its collapse would have on the nation, there was an almost surrealistic unconcern in Washington. Treasury Secretary William Simon suggested that a New York City default would cause only "moderate and relatively short-lived disruption" while the President himself disclaimed all interest in the proceedings. Yet on October 2 the unending crisis caused Moody's Investor Service to downgrade both New York State and City securities, as well as to totally withdraw its ratings for other state agency bonds. Analysts estimated that a hundred banks across the nation might fail after a New York default and all other states and cities were themselves experiencing the ripple effects of the crisis; they were being forced to pay higher interest rates in order to market their own securities. A delegation of fifteen mayors visited President Ford to warn him of a "domino effect" should the "Big Apple" fall and West German Chancellor Helmut Schmidt said the crisis clearly would disturb financial centers such as Zurich and Frankfurt. Vice-President Nelson Rockefeller, who as Governor had approved much of the shoddy financing, now argued that the threat of default was causing the value of the dollar to decline on international exchanges. On October 18, "Rocky" became the first administration official to support a direct federal aid or loan guarantee program for New York! Had anyone doubted the enormous importance of the metropolis in both national and world markets, the virtually unanimous chorus of gloom voiced in September and October should have convinced them. *Business Week* summed it up on October 13; "New York is like a disease that is contaminating all. . . . The City has taken the state down with it, and if the state goes, others will follow." The October 20 edition of *Time* featured a cover showing a bedraggled Beame holding a tin cup and asking, "Brother can you spare $4 billion?"

The crisis seemed to intensify in October. On October 17 the City's cash needs totalled $477,000,000 but it had only $34,000,000 in all its current accounts. That afternoon New York was only 53 minutes from defaulting on its obligations when an eleventh-hour infusion of cash from teacher pension funds completed yet another complex financial package. Offices stayed open late into the evening so that the City could redeem $453,100,000 of its notes as they were presented. MAC Chairman Felix Rohatyn lamented that "the dikes are crumbling and we are running out of fingers." Governor Carey cabled President Ford asking that he recognize New York as "part of the country." The EFCB on October 20 gave its final approval to a three-year City austerity plan but ordered Beame to further reduce his capital-spending projections for that period. Slowly and reluctantly Congress moved to consider the City's plight but the movement seemed to halt when the President, on October 29, vowed to veto any federal "bailout." Ford suggested that Congress adjust existing bankruptcy statutes so that there could be an "orderly reorganization" of the City's obligations after it defaulted. He took the occasion to specifically criticize the high wages and pensions of City workers, CUNY, the eighteen-unit municipal hospital system, and the fact that there were ineligible recipients on the welfare rolls. The President's unyielding National Press Club address led the *Daily News* to headline its next edition, "Ford to City, Drop Dead." Carey said the City would lapse into bankruptcy by December 1 and bitterly remarked that "it isn't fair when the President . . . kicks the people of . . . New York in the groin." October 1975 was perhaps the first time in two centuries that the metropolis on the Hudson was clearly an underdog.

Although many in Washington embraced Ford's "no bailout" position, the weight of informed opinion and the wisdom of necessity clearly indicated that some federal action was needed. On November 1, the Joint Economic Committee of Congress declared that a default would add 300,000 workers to the jobless rolls and reduce America's real GNP by a full percentage point. The results of three separate polls taken after Ford's speech all disagreed with his hard line; respondents believed the entire nation would suffer. Since 29,000 City workers had already been dismissed by the end of October and the millions of subway riders were paying higher fares, no one could legitimately argue that the City was not beginning to reform. Gradually, the administration eased its intransigence. On November 26 the President asked Congress to consider a measure granting $2.3 billion in direct federal loan guarantees to New York on a "seasonable basis." Harsh repayment conditions would be exacted and there would be "no cost" to taxpayers because all outstanding loans from one year would have to be repaid before new moneys became available. Indeed, in the final analysis the U.S. Treasury made millions on the loans.

Several additional measures orchestrated by Governor Carey preceded the final federal turnabout. On November 14, the legislature passed a controversial debt moratorium procedure which enabled the City to postpone repayment of up to $1.6 billion of its short-term notes. Under its aegis the City was permitted to suspend paying the principle on these issues for three years; bondholders were offered the option of receiving ten-year 8-percent Big Mac bonds or holding their existent notes at 6 percent. In either case, they would not be permitted to regain their principal. In point of fact this was default though no one admitted it! Carey's second great achievement was to put in place a $200,000,000 tax package on the eve of Ford's November 26 address. This measure brought to completion an elaborate $6.6 billion three-year financing program which once again drew on the resources of municipal pension systems. In addition, the City's largest financial institutions agreed to extend the maturity dates of their notes at a lower rate of interest. It thus became inevitable that Congress approved and Ford signed on December 9 a seasonal loan guarantee program for New York City. After months of crisis the solvency of the City was saved. All that remained to be done was to implement the budget cuts and suffer.

The fiscal crisis abated temporarily after a state court decision upheld the moratorium in December 1975, but it was by no means over. After a year of appeals, lawyers for the Flushing National Bank convinced New York's Court of Appeals that the moratorium indeed was unconstitutional and the City had to find a quick billion dollars early in 1977. However, after the trauma of 1975 such an operation was relatively simple because, as Mayor Beame said, "We looked in every pocket." More serious was the continued deterioration of the City economy. From December 1974 to December 1975 another 143,000 jobs had been lost in New York and important political leaders still argued publicly that the City should officially default rather than inflict continued sacrifice upon its citizenry. Their counsel was ignored.

As the course so painfully established in 1975 remained steady, there were some glimmers of hope amid the debris. Statistics showed that in 1974 the long-neglected Port of New York handled more long tons of cargo than in any year since 1941. While long-needed modernization and containerization facilities were rapidly being completed, the vast harbor still remained America's busiest port with about 600 ship clearings per month. Despite the constant attrition of middle-class families of all races, the City in 1975 still had 172,000 taxpaying business enterprises of all types. And the resilience of the populace even in the face of reduced services was amazing. Up to 10,000 block associations were reported to exist during the bleak 1970s and community spirit and pride began to resuscitate areas as disparate as Little Italy and Soho in Manhattan, Belmont in the Bronx, Long Island City and Astoria in Queens, and Park Slope in Brooklyn. A renewed sense of appreciation for the past glories of the City led to a preservationist spirit which achieved the creation of Special Historical Districts which today number 42. At Harlem River Houses, the first federally financed and built public housing in Manhattan (1937), tenant groups in October 1975 were successful in obtaining landmark designation from the Preservation Commission. Moreover, the office space glut of the early seventies gave signs of finally ending and plans for new construction suddenly began to be discussed. In small but important ways the City began to prove that its vitality had not yet been destroyed.

What seemed to be needed was a psychological revival after two years of trauma and this fittingly was provided by the Bicentennial of 1976. Although celebrations were held across the nation, the one image that seems to have been indelibly imprinted upon the national memory is the sight of the parade of "tall ships" through New York Harbor and up the Hudson River. The beauty of the modern skyline behind acres of sail brought home to the nation the enduring value and historical importance of the great metropolis. Specialists might note that a more important nautical fact was that the foreign trade of the port had increased by

9.46 percent in the fiscal year ending on June 30, but to Americans that was irrelevant and unknown. The real triumph was the surge of emotion caused by that magnificent procession on the Fourth of July. That spirit intensified in August when the City played host to the Democratic National Convention; up to 20,000 delegates and visitors were practically overwhelmed with attention. Moreover, the nomination of Jimmy Carter gave New York hope for the future because Abe Beame had been one of the first politicians to join his bandwagon. Tourists again began to flock to Manhattan and in 1976 they constituted the City's second largest industry as 834 conventions were held. And if that were not enough, the Yankees moved into their renovated stadium, a job which typically had been completed only after quadrupled costs. The team promptly won a pennant preparatory to winning World's championships in 1977 and 1978. Thus on many levels the turnabout had begun.

Early in 1977 the Big Mac bond issues that had saved the City were selling at a premium and the City successfully met the emergency created by the invalidation of the bond moratorium. Optimism was in the political air and, after the election of Jimmy Carter, anything seemed possible. Thus it was in March of 1977 during his State of the City speech that Abe Beame announced that he, as a "dynamic" leader, had decided to run for another term. He claimed to have made the "tough decisions" that saved New York. The incredulity with which this statement was greeted is difficult to imagine since even the most obtuse voter recognized that all those "tough" decisions had been forced upon a protesting Mayor. Beame pressed forward, however, and in April the EFCB approved his proposed $13.9 billion budget. It was not so much the size of the budget which was striking but rather that it was so pre-crisis in attitude. Everyone, it seemed, would benefit; proposed were higher municipal salaries, more capital construction, and an end to reduced services. Beame also promised to hold property taxes level for the next five years. Despite the budgetary largess, there was nonetheless a veritable stampede of Democrats anxious to oppose Beame. Yet, since the Mayor held the support of the remnants of the machine vote, it seemed possible he might be victorious in a crowded primary field. Perhaps no individual was as shocked by Beame's decision as was Hugh Carey but the Governor moved decisively to prevent a farcical renomination. Not only did Carey openly endorse his own candidate but also he decreed that the Democratic primary date should be pushed back to September. By that date, he was certain, a long-delayed SEC investigation into the causes of the New York crisis would be published. When the report was issued in August it laid much responsibility at the door of City officials who had not informed investors as to the decrepit reality of municipal securities. Beame's campaign people were outraged at the timing of the report and believed they had been sabotaged. The Mayor himself admitted he had lied but only to protect the City. Besides, since everyone in authority had perpetuated the illusion of solvency then no one really was guilty of fraud! The voters—aware that they were ruled from afar, were paying higher transit fares and tuition to send their children to CUNY, as well as receiving less service for more dollars—disagreed!

After a marvelously complex political season, the citizens of New York turned for leadership to the official nominee of the Democratic party—not Abe Beame but Edward Irving Koch, a Reform Democrat who boasted of being a "capital punishment liberal." Koch had won the party nomination with a no nonsense, abrasive, confrontational style which the voters found immensely attractive. Prior to his election he had demonstrated his independence when, during Jimmy Carter's excursion to view the devastation of the South Bronx, he had handed the President a letter protesting administration policies toward Israel. Victorious in a four-way race against Conservative, Liberal, and Republican candidates, Koch declared he intended to be a three-term Mayor and restore prosperity and social idealism to New York. His Inaugural Address voiced the faith of millions when he asserted that "New York is unique in the history of human kindness"; the Mayor argued that "New York is not a problem. New York is a stroke of genius. From its earliest days this City has been a lifeboat for the homeless, a leader for the hungry, a living library for the intellectually starved, a refuge not only for the oppressed but also for the creative." As leader of the greatest and most open City in the world Koch confessed its past errors, "but our mistakes have been those of the heart." Nevertheless he pledged to be tough enough to sustain the recovery process.

Recovery was indeed in the air in 1978. Labor statistics indicated that (after eight years of decline) New York did not experience a decrease in manufacturing jobs in 1977. Even more encouraging was the fact that the hemorrhage of jobs, after having drained almost 650,000 jobs away since 1969, had finally been cauterized. During the remainder of the decade there would be slight but nevertheless real gains in employment each year although they were largely confined to service areas. Cost-of-living indexes proved that the City was no longer the most expensive place to live in the United States; indeed it had dropped out of the top ten. Moreover, the massive influx of minorities seemed to have platformed while welfare rolls were reduced to 907,126 in June with more effective management of the system. The previous inventory of surplus office space had been eliminated and a building boom seemed in the air. Symbolic of the new activity was the opening of the City Corp Building on Lexington Avenue just as Koch took office. Hugh Stebbins's 915-foot tower was designed to be a functioning element of its neighborhood on a 24-hour basis and was to prove a commercial, if not unanimously critical, success. Similar headquarter structures for ATT and IBM were also planned. Although the Citizens Budget Committee alerted Koch that budget problems still loomed, the Mayor clearly preferred to remember that more than 100 Manhattan real estate sites were worth over $10,000,000 and that no fewer than 16 Nobel Prize winners made New York their home. With such credentials, the commercial and cultural dominance of the metropolis was certainly secure.

Yet in the face of a brightening prognosis, the Koch administration's first priority remained money; a campaign to secure extended federal loan guarantees had to be waged and won. All participants in the rescue operation of 1975 had vehemently sworn that a one-time infusion of federal support would be sufficient to save New York but they all had dissembled. The City had successfully repaid all federal seasonal support and added $12,000,000 in interest, but its cash flow problems necessitated the continuation of Washington's assurances in order to soothe the nerves of an admittedly skittish investment community. In 1978, with a Democratic President in power, the task was easier to accomplish. After a three-month campaign, Jimmy Carter came to New York, where he signed legislation extending the Loan Guarantee program to 1982. While approving the bill, Carter praised the resilience and spirit of a City which has served as the nation's "Big Apple for more than two centuries."

Koch, who often displayed a tendency to euphoria, was already trumpeting that New York was experiencing a Renaissance. In the elation of financial success, he seemed temporarily to forget that he had been elected to put things right in the City, not continue business as usual. Welfare rolls might be the lowest they had been since 1969 but they still contained 907,126 clients. Thus in June, a new contract was negotiated with a coalition of City workers which provided for only a 4-percent pay raise, a meager one indeed considering the growing inflation rate. However the Mayor failed to obtain "give backs" as promised, and his claim that productivity gains would flow from higher wages was more wishful thinking than reality. Critics of Koch's cave-in abounded but they themselves seemed to forget that union investments and worker sacrifices had been of fundamental importance in saving the City. Perhaps it was too much to expect that either the unions or the Mayor for whom many of them voted could avoid the practices of the past. Far more difficult to justify was the sweet "catch-up" contract the Mayor agreed to in 1980.

As improving economic conditions increased City revenues and the retirement of short-term debt continued, a definite optimism became evident. In July 1979 the City began its fiscal year with a budget of only $12.8 billion, an increase of merely 7 percent since 1975. Fiscal monitors for Albany and the General Accounting Office (GAO) in Washington constantly chorused the need to "face up" to budgetary restrictions in order that 1982's spending might be balanced according to generally accepted accounting principles. A report issued by the Planning Commission virtually conceded that the New York of the future would be smaller but it was nevertheless proving immensely attractive to foreign-based corporations seeking secure havens for their money. Although the City's agony had reduced the number of headquarter operations to only 80 of the Fortune 500, the gap was now being filled by foreign corporations and banks anxious to take advantage of the dollar's weakness abroad. Moreover, business labor costs were suddenly discovered to be cheaper in New York while the improvement in harbor facilities meant more expeditious handling of greater cargo volume. Thus it was in July 1979, for the first time in four years, that a consortium of banks agreed to market $600,000,000 in City revenue anticipation notes without any participation by pension funds. It was a tentative step toward monetary responsibility. Budgets remained spare and the lack of money to rebuild a crumbling infrastructure continued for several more years, but New York once again was back in the fiscal game.

By early 1980 it was obvious that a corner had indeed been turned. Not even a rerun of the subway strike which had so damaged Lindsay could halt the City's revival. Mayor Koch stood up to an eleven-day stoppage in April 1980 with strength and good humor that infected the entire town. His query "How am I doin'?" was heard in every borough. The answer seemed to be "Fine," even though fares increased once again! New construction seemed to proliferate and no fewer than five major hotels were opened to cope with the flood of tourists and business visitors which had increased each year since 1975. Prices for a night's accommodations passed $100, but delegates such as those at the Democratic National Convention of 1980 did not seem to mind. The theater, always a fabulous invalid, was selling more tickets than ever at prices up to $40 and opera goers had their choice of two companies which challenged each other across the battlefield of a completed Lincoln Center. Welfare clientele continued to decline and the resident magicians at Big Mac had refinanced the bulk of the short-term debt. The City's life signs were all highly positive.

It was not that citizens were unaware of the fundamental changes. There seemed a weary acceptance that the future New York would have to be smaller, with fewer schools, hospitals, and corporations than it had boasted in the past. Although some marginal gains in factory jobs were reported at the end of the 1970s, it was evident that the metropolis could never regain its manufacturing primacy. A changing economy represents one of the most essential problems facing the City for it must somehow learn to utilize unskilled portions of its population. In the past, manufacturing jobs, the "smoke" and product creators which had fueled New York's greatness, had always been available to its aspiring poor. For the 1980s and beyond, the City would offer only a service-oriented economy requiring more educated and skilled workers. "Nitty gritty" labor had been essential to New York's past, but that kind of economy did not appear recapturable. One major exception to this thesis must be mentioned. The financial crisis obliged the City to ignore the pressing needs of refurbishing its often crumbling infrastructure; billions of dollars worth of rehabilitation was necessary for roads, bridges, sewers, and so forth. If the money can be found to create jobs for renewal, waste recycling, waterfront improvements, and industrial park projects, perhaps the unskilled can once again find in New York the ladder to success. By 1981 a construction boomlet had restored new office space construction to the level of 1975 and, ever more impressively, it was expected that 8,504,000 square feet of office space would be completed in 1982. The critical weakness of course was that the office space demanded workers of a type that New York did not yet have in great supply.

In addition to office construction, the reappearance of large-scale projects even despite national recessions in 1980 and 1981 gave promise for future growth. Vast residential complexes at Waterside on the East River and Battery Park on the Hudson were underway as was a new Convention Center whose completion was expected to revitalize the West Side of Manhattan. Zoning changes had been enacted to shunt new construction away from the overbuilt confines of Midtown toward the Upper West Side of Manhattan and to the outer boroughs as well. An industrial park opened in the blighted South Bronx while a complex program of $7 billion in mass transit aid was finally in place. The despised subway system, for all its smell and graffiti, remained one of the City's greatest potential strengths in delivering labor to employment; in 1982, however, the ridership fell below a billion for the first time since 1917. It was undeniable that even despite the long manufacturing slide, Manhattan remained the apparel center of the nation and 140,000 legal workers—there were thousands of underpaid illegal garment workers—daily created "union label" goods. The census of 1980 revealed that 3,298,400 persons held jobs in New York —the total rose by 57,000 in 1981—and that the City, despite all its woes, retained 11,321 manufacturing establishments. In fact, if combined with its Long Island "bedroom," the City would still be the largest manufacturing center in the nation.

The census graphically revealed what everyone understood to be true; the metropolis was shrinking rapidly. Although it still had more Jews than Tel Aviv, more Irish than Dublin, and more

Italians than Florence, the population total had been reduced by white flight and economic distress to only 7,071,030. The proportion of its minority residents had risen to almost half. There were 1,723,124 blacks and 1,405,957 Hispanic citizens in the City, a vast group that demanded not only social services but also a share of political power. It has been undoubtedly true that for the last twenty years Italian, WASP, and Jewish politicians, who agreed on little else, managed to keep New York's latest minorities from fully enjoying political power. Yet the lesson of New York's past is that the shifting tides of ethnicity and demography ultimately result in political change. Black and Puerto Rican candidates participated in the Democratic mayoral primary in 1977 and both groups believe that a political breakthrough will occur in the 1980s.

For the present, however, New York remains under the benevolent leadership of Ed Koch, a man who was deeply criticized in his first term for being insensitive to his City's minorities. Koch's reply was that he had been given a mandate to save New York and that he would do so regardless of who he had to oppose. New York could not be salvaged by "business as usual" politics and it was an unfortunate fact that services most affected by budgetary pruning were those most obvious to blacks and Hispanics. Only by the most narrow of margins did Koch avoid violence in 1979 when he attempted to close Sydenham Hospital, a facility that served a basically minority population. That action caused the resignations of Koch's black and Hispanic deputy mayors and caused him irreparable damage among the City's minority groups. When transit fares increased again, to 75 cents in July 1981, it was those same minorities who most felt the effect; that fares no longer were the Mayor's responsibility was irrelevant. Koch's first term, with all its statistical and budgetary gains, was a continuing exercise in cost control; New York struggled toward respectability on the backs of all its sacrificing citizenry.

But the payoff was tangible. In February 1981 the City sold $100,000,000 in short-term notes at less than 8.5 percent interest, its first sale based solely on future tax revenues since 1974. Then in the spring, the comptroller's office was able to market 20-year "investment grade" bonds for the first time since the crisis. Most impressive was the fact that fiscal year 1981 (July 1, 1980–

June 30, 1981) ended with a true budgetary surplus according to accepted accounting procedures. Critics of the Mayor, and there were many, argued that the accomplishment was tainted by tax revenues increased by inflation alone—but they did not deny that Koch had tamed the budget monster a full year before he was obligated to do so. Indeed by 1982 the unimaginable short-term debt of 1975—almost $6 billion—had been eliminated and by that June the City expected its second consecutive balanced budget. Early in 1982 the City requested its last federal loan guarantee and by the end of the year it would stand alone before the financial markets. Projections indicated that future fiscal troubles might still be encountered but, temporarily at least, acerbic and contentious Ed Koch, along with Big Mac and the EFCB, had made the "rotten apple" presentable again.

It was as a hard-nosed, exuberant yet thrifty miracle worker that Ed Koch announced for reelection in 1981. From the outset of the campaign he had little opposition and his budget proposals promised more cops, sanitation men, and teachers in order to rebuild lost services. On September 22, Koch scored a coup unprecedented in New York's turbulent political history—he won the nominations of both the Republican and Democratic organizations. On November 3, the man who had "promised God" to serve three terms as New York's Mayor was triumphantly reelected; 1977's underdog without a power base suddenly was the choice of practically everyone. In a sense his victory completed the process of party decline that had been evident for two decades. Middle-class white voters of both parties appreciated that he had supervised the procedures which had restored budget balance to the profligate metropolis. Minorities, who had borne a disproportionate share of the reductions in City services and payroll parings, voted for Koch because they had no real alternative but to trust his fundamental political philosophy. All New Yorkers seemed proud of the tremendous salvage job that the City had lived through and looked forward to a restoration of influence and prosperity. Future budgets might be questionable, but the Great Metropolis had been saved and seemed certain once again to be in the vanguard as America and its people searched for their destiny.

* * * * *

New York is the world's greatest City, a complex organism always in the process of disintegration and rebirth. In 1980 even after losing 900,000 residents in a decade, its population was still twice that of Chicago the perennial "second City." Across the globe other cities could achieve larger populations but none symbolize the spirit of their society as does New York. Despite the disasters of the 1970s its economic domination of the American scene remains unassailable. Its great port handles more than 50,000,000 long tons of cargo annually; retail sales in 1980 rose by 20 percent to $24.5 billion; Wall Street remains the symbol of world finance, and New York's 202 commercial and 82 savings banks have combined assets of $197.6 billion. The New York Clearinghouse for checks made 38.2 trillion transactions in 1980. And with a gross City product of over $100 billion annually the metropolis is bound to maintain its extraordinary commercial lead. Half of New York's present economy is tied to the emerging business of providing information and thus its domination is bound to increase. The metropolis is rapidly moving into a "post-industrial" position which will further enhance its role in world marketing. But as always the story of New York is more than commerce for it remains the national center for culture and education. Twenty-nine universities, 65 museums, and over 1,500 galleries, dance companies, and theaters maintain that supremacy today. Its population may be only 3.1 percent of America living on a tenth of 1 percent of its land, but the encomium of Steinbeck still rings true: "All of everything is concentrated here."

If the fiscal crisis can be said to have a silver lining, it may well be that its rigors regained for New York a competitive edge which it had lost. The high costs of doing business in Gotham became outrageous in the early 1970s and drove corporations away. After retrenchment and a series of tax cuts, a more favorable business climate has been created. The City remains a Mecca for the highly skilled and educated white-collar worker but its ability to employ the "redundant underclass" which populates its ghetto areas remains a major issue. Certainly the greatest challenge of the 1980s will be creating a decent life for these latest strivers, as earlier versions of New York had provided opportunity for so many others in the past. If the black and Puerto Rican migrations have come to an end, the hegiras of other Caribbean peoples and thousands of others from across the earth continue. Can the metropolis meet their needs with an infrastructure and service base neglected for six years? If the history we have studied is any guide, it would be foolish to underestimate New York. It will probably stand once again, bloodied but triumphant, as the most enduring symbol of what America is all about.

BRIEF BIBLIOGRAPHY

Abrams, Charles. *The City Is the Frontier.* New York, 1965.*
Auletta, Ken. *The Streets Were Paved With Gold.* New York, 1979.
Ferretti, Fred. *The Year the Big Apple Went Bust.* New York, 1976.
Gittel, Marilyn, and Berube, Maurice R. *Confrontation at Ocean-Hill-Brownsville.* New York, 1969.*
Gottmann, Jean. *Megalopolis: The Urbanized Northeastern Seaboard of the United States.* New York, 1961.*
Hall, Max, ed. *Made in New York.* Cambridge, Mass., 1959.
Lindsay, John V. *The City.* New York, 1969.*
Morris, Charles R. *The Cost of Good Intentions: New York City and the Liberal Experiment.* New York, 1980.
Newfield, Jack, and Du Brul, Paul. *The Abuse of Power: The Permanent Government and the Fall of New York.* New York, 1977.*
Ravitch, Diane. *The Great School Wars: New York City, 1805–1973.* New York, 1977.*
Vernon, Raymond. *Metropolis 1985.* Cambridge, Mass., 1960.
White, Norval, and Willensky, Elliot. *A.I.A. Guide to New York City.* rev. ed. New York, 1978.

*Paperback

General Works

In the study of urban history in general and that of New York City in particular, the secondary literature alone is so voluminous that no attempt will be made here to be inclusive. What follows is a sampling of the great variety of materials, old and new, that deal with the history and development of the Empire City.

Allen, Robert S., ed. *Our Fair City*. New York, 1947.

Atkins, George. *Health, Housing and Poverty in New York City, 1865–1898*. New York, 1947.

Bakeless, John. *Eyes of Discovery*. Philadelphia, 1950.

Beggs, Donald, ed. *New York; The City that Belongs to the World*. New York, 1956.

Bercovici, Konrad. *Around the World in New York*. New York, 1924.

Berger, Meyer. *The Eight Million*. New York, 1942.

———, and Busse, Fritz. *New York: City on Many Waters*. New York, 1955.

Blake, Nelson. *Water For the Cities*. Syracuse, 1956.

Booth, Mary L. *History of the City of New York*. 2 vols. New York, 1867.

Brace, Charles L. *The Dangerous Classes of New York*. New York, 1872.*

Brown, Henry C. *From Alley Pond to Rockefeller Center*. New York, 1936.

Churchill, Allen, *The Upper Crust: An Informal History of New York's Highest Society*. Englewood Cliffs, 1970.*

Costello, Augustine. *Our Firemen; A History of the New York Fire Department*. New York, 1887.

———. *Our Police Protectors; History of the New York Police*. New York, 1885.

Ellis, David M.; Frost, James A.; Syrett, Harold C.; and Carman, Henry J. *A Short History of New York State*. New York, 1957.

Federal Writers' Project of the Works Progress Administration in New York City. *New York City Guide*. New York, 1939.

Flick, Alexander, ed. *History of New York State*. 10 vols. New York, 1933-1937.

Griscom, John H. *Sanitary Condition of the Laboring Population of New York*. New York, 1845.

Hawkins, Stuart. *New York, New York*. New York, 1957.

Headly, Joel T. *The Great Riots of New York, 1712—1873*. New York, 1873.*

Janvier, Thomas A. *In Old New York*. New York, 1894.

Klein, Alexander. *The Empire City: A Treasury of New York*. New York, 1955.

Kouwenhoven, John. *Columbia Portrait of New York City*. New York, 1951.*

Lamb, Martha. *History of New York City*. 2 vols. New York, 1880.

Leonard, John W. *The HIstory of New York City*. New York, 1910.

Limpus, Lowell. *History of the New York Fire Department*. New York, 1940.

Lossing, Benson J. *History of New York City*. New York, 1884.

Maurice, A. B. *New York in Fiction*. New York, 1899.

Morris, Lloyd. *Incredible New York*. New York, 1951.

Myers, Andrew B., ed. *The Knickerbocker Tradition: Washington Irving's New York*. New York, 1974.

O'Callaghan, E. B. *History of New Netherland*. 2 vols. New York, 1846-1848.

———, ed. *The Documentary History of the State of New York*. 4 vols. Albany, 1950–1951.

Richardson, James F. *The New York Police: Colonial Times to 1901*. New York, 1970.*

Richmond, J. F. *New York and Its Institutions*. New York, 1873.

Rodgers, Cleveland, and Rankin, Rebecca B. *New York: The World's Capital City*. New York, 1948.

Rothery, Agnes E. *New York Today*. New York, 1951.

Sayre, Wallace S., and Kaufman, Herbert. *Governing New York City: Politics in the Metropolis*. New York, 1956.*

Simon, Kate. New York: *Places and Pleasures*. New York, 1959.

Stiles, Henry M., ed. *The History of the County of Kings and the City of Brooklyn, New York, from 1683–1884*. 2 vols. New York, 1884.

Still, Bayrd. *Mirror for Gotham: New York as Seen by Contemporaries from Dutch Days to the Present*. New York, 1956.

Stokes, I. N. Phelps. *New York Past and Present*. New York, 1939.*

———, ed. *The Iconography of Manhattan Island, 1498–1909. . . .* 6 vols. New York, 1915–1928.

Syrett, Harold. *The City of Brooklyn*. New York, 1944.

Tunnard, Christopher, and Reed, Henry H. *American Skyline*. New York, 1953.*

Van Pelt, Daniel. *Leslie's History of the Greater New York*. 2 vols. New York, 1899.

Werner, Morris R. *It Happened in New York*. New York, 1957.

White, E. B. *Here Is New York*. New York, 1949.

Wilson, James G., ed. *The Memorial History of the City of New York*. 4 vols. New York, 1892–1893.

*Paperback

Bibliographies of New York City

Brooklyn Public Library *List of Books on Greater New York in the Brooklyn Public Library.* 3rd rev. ed. The Library, Brooklyn, 1909.

Dunn, James T. "Masters' Theses and Doctoral Dissertations in New York History (1897–1951)." *New York History.* vol. 33, 1952.

Eiberson, Harold, and Ditzion, Sidney. "Sources for the Study of the New York Area; A Bibliographic Essay." *The New York Area Research Council.* The City College, New York, 1957.

Government Affairs Foundation. *Metropolitan Communities: A Bibliography.* Public Administration Service, Chicago, 1956.

Institute of Public Administration. *Selected Recent References on Materials Relating to the Operation of the Government of the City of New York.* The Institute, New York, 1959.

Municipal Reference Library *Notes.* 1914 to Date (Indexed).

New York Historical Society "Books about New York City, Primarily History, Published from 1898–1947." *The Society,* New York, 1948.

New York Public Library "Selected List of Works Relating to City Planning and Allied Subjects," *New York Public Library Bulletin,* vol. 17, 1913.

Port of New York Authority. *A Selected Bibliography of the Port of New York Authority, 1921–1956.* The Authority, New York, 1957.

Reynolds, James B., ed. *Civic Bibliography for Greater New York.* Charities Publication Committee, New York, 1911.

Selected Bibliography on Revision of the New York City Charter. School of Public Affairs, Princeton, New Jersey, 1933.

Shaw, Thomas S. *Index to Profile Sketches in the New Yorker Magazine.* Boston, 1946.

Spielvogel, Samuel. *A Selected Bibliography on City and Regional Planning.* Washington, D.C., 1951.

United States Works Progress Administration, Division of Professional and Service Projects *Guide to Manuscript Depositories in New York City.* Historical Records Survey, New York, 1941.

Vormalker, Rose L. *Special Library Resources.* Special Library Association, New York, 1941.

317